M

1/2/2/09

Entrepreneur
MAGAZINE'S

LEGAL
GUIDE

Sm
Cou
Gui

Ep
Entrepreneur
Press

MAR 12 2008

Publisher: Jere L. Calmes
Cover design: Desktop Miracles, Inc.
Composition and production: MillerWorks

Advisory Editor for the Entrepreneur Press Legal Guide Series: Helen Cicino

This publication is designed to provide accurate and authoritative information in regard to the subject matter covered. It is sold with the understanding that the publisher is not engaged in rendering legal, accounting, or other professional services. If legal advice or other expert assistance is required, the services of a competent professional person should be sought.

Unless otherwise specified in this book, any reference to individuals, entities, incidents, or situations is fictional, and any resemblance to actual persons, living or dead, businesses, companies, events, or locales is entirely coincidental.

Scales ©Rzymu

Library of Congress Cataloging-in-Publication Data

Spadaccini, Michael, 1964-
    Small claims court guidebook / By Michael Spadaccini.
        p. cm.
    ISBN-13: 978-1-59918-154-7 (alk. paper)
    ISBN-10: 1-59918-154-1 (alk. paper)
        1. Small claims courts--United States--Popular works. I. Title.
KF8769.Z9S68 2008
347.73'28—dc22   2007027557

Printed in Canada

12 11 10 09 08 07   10 9 8 7 6 5 4 3 2 1

Entrepreneur
MAGAZINE'S

LEGAL GUIDE

Michael Spadaccini
Attorney at Law

Small Claims Court Guidebook

Ep
Entrepreneur.
Press

- How to Evaluate, Research, Plan, File and Execute a Successful Case
- Instruction and Advice for All 50 States

Additional titles in Entrepreneur's *Legal Guides*

Helen Cicino, Esq.
Managing Editor

Bankruptcy for Businesses: The Benefits, Pitfalls and Alternatives

Business Contracts: Turn Any Business Contract to Your Advantage

Business Structures: How to Form a Corporation, LLC, Partnership, Sole Proprietorship (Available December 2007)

Estate Planning, Wills and Trusts

Forming an LLC: In Any State

Forming a Partnership: And Making It Work

Harassment and Discrimination: And Other Workplace Landmines (Available December 2007)

Hiring and Firing

Incorporate Your Business: In Any State (Available October 2007)

Intellectual Property: Patents, Trademarks, Copyrights, Trade Secrets (Available December 2007)

The Operations Manual for Corporations (Available December 2007)

Principles of Negotiation: Strategies, Tactics, Techniques to Reach Agreements (Available December 2007)

The Small Business Legal Tool Kit

Tax Planning for Business: Maximize Profit, Minimize Taxes (Available December 2007)

Contents

Preface

S mall claims courts are courts of limited monetary jurisdiction that are utilized for the resolution of smaller disputes. The monetary limit in small claims courts varies by state. On the low end, Massachusetts allows awards of up to $2,000, while on the high end, Tennessee allows awards of up to $25,000 in some of its counties. Generally, most states allow awards of around $3,000 to $5,000.

Small claims courts operate much more informally and more simply than regular civil courts, and decisions are speedy. The entire process, from filing a claim, to getting a hearing, to getting a judgment

Definition: Plaintiff

A plaintiff in a lawsuit—small claims or otherwise—is the party that is seeking relief by bringing the legal action.

(or losing and getting nothing) can usually be accomplished in 60 days. In a regular civil court, litigants rarely can get to trial within a year and a half from filing.

Like most Americans, you've probably seen one or more of the television shows that showcase small claims cases. These shows are obviously not real courtrooms; they are arbitrations—informal dispute resolution procedures before a third party—and the awards are real. The conduct of these televised "trials" is actually quite close to what one might see in a real small claims case—I recommend watching those shows as a "warm up" for your own case. The level of formality in the televised trials is fairly accurate, and the judge's degree of inquiry into the facts is also fairly equivalent. One of the pieces of information I will offer here is that if you have a pending small claims case, you should attend a small claims case and observe the conduct.

Definition: Default

Default is relief granted by a court when an opposing party fails to answer a complaint or appear for trial.

If you're a plaintiff or defendant in small claims court, you are going to get about ten minutes to speak. Sometimes, a case will be more complex, and will take a bit longer. Also, only about 80 percent of the defendants bother showing up. Defendants who don't show up will lose their case by "default." We'll discuss the procedures and issues surrounding default throughout this book.

Easy Liability, Low Damages

There are two very important insights that I want to bring up regarding small claims court:

1) The logistics of small claims courts tend to favor plaintiffs. In fact, as a lawyer advising small claims litigants, I would often jokingly refer to small claims court as "plaintiff's court." There are a few reasons for the plaintiff's advantage. The speed and ease of entry to the court is an obvious tactical advantage. If a plaintiff is forced to bring his or her claim in a standard civil court, the defendant can maneuver for months

or even years to postpone final judgment. In civil litigation, it is the plaintiff who wants to move the matter forward as quickly and easily as possible. Conversely, the defendant will usually want to slow the matter down, and complicate the legal process as much as possible; this frustrates the plaintiff's attempt to get an award. There is another side, however, to the plaintiff's advantage—small claims courts tend to keep damages low. Small claims courts tend not to extend damages into areas of consequential damages; they tend to stick to the tangible, easily provable damages. In this respect, small claims courts honor the principle of "easy liability, low damages." If your case relies heavily on consequential or intangible damages, you should consider seeking redress in an upper court.

> **Definition: Defendant**
>
> The defendant is the party that opposes a plaintiff in a lawsuit. The plaintiff in a lawsuit seeks compensation from a defendant.

2) The second insight into small claims court is that in my experience, small claims court judges have a natural bias in favor of plaintiffs. This bias is understandable. Truly, most plaintiffs in small claims court have been wronged to some degree. Beyond that, by the time the plaintiff gets to court, he or she has probably endured some unpleasant wrangling with the defendant. Defendants have a natural tendency to appear and act evasively. So, generally, small claims judges will strain to find a way to get the plaintiff some sort of award.

In addition to these two insights, in my experience there is a small minority of small claims judges that are simply poor adjudicators, or worse. Small claims judges are not particularly well paid, nor particularly well respected by their peers. They possess all the faults, limitations, and prejudices of ordinary folks and they take those limitations with them to work. And, even if the judge is thoughtful and competent, he or she will be overworked, and there is precious little time to hear every facet of every case. All this adds up to an inherent unreliability in small claims decisions. We'll talk about the unreliability of decisions throughout this book, and how to deal with it.

In California, small claims is further complicated by the fact that a defendant can appeal a small claims judgment brought against him, while a plaintiff cannot—the plaintiff only gets one shot. As a young lawyer in San Francisco, I occasionally represented clients in small claims appeals at the superior court level. The superior court judges are simply more experienced and more thoughtful than small claims court judges. In the small claims appeal cases that I tried before the superior court, I recall clearly that I won two of the three cases. The superior court rulings were "reversals"—decisions that reversed the order of the small claims court judge. The litigants that opposed me in all three cases were absolutely convinced of the strength of their position and were absolutely certain they would win. It's likely that their victory before the small claims judge gave them confidence in the strength of their cases.

My clients' success rate is obviously not a scientifically significant sample. Since only defendants can bring appeals from small claims court in California, the actual reversal rate of small claims judgments in San Francisco is probably more like 25 percent. That's a fairly dismal statistic; it means that many litigants are getting bad or unfair rulings in the small claims court. These reversals also highlight the "plaintiff bias" of the small claims court—the Superior Court does not always share that bias. The high reversal rate on appeal also shows the inherent unreliability of small claims awards.

Clearly small claims courts are not perfect. But the idiosyncrasies of the small claims court can perhaps be used to your advantage. For example, assume that you have a plumbing business and you did some work for a client and the client didn't pay you. You decide you want to collect via small clams court. On the other hand, assume that there is a gouge in the client's granite countertop, and he claims that you made the gouge while performing your work and he doesn't feel he owes you the money because of your poor workmanship. Your case, therefore, is not a sure winner. You both have a good argument, and there would have to be some back and forth in the court to get down to the facts of whether the countertop damage was your fault. In this instance, I'd recommend first sending a demand to the client for payment and point out to him both the unreliability of the small claims court and the plaintiff's bias. This might be enough to bring the client around. You might, in some cases, have to settle before going to court for less than the full amount that is owed to you. Settling is part of the lawsuit game, and sometimes a settlement can be a good deal for all.

If you or your business is facing a small claims case, either as plaintiff or defendant, I recommend that you read this book through, and then focus on certain areas that are pertinent to your case.

My Goal: To Help You Win

My goal in this book is, quite simply, to help you win. I want you to get the best result possible in your case. That may mean going to court to either pursue or defend an action; we'll cover both sides. You might also achieve victory by making an effective demand for payment, or by making an effective rebuttal to a demand; again, we'll cover both sides.

This book is designed primarily for the business owner. Business owners are more likely than most to either become a defendant in a small claims case, or to have a need to bring a small claims case. As a business owner myself, I have often come close to filing a small claims case on my own behalf, but have managed to avoid it by using some of the techniques in this book. There are many steps through which you should pass before actually going to trial at small claims court. Remember always that the threat of bringing a lawsuit can sometimes induce a reluctant debtor to pay up.

Our Road Map

If you follow the instruction and guidance in this book, you'll increase your chances of winning your case tremendously. All small claims court litigants think they are prepared—but only a small minority actually are prepared for their hearing.

So let's set out a road map for what we'll cover in this book. We'll begin with the all-important process of evaluating your case. This is the first step, and it colors every subsequent step. If you misjudge your likelihood of victory, you might get burned in court or miss an opportunity for settlement.

Definition: Jurisdictional Limit

The jurisdictional limit in small claims court is the maximum dollar amount that a small claims court is empowered to award. Cases that exceed the jurisdictional limit can typically be brought in small claims court, but the amount of the award in excess of the jurisdictional limit cannot be awarded and will be permanently waived.

You evaluate your case first by research, and then by consultation. I once witnessed a small claims court hearing where a plaintiff attempted to collect a judgment on a gambling debt; he claimed "breach of contract." Well, gambling is illegal, and illegal contracts cannot be enforced in a court of law. While he was not charged with a crime, he did lose the small claims case. If he'd bothered to research, or to even think for just a moment, he'd have saved quite a bit of time. Also, the internet offers many free resources to research claims and defenses. I will outline how to go about doing research for your case.

After research, I highly recommend consulting with someone about your chances of victory. Outline your case and ask "would I win?" Preferably, you'd wish to consult with a lawyer. You might have to pay for that service, or maybe you have a relative or friend who is a lawyer that you could ask.

Then we'll move on to how to get help with preparing your case. Some states mandate free assistance for small claims litigants. Also, some law schools offer free assistance programs. I'll cover how to find and take advantage of free programs.

In Chapter 3, we'll examine some specific types of cases and claims, such as cases involving negligence and motor vehicles, contract disputes, landlord-tenant disputes, bounced checks, dog bite cases, and libel, slander, and defamation. Each of these types of common cases requires some special treatment. We'll take a close look at how to win.

Then we'll briefly cover some procedural matters. First of all, is small claims court the right court for your claim? What if the total amount of the claim exceeds the jurisdictional limit of the small claims court? What if the other party is in another state? That might present an opportunity to "shop" for a better court in a better state. Also, there are statutes of limitations that dictate that certain cases are brought within a certain time. Statutes of frauds (it's a misnomer, it has nothing to do with fraud) dictate that certain contracts be committed to writing to be enforceable. These statutes are ripe ground for defendants to defeat claims.

Then we'll cover pre-litigation maneuvers. Court should be your last resort—but you might not want to say that to your opponent. All litigants should always endeavor to settle their claims if possible. We will cover settlement techniques, negotiation techniques, and how to draft an effective final demand letter. This chapter will also cover how to evaluate a weak case—how much should one accept if their case has problems?

In Chapter 6, we will cover the problems with parties to lawsuits. First of all, if you run a business, and you wish to sue a client for non-payment, who is the plaintiff? Is it you personally, or is it your business, or perhaps it's both? Likewise, a small claims suit may have one defendant, or it may have several defendants. Do you sue the client personally, or do you sue his company? Do you sue his wife or his business partners? This is a deceptively tricky component to pursuing a case. If you bring the case against the wrong party, you can actually lose or you might even trigger counterclaims against you, the plaintiff. Counterclaims are covered in Chapter 7.

In case all of your settlement efforts fail, you'll need to learn how to proceed as a plaintiff. You'll learn the preparation, drafting, and filing of the complaint.

We'll take a close look at serving the defendant in Chapter 8. Once a defendant is served, the case is ready to proceed. However, defendants can raise objections based upon a multitude of technical defenses such as failure of service, failure of the statute of limitations or statute of frauds, or improper court. Defendants can also

> ## Definition: Statute of Limitations
>
> A statute of limitations is a law that dictates the number of years in which a claim must be brought for liability to attach to a defendant. If a plaintiff waits beyond the expiration of the statute of limitations to bring his claim, the claim is lost forever.

> ## Definition: Statute of Frauds
>
> Laws that require that some contracts be committed to writing and signed by the party against whom enforcement is sought in order to be enforceable. The term statute of frauds comes from an English law passed in 1677 called the Statute of Frauds and Perjuries.

> **Definition:**
> **Counterclaim**
>
> A counterclaim is a claim brought by the defendant against the plaintiff that is filed and served following the plaintiff's original claim.

file counterclaims—that's probably the defendant's most powerful weapon.

We'll then move on to how to organize and gather evidence and witnesses, and how to compel oral and written testimony by subpoena. Then of course, we'll go over the conduct of the actual small claims trial or hearing. You'll find out what to expect, and how to deliver the most effective presentation. And you'll learn about certain types of common cases, such as motor vehicle cases, property damage and theft, contracts, and landlord-tenant cases.

Finally, we'll discuss the post-trial workings, either through appeals or collections. We will examine the collections process step-by-step. The appendices provide reference information, including maximum jurisdictional amounts, filing and service procedures, appeal rules, and procedural rules and requirements, for all 50 states.

Acknowledgments

I'd like to thank Jere Calmes, editorial director of Entrepreneur Press, for giving me the opportunity to write this book. I am also grateful to:

- Attorney, friend, and fellow golfer Dan Sweeney, who contributed to this volume by providing invaluable legal research.
- My law professors at Quinnipiac University School of Law, who taught me the foundations of corporate and business law which I now offer to you.
- My family and friends, who offered their support throughout the drafting of this volume.

- All the clients who have sustained my law practice throughout the past ten years and whose support helped me grow to become an expert in my field, with special thanks to Don LeBuhn and his family's business, Evolution Furniture of Berkeley, California (my first clients) for whom I organized my first corporation back in 1993.
- Emmett Ramey, president of Oasis Press, who gave me my first book contract based not upon any experience I could demonstrate, but solely upon my repeated and vehement pronouncements that I would do a fine job.
- Finally, and most importantly, my wife Mai, for enduring an admittedly imperfect man.

CHAPTER 1

Evaluating
Your Case

Most people make their greatest error in the evaluation of their small claims case. Be careful. When you misjudge your case, you run terrible risks. You might miss an offer for settlement or resolution, or you might waste time pursuing a loser case. Remember, nearly every case has a winner and a loser. Thus, in nearly every case, someone did not evaluate their case properly and went ahead anyway and lost. (There are some cases in which both sides win, as when a judge gives a partial recover to a plaintiff.)

All the decisions you'll make in pursuing or defending your case will rest upon your initial evaluation of the case. So a small error here will mean large errors later on. Despite the importance of properly evaluating a case, it's where most people focus the least effort. It's also one of the easiest steps in the process, so it makes sense to do it right.

You evaluate your case in two steps. First, you evaluate by researching both the law and the likelihood of recovery. Both are important. And second, you confirm your research through consultation with an attorney (preferably) or by presenting a sample of your case to others to establish their evaluation. Lawyers use the basketball term "slam-dunk" to refer to cases that are absolute 100 percent winners. Slam-dunk cases are rare. Most cases have some shade of uncertainty to them. That uncertainty might simply come from a defendant that is willing to lie to bolster his or her defense. Examples of slam-dunk plaintiff's cases would be the following:

- Someone wrote you a check and the check bounced. You have the physical check with "Non Sufficient Funds" stamped on it by the defendant's bank, and you bring that check to court. This is called "suing on the check" or "suing on the draft," and theoretically does not require any additional proof of what services or goods the check was written for.
- You have an unpaid promissory note in the amount of $3,000 bearing the defendant's signature, and you were present when he or she signed it. You also have evidence that you loaned $3,000 to the defendant on or about the time the promissory note was signed.
- Your parked car was rammed by a driver, who later confessed to being drunk at the time. You obtained the police report by going to the records department at the police station near where the accident happened, and the report clearly shows the defendant was at fault.

A defendant can have a slam-dunk case as well. Here are some examples:

- A plaintiff brings a claim against a defendant based upon a contract that was signed twelve years ago. That claim would clearly be barred by the statute of limitations.
- You had a poker night with your friends, and went in the hole to a friend by $500. Your friend brings a suit against you to recover the $500. This gambling debt is the result of an illegal contract and is not enforceable.

- A plaintiff will sometimes bring a claim against the wrong party. For example, a plaintiff might serve the wrong person with the same name, or sue the owner of a corporation when the corporation clearly was the appropriate defendant.

Most cases though, have arguable points on both sides. Typically, most slam-dunk cases settle, because they are so certain to result in victory for one side or the other. If you have the more likely situation of a case with some shade of argument that can be offered by either side, you should evaluate your case to determine your chances of victory.

Evaluating the Legal Merits of Your Case

The underlying legal merits of your case are important. Most experienced lawyers, though, might say that these merits aren't everything—and they'd be right. There is always some maneuvering that can and should be done, and there is always the problem of collecting on judgments. You may have the best case in the world, but the defendant might be dead broke. In that case, you might as well have no case at all. But certainly the place to start is to evaluate the legal merits of your case.

Finding "The Claim"

When lawyers use the term "claim," they are using the term as a term of art. A "claim" means a specific cause of action; a defined lawsuit founded on legal grounds and alleged facts, which, if proved, would con-stitute all the "elements" required by statute or common law. For example, to have a cause of action for breach of contract, there must have been an offer and acceptance by the other party, and a breach of obligations under that contract. For a tort claim, a party must have been negli-gent or intentionally wrongful, and that party must have caused injury. Claims are specific and defined. A plaintiff must fit his facts into a claim in order to be successful.

| **Definition: Term of Art** |
| A word or phrase used by legal professionals that has a precise meaning in a particular subject area. |

Definition: Common Law

Common law is the collective body of law that is established by precedent, from judicial court cases and judicial decisions within a jurisdiction.

Now some lawsuits can have several separate causes of action, such as fraud, breach of contract, and debt, or negligence and intentional destruction of property.

In upper courts, the rules of pleading are formal, and in some cases, you would have to define your claim with more particularity and formality. Luckily, small claims courts are informal, so you'll never need to use the term "negligence" to define your claim for the court. In small claims court, you'll just need to state facts sufficient to raise a claim and the judge will see if your facts fit an existing claim.

You need to figure out ahead of time if your case constitutes a claim, or fails to constitute a claim. You begin to do this by performing legal research. In small claims courts, cases for breach of contract are the most common. And a large majority of contract cases are simply collection cases. Collection cases are found where the breach of contract is clearly obvious, and the plaintiff is simply coming to court as a matter of course, to convert an overdue debt into judgment. In collection cases, often the defendant does not appear at the hearing. He or she recognizes the debt and does not object to it, but he or she simply does not have the money to pay, and so chooses to ignore the debt and the case.

Breach-of-contract cases are fairly easy to evaluate. First, there must be an offer and acceptance by two parties to enter into a binding agreement. That agreement must possess a degree of certainty. In other words, a contract to "build an addition to my house for $20,000" is probably not certain enough.

Definition: Tort

A civil wrong or breach of a duty to another person, as outlined by law.

The more professional and complete a contract, the more actionable it will be. Then, of course, someone would have to breach the contract by not performing his or her end of the bargain.

Or your claim may be a negligence claim, where someone's improper actions caused damage to either your business' property and/or your person. Automobile accident cases are almost always negligence claims. A more formal definition of negligence is "the doing of an act that a reasonably prudent person would not do," or the opposite, the failure to do something that a reasonably prudent person would do under like circumstances. Another manner of expressing it would be "a departure from what an ordinary reasonable member of the community would do in the same circumstances."

Now, you may face a set of facts that do not constitute a claim. For example, perhaps someone insulted your business at a cocktail party by saying "Jack's Plumbing is run poorly and they do shoddy work." That just an expression of opinion and doesn't rise to the level of libel or slander. You may be hurt by it or harmed by it, but that doesn't mean it rises to a legal claim. Similarly, "taking" clients away from your business by underbidding you or through regular competitive practices does not rise to the level of an actionable claim.

> **Definition: Actionable**
>
> An actionable claim is one that has grounds for legal action.

It may be plainly clear that you have a contract claim or a negligence claim—and those two causes of action represent 80 percent of all small claims cases. But if you think there are some problems with your claim, you may need to do further research. Now may be the time to talk to a lawyer to see what he or she thinks about your claim. Or, first, you can do further research yourself.

Researching Your Case Through the Internet

A basic internet search is a great place to start researching your case. If you type a simple clause into a search engine, such as "California contract law," you'll get back a list of legal summaries drafted by lawyers. There are also specific legal web sites with helpful information for non-lawyers. Listed below are some of the most useful sites that I have used in my practice:

- **LearnAboutLaw.com** (www.learnaboutlaw.com) is a site operated by this author. There you will find periodic updates of the summaries found in the appendix in Table A-3: Small Claims Court Summaries for All 50 States. Be sure to check here during your research, because laws change frequently. You will also find dozens of summaries on various legal topics, as well as model documents. LearnAboutLaw.com also maintains online question and answer forums operated by several practicing attorneys. Follow the links to "forums"—you can post questions for free and practicing lawyers will answer your questions. Or, you can search the existing topics. This might be a good place to look if your research reaches a dead end.

- **The 'Lectric Law Library** (www.lectlaw.com). This site has hundreds of useful summaries on a wide variety of legal topics.
- **FindLaw** (www.findlaw.com) is the largest of the online legal sites. It's designed for legal professionals as well as non-lawyers. It's essentially a search engine with a focus on legal information. It's crowded with ads, and can be hard to navigate.

Or your research may require that you research statutes. A perfect example of when such an inquiry would be necessary would be if you needed to search for the statute of limitations applicable in your state. In the appendix, you'll find the web address of state statutes for all 50 states. Or you can find a handy reference table (that is periodically updated) at the author's web site at www.learnaboutlaw.com. Follow the link under "Research."

Researching Your Case at a Law Library

When it comes to legal research, the internet has its limits. The internet lacks consistent and comprehensive case law. Small libraries of case law are beginning to appear on the internet, but for the most part, you'll need to visit a law library to research case law. Another resource that you'll find in a law library but not on the internet are case law digests. Case law digests are multi-volume, encyclopedic, indexed summaries of case law decisions. Digests compile the laws of an entire state into one easily researchable set of books. Digests exist for every state, and for the federal system.

> **Definition: Case Law**
>
> Case law refers to the collective body of written court decisions that comprise the common law of a jurisdiction.

Using Digests

To use a digest for the first time, you'll likely need some help. Law libraries are always staffed by experienced librarians or law students, and you'll find the assistance both free and useful.

Digests are typically comprised of 30 volumes, with the last volume being the index. You begin by using the index, and looking up your topic, such as "contracts." The index will guide you to the volume number and paragraph number. When you look up the paragraph number, you'll find a small summary of a case (called a headnote), and a citation number where you can look up the entire case.

> **Free Research Tool**
>
> The California state library system offers a free service called "Ask Now," where users can make direct, web-based inquiries of librarians. You can find the service at www.asknow.org/, and follow the link for "Law Librarian."

Let's say your case is the result of your company's delivery truck driving during a snowstorm, and your driver struck a snowmobile that was stopped in the road. Your research would probably lead you to try to answer the question, "Is a snowmobile allowed on a road?" You would look into the index to the digests and look up a definition of "motor vehicle" or "snowmobile." The index would lead you to a set of headnotes. A sample headnote might look something like this (this one is not real):

1411.3. What Are Automobiles or Motor Vehicles.

Cal. App. 4th Dist. 1958. A "snowmobile" is a self-propelling vehicle, but is not suitable for use on public street or roadway.

Williams v. Standard Acc. Ins. Co., 322 P.2d 1026.

That headnote expresses a single idea or ruling made in a legal case. In this case, it supports your suspicion that the snowmobile that your company's driver hit should not have been on the road. That would tend to mean that the accident is the snowmobile owner's fault, and not the fault of your driver. If that case has not been overturned, you can then go look up the case and read more about it. If the case is favorable, you'll want to photocopy it to either persuade your opponent to see the case your way and settle out of court, or perhaps to show to the judge. That headnote also has a bunch of confusing symbols and numbers. Let's break it down to see what all the numbers and abbreviations mean:

- "1411.3. What Are Automobiles or Motor Vehicles." This is the topic heading or title of that section of headnotes. You'll typically see many headnotes for many cases from different courts under that title.

- "Cal. App. 4th Dist. 1958." This shows the court that decided the case (the California Appeals Court for the 4th District) and the year the case was decided.

- "A 'snowmobile' is a self-propelling vehicle, but is not suitable for use on public street or roadway." This is the actual principle of law expressed in the case. Editors write the summaries that ultimately become headnotes, but if you look to the case upon which the headnote is based, you'll find the same or similar language expressed by the court.

- *"Williams v. Standard Acc. Ins. Co."* This is the title of the legal case. Someone named Williams was the plaintiff, and Standard Acc. Insurance Company was the defendant.

- "322 P.2d 1026" This seemingly confusing set of numbers and letters is actually a very meaningful case citation. These citations are the "address" where you'll find the actual text of the court's decision in that case. This part is actually quite easy. Let's start with the letters in the middle, P.2d; this means the Pacific Reporter, Second Edition. The Pacific Reporter is a set of law books where cases are compiled. If you can't tell from the abbreviation what set of books are referenced, ask a librarian; he will know off the top of his head. The first number, 322, is the volume number—the Pacific Reporter has hundreds of volumes, and they'll be neatly arranged in the law library in sequence. So, you simply go down the aisle until you reach volume number 322. The last number, 1026, is simply the page on which you'll find the case. See, not so hard, right?

Through your research of statutes and case law, you should be able to pin down the relative strength of your case or your defense. Collect statutes and the strongest case law that supports your position. You'll need to bring photocopies to the court, if your case goes that far. Don't expect the judge to go looking in a law library to research your case; you'll need to show statutes and case law at the hearing—within reason. For example, you don't need to show the judge law that says that a person who runs a red light is liable for negligence; the negligence is presumed because the conduct is so obviously a breach of public safety. You simply need to demonstrate that the driver ran the red light.

Often, your opponent will not be as prepared as you are. If you come to court with relevant and persuasive statutes and case law, it may be the edge you need.

Researching the Likelihood of Recovery

Now you must research the question of whether a judgment can ever be collected from the defendant. If the defendant does not pay a judgment voluntarily, the plaintiff is then forced to resort to time-consuming collection efforts such as placing liens on property or garnishing wages. A crafty defendant can dodge legitimate collection efforts for years. And, of course, a plaintiff cannot get blood from a stone. A person or company against whom a judgment cannot be collected due to poverty or insolvency is known as "judgment proof." A person or entity is said to be judgment proof when it is immune from collection activity.

There are many reasons why a person or entity might be judgment proof.

- The person or entity might simply be insolvent or poor.
- An entity may be a corporation with only a business name, and no meaningful assets.
- A person or entity may have an effective asset protection plan in place (asset protection is covered in Chapter 12).
- A person or entity may be judgment proof because they are in a foreign country.

> ### Expert Tip:
> ### Never Tell a Judge You Are Judgment Proof
>
> While you may wish to point out to a plaintiff that you are a judgment-proof defendant, you should never tell a judge that you are judgment proof. That is just like saying to the judge, "I will not abide by any judgment issued by this court." A judge may see it as an affront to his or her authority. If you must convey your financial situation later in court, say "I do not have the resources to pay a large award."

If you (or your company) are a judgment-proof defendant, you may wish to communicate that to the plaintiff. If you can convince a plaintiff that their case—however strong—will never result in a recovery, you may be able to shake them off you. A plaintiff might have a slam-dunk case, but that case may not ever yield any recovery because the judgment cannot be collected, making it a waste of time to proceed.

Who is the Defendant?

First, you need to determine who the defendant is going to be. Is the defendant an individual, or a corporation or LLC? Individual defendants are generally easier targets for collecting judgments. Nevertheless, many individuals are judgment proof. Corporations and LLCs are generally harder to collect judgments from. Here's why:

First of all, LLCs and corporations are liability-shielding entities—they protect their owners from the debts of the company.

Individuals must maintain a good credit rating in order to have access to home loans, car loans, credit cards, and other credit privileges. Thus, individuals tend to care much more about having an unpaid judgment appear on their credit report. Corporations and LLCs don't require a good credit rating to the same extent as individuals, so the threat of a lingering judgment won't necessarily influence a corporation or LLC.

Individuals are more likely to own tangible property that can be attached for collection, such as houses and bank accounts. Corporations and LLCs typically rent their office space rather than own, so they generally have no real estate to attach. Furthermore, corporations and LLCs tend not to maintain large amounts of cash in bank accounts. Corporations and LLCs that fall into financial trouble will simply shut their doors, leaving creditors in the lurch. Individuals do not have that option.

So what is the lesson here? There are several. First of all, as a potential defendant, you should never run any business outside of the protection of an LLC or corporation—the liability exposure is just too great a risk to take. LLCs and corporations protect your personal assets from the reach of lawsuits and creditors. Entrepreneur Press offers many books on setting up your own LLC or corporation. For plaintiffs, the lesson is that you want to bring your case against individual defendants if you can. Furthermore, you can engage in what is thought of as a "pre-litigation planning" by contracting with an individual rather than with a corporation, or by insisting that an individual personally guarantee performance under the contract. Then if a lawsuit arises, your will be dealing with a defendant who is not shielded by a corporation. This practice is universally followed by commercial landlords. They nearly always require a personal guarantee when they lease commercial space. Their reasons are obvious; they want to avoid collection difficulties against a corporation or LLC in the event the tenant goes out of business.

As a plaintiff, you want to bring your suit against individual defendants. To bring a case against an individual defendant, that individual defendant must have been an actor in the underlying claim. For example, the individual defendant must have signed a contract in his or her own name. Or, the individual must have caused the harm to you or your business.

If you cannot by any reasonable argument bring your claim against an individual defendant, you may be forced to bring your case against a corporate or LLC defendant. An alternative, however, is to check out the corporation to make sure it is up-to-date with its required filings and in good standing. Perhaps the corporation or LLC is dissolved for failure to pay taxes. Research the corporation or LLC at the web site of the secretary of state in the entity's state of incorporation. If the corporation is not in good standing, you can bring claims against the individual owners, but be prepared to prove it to the judge.

Potential plaintiffs should also investigate whether the potential defendant has insurance for the plaintiff's losses. If the defendant is insured, that's good

> **Expert Tip:**
> **Is Your Opponent's Corporation**
> **or LLC in Good Standing?**
>
> When pursuing a corporation or LLC defendant or
> when defending against a corporation or LLC plaintiff,
> always check to be sure that the corporation is
> 1) in good standing in its state of incorporation, and
> 2) properly qualified and registered to do business in
> a state other than its state of organization.
> Look for blemishes in the corporation's (or LLC's) fil-
> ings with the state. You can use this information to
> go around the entity to reach its owners—you can
> argue before the court that because the corporation
> or LLC is legally void, the corporation or LLC does not
> even have the legal right to appear in court and its
> owners must answer for the debts of the entity.

news for both the plaintiff and the defendant. Motor vehicle insurance is legally required in most states, although some drivers violate the law by not keeping up with their premium payments. Most businesses carry some form of liability insurance that cover accidents and some business-to-business lawsuits. It is in the defendant's interest to disclose insurance coverage to a plaintiff, so plaintiffs should ask the defendant whether or not they have insurance coverage. Most defendants will answer that inquiry. If the defendant is insured, the plaintiff will negotiate with the insurance company, rather than directly with the defendant.

If your research into the likelihood of recovery leaves you with no clear answer, you can always do an asset search. There are dozens of firms that perform these searches, and the prices range from about $50 to $80 per search for very comprehensive asset searches. Two of the largest and most successful are ZabaSearch.com and Intelius.com. You'll discover any other judgments against the defendant. A debtor with too many outstanding judgments may be judgment proof. You won't collect a judgment from a judgment-proof debtor, but at least you won't waste time and money trying to pursue the claim. These searches will nearly always reveal land and homes owned by the target defendant, and some searches even yield bank accounts. Experienced lawyers use these searches before agreeing to take on cases. For defendants, always consider that such searches can find your property, if the plaintiff is resourceful and determined enough to use such searches.

Confirming the Strength of Your Case

Once you have completed the initial evaluation of your case as outlined above, it's a good idea to do a test run of your case on a neutral party. The best person to confirm or refute the strength of your case is an attorney. Better yet, maybe there is a judge in your family. If you don't have a family member or friend, you might wish to call a local attorney and offer them their hourly rate for 15 minutes to discuss your case and give their opinion. If your case is too small to warrant the expense, try posting a summary of your case on the forums at www.LearnAboutLaw.com. Typically, a lawyer will answer back in a day or two.

I generally recommend confirming the strength of your case because you'll make big decisions based on the likelihood and size of your potential recovery or exposure. You will develop a settlement figure based on the strength of your case. You will also commit time and resources to your case based on its strength. Thus, you need to get an accurate read on your case. This is an important step, but it's also one of the easiest. You don't want to throw a lot of time and money into a losing case. And the more accurate your evaluation, the better off you'll be. Keep in mind that you need to re-evaluate your case constantly. Say you have a solid case of liability, but then you later learn that the defendant just lost his job. That weakens your likelihood of possible recovery, so you'll need to adapt your strategy as your case unfolds.

Is Small Claims the Right Court to Bring Your Case?

Small claims may or may not be the right court to bring your case. There will be many cases that can be brought to more than one court in more than one place. As a plaintiff, you may need to strategize to select the right court. Let's begin by examining when a case might be brought in either small claims court, or in a higher court. We'll use California as an example—statistically, the most lawsuits are brought and defended there. California's small claims court jurisdictional limit is $7,500—that's the most an individual person can receive in small claims; corporations are limited to awards of $5,000 per claim. California's superior court is of unlimited monetary jurisdiction, which means that any amount of damages can be awarded.

Where to Bring a Case that Exceeds the Jurisdictional Limit of the Small Claims Court

Say you have a contract dispute where you are owed $5,750, and the liability is quite certain; you have a written contract outlining that you are owed that sum, and you did not breach your end of the bargain. You are faced with a choice of bringing the suit in small claims court—but you'll only get a maximum of $5,000. Even if you win your case, you'll lose the excess $750 forever. You can't bring a separate suit to recover the $750, the matter will be *res judicata*, or "the thing was adjudicated." You can only sue once on a single legal claim.

Your other choice would be to seek the full amount of the claim, $5,750, in superior court. In California superior court, you can collect the entire amount of the judgment without limitation. Every state has civil courts where the jurisdictional amount is unlimited. And you might be able to supplement your award with attorney's fees, consequential damages, and punitive damages. So the ceiling on the award will be higher. That's a clear advantage. The disadvantage to superior court is that you'll work much harder to win and you'll wait much longer to get resolution. Superior court is a standard civil court with formal and complex rules of pleading and discovery and trial conduct. Have you ever conducted a deposition of an opposing party? It isn't easy. You won't get to trial for at least a year in most places. And you'll likely need a lawyer to navigate the procedural complexities.

I have heard of cases where people have brought claims in the area of $25,000 into California small claims courts just to get a quick $5,000 judgment. In those cases, the decision was made to ensure speed of recovery. But consider also that you never want to push a defendant into bankruptcy. If you have a $30,000 claim against someone, but you know the defendant can't afford that judgment, then you might trigger the defendant to seek bankruptcy protection. If he or she goes into bankruptcy, the bankruptcy court will likely wipe out your entire claim. So it may make sense to bring your case in small claims

---

Definition: Punitive Damages

Punitive damages are monetary awards made to a victim that are intended to punish a defendant and deter the defendant from repeating the conduct that injured a victim. Punitive damages are intended to deter others from similar conduct.

court to secure a smaller judgment that does not trigger bankruptcy and the eventual discharge of the entire obligation to you.

The limited jurisdictional amounts in small claims courts are the trade-off that one must accept for ease of entry and speed of resolution. You just need to weigh the options and pick a path to resolution. Even if you are forced to accept a lesser amount than you are due, you must keep in mind that

> ### Definition: Discovery
>
> Discovery is the phase of the pre-trial litigation process during which each party requests relevant information and documents from the other side in an attempt to "discover" pertinent facts. Such devices include depositions (oral interviews), interrogatories (written questions), requests for admissions, document production requests, and requests for inspection. Discovery is limited in small claims court.

claims are settled for pennies on the dollar every day, and they will continue to be forever. You must strategize your legal claims to be effective.

Taking Small Claims Cases into Upper Trial Courts

Would you ever bring a small claims-sized case into an upper court? Actually, yes. Small cases are often brought into upper courts. There may be advantages to bringing the case into an upper court. Recall from the section above that a standard trial court involves very technical and time-consuming rules of pleading and discovery and trial conduct. This complexity is a burden on a plaintiff—but it is equally burdensome on a defendant. Often, a defendant would rather pay a judgment than participate in a pre-trial deposition. As a plaintiff, you are entitled to inquire to the defendant in a deposition as to a fairly broad range of facts. Defendants never like depositions. Depositions are invasive procedures, they take one away from work or family, and depositions are given under oath, so there is always a risk of perjuring one's self. So the procedural burden can be used as a weapon against defendants. If your case is weak, you might bring the defendant to his or her knees more easily if you bring your case in a standard trial court.

> ### Definition: Deposition
>
> The oral examination of a witness, taken under oath and recorded for use in court at a later date.

In addition, some small claims courts do not allow parties to be represented by attorneys. If you'd rather send your attorney to court than appear yourself, you'll need to bring your claim in an upper court.

"Shopping" for the Best Forum

Also consider that you may be able to bring your case in more than one geographic location. While most small claims cases tend to be local, there are undoubtedly instances where a case could be brought in more then one place. For example, if you are a resident of New Mexico, and you enter a contract with a resident of Arizona to be performed in New Mexico, you can bring suit on that contract in either Arizona (where the defendant resides) or in New Mexico (where the contract was to be performed). If the amount in dispute is $10,000, then your choice of forum will be quite easy: New Mexico's small claims jurisdictional limitation is a generous $10,000, while Arizona's limit is $5,000. Not only that, but some judges might tend to favor a local party over an out-of-state party.

Here's another example. In Arizona, the statute of limitations (the time limit in which a plaintiff needs to bring a case) is three years for oral contracts. In New Mexico, the statute of limitations is four years. So if your claim on an oral contract is more than three years old, but less than four years old, you'll bring your claim in New Mexico. The process of picking a court for a strategic advantage is known as "forum shopping." Good lawyers always forum shop. As a plaintiff, you should forum shop as well. As a defendant, you should hope that your plaintiff does not engage in forum shopping effectively.

Special Types of Cases

You should also consider that some small claims courts do not hear particular sorts of cases. Libel and slander cases often cannot be heard in small claims courts. Also, eviction cases often cannot be heard in small claims courts. The state reference tables at the back of this book have summary information for the small claims courts in all 50 states, but you should always check with the clerk of the small claims court to see if your type of case can be heard in the small claims court.

CHAPTER 2

How to Get Help with Your Case

There are many ways to get help with your small claims case; some methods are free, some are not. This chapter covers both, but we'll focus on ways to get free help. There's plenty of free assistance out there, if you know where to look.

Start with the small claims court itself. It's always best to make one trip in person to the court to get help at the beginning of your case. There, you'll be able to inquire directly as to what programs are available to assist litigants. You will likely find that there are several avenues for free assistance.

Assistance from Court-Appointed Representatives

When you go to the counter at your local small claims court, you'll speak with a clerk or assistant clerk. Clerks are employees of the state or county court and are not allowed to give direct legal advice. But what constitutes legal advice is a tricky question. Clerks sometime will discuss your case in rough terms, but most will be uncomfortable digging into the details. Clerks will, however, advise you of filing procedures and fees and direct you to the proper forms for filing complaints and compelling witnesses and subpoenaing documents (more on these details later).

Clerks can also direct you to free advice. In California, and some other states, the county is required by law to provide legal assistance to small claims litigants. So every small claims court in California has an office adjunct to the court. Small claims assistance is given to litigants, free of charge, by a "small claims assistance office," or a similarly named department. Assistance offices sometimes carry strange or part-time hours, and the phone lines can get clogged, but the assistance is valuable. Check with your local court to see if it offers assistance to litigants free of charge.

You'll want to find out if you can get help over the telephone or if you need to appear in person. Court liaison assistance is precious. The court liaison might actually know the particular quirks of individual judges, if you can get them talking openly. You should ask the representative about any special filing procedures, such as how to compel witnesses to appear at the court hearing, or how to subpoena documents from witnesses or other parties. You should also be prepared to outline your case to the representative. It might be helpful to ask the following sorts of questions of the representative while you present an outline of your case:

- Is my case strong or weak?
- How can I improve my case or improve my chances of winning?
- What evidence is lacking in my case, and how can I go about obtaining such evidence?

The court's assistance office is where you want to start, if such an office is available in your state. If no such office exists in your state, there are many other avenues to pursue to get free help.

Assistance from Non-Profit and Volunteer Programs

Another great resource for free small claims assistance is a local law school or legal aid office. Many law schools have volunteer assistance programs for small claims litigants. The county small claims clerk will know about any such programs or you can search the internet for assistance. There are also non-profit legal aid departments in some areas that offer free or nearly free assistance to small claims litigants. Again, ask the clerk of the small claims court about any such programs. If the court clerk doesn't know, try an internet search. There is free help available through one means or another for nearly every small claims litigant in this country.

Getting Assistance from a Lawyer

Remember that small claims court is intended as a forum for litigants to resolve smaller disputes in an informal forum without necessarily requiring a lawyer. Some states allow attorneys to represent clients at small claims hearings, and some states do not. For example, California does not allow attorneys to represent clients at small claims court hearings. Of course, an attorney can appear on his or her own behalf when he or she is personally sued, just not on behalf of a client. The prohibition against attorneys appearing at hearings, however, does not mean that you can't get an attorney to help with your case generally. Even in states with a prohibition against attorney appearance, you are free to hire an attorney to help you prepare your case. Your attorney can even go to court with you and consult with you privately during the hearing; he or she just cannot speak to the judge. If your case has $10,000 or $15,000 on the line, you might be wise to pay an attorney to help you. An attorney will likely charge you by the hour, and typically it would require two or three hours of an attorney's time to help you prepare your case and meet with you.

Some states do allow attorneys to appear in small claims court on behalf of their clients. You may wish to simply hire an attorney to handle the entire matter for you, including appearing at the hearing. Hiring an attorney may be necessary if you are a defendant being sued in another state. Of course, attorneys must be paid, so you'll obviously spend more. A good rule of thumb to follow is to spend up to, but not more than, one third of the amount in dispute—but only when you have either a moderate or high risk of losing. If you have a very low risk of losing, you'll probably be fine without a lawyer. This is where the evaluation of your case becomes important. If the evaluation you make of your case is accurate, then your decision of whether or not to spend money on an attorney will be sound. We'll see repeated examples where an accurate evaluation of your case will help you make sound decisions as you proceed through your case. Be prepared to be a little flexible in applying the one third formula, but don't stray too far from it. In other words, it makes no sense to pay an attorney $5,000 to defend a $5,000 claim; you could probably settle a $5,000 claim for $2,000 on a good day. If the claim is $5,000, and you have a moderate chance of losing, consider spending no more than around $1,500. If you have a very high risk of losing, then you might consider spending a bit more.

Assistance Through the Internet

If you feel you need just a bit of advice from a lawyer but don't want to pay substantial fees, you can join one of several community forums on the internet where you can pose questions about your case to lawyers for free. Typically, you'll hear back in a day or two. You might get pitched on paid services by one or two lawyers, but you can ignore those posts if you want to. The two most active forums are the following:

- **Lawyers.com** operates a community message board that has fairly heavy traffic and good advice. You can find the forums here, just following the link for "small claims": http://community.lawyers.com/messageboards/list.asp

- **LearnAboutLaw.com** also maintains online question-and-answer forums operated by several practicing attorneys. Follow the links to "forums"—you can post questions for free and practicing lawyers will answer your questions. Or you can search the existing topics. This might be a good place to look if your research reaches a dead end. Keep in mind also that you can search the forums at www.freeadvice.com to see if another person has already posted your question.

CHAPTER 3

Specific Types of Cases and Claims

When lawyers talk about lawsuits, they speak in terms of a "claim" or "claims." A claim is a specific legal theory or principle upon which court-sanctioned relief can be granted. Examples of specific claims that can ripen into cases are:

- Breach of contract
- Negligence that causes either damage to person or to property
- Conversion, the wrongful taking of goods or property
- Libel and slander
- Trademark and copyright infringement

A claim is a formal concept in the law. You must conform your case to a legally recognizable claim but you need not make a formal declaration of each specific claim in small claims court; the court will do that for you. The claims that American courts recognize are, for the most part, hundreds of years old. The claims of breach of contract, negligence, conversion, and libel and slander are examples of "common-law" claims. Common law is the system of law developed by courts applying precedent, tradition, and settled case law, and not necessarily following written codes or statutes. *Stare decisis* is the policy of a court to stand by precedent; the term is an abbreviation of *stare decisis et non quieta movere*, which means "to stand by and adhere to decisions and not disturb what is settled." Common law is simply law that is made by courts.

The American system is a blend of common law and statutory law. Statutory law is the codified set of laws that is drafted and enacted by state and federal governments. Trademark and copyright infringement claims are claims that arise from rights found in statutes. These claims can be brought in court because a statute says so. Whether a plaintiff pursues a statutory law claim or a common law claim, the plaintiff must conform his case into a claim for which the law affords a remedy.

All claims are comprised of "elements," specific components or parts that must exist for a claim to be recognized. For example, a breach of contract requires that two persons agree to enter a contract, and one of those persons must materially breach the agreement. The individual components of the claim are the elements. Negligence has elements too; a negligence claim requires that some person had a duty to perform some act in a particular way, the person must have failed to act appropriately, and the failure to act must have proximately caused the damage of which the plaintiff complains.

In legal claims, *all* of the elements must be met; the failure of one element means the entire claim fails. You can't claim breach of contract unless there were two parties that agreed voluntarily to enter a contract. As a defendant, you can attack any one of the elements of a claim. In a contract dispute, a defendant might try to argue that no contract was ever entered into. In a negligence dispute, a defendant might try to argue that the damages were not a proximate result of his or her failure to act.

In practice, to conform your case to a legally recognizable claim, you must first "think inside the box." Because claims are somewhat formal, and have recognizable elements, you must mentally fit your case into the claim. Here is an example of conforming a set of facts to a claim:

> Peter is fired from his sales job because his manager, John, suspected Peter of stealing from the company. John told some of Peter's co-workers that "I suspect, but am not sure, that Peter might have stolen some money. I wasn't sure, so I just fired him." Peter was innocent and wants to bring a claim. Peter must now analyze the facts to find a claim.

> Because there was no evidence of racial or age discrimination against Peter, the claim does not fall into those categories of federal employment discrimination claims. But Peter may have a breach of contract claim. Peter and the company entered into an employment contract, and the company, through its manager, John, breached that contract by wrongfully firing Peter.

> There may be another claim as well. John's comments to co-workers might constitute slander, a false defamation, spoken to others, that injures the character or reputation of another.

> By conforming his facts to specific claims, Peter accomplishes a few important goals. First, he avoids the obvious error of mischaracterizing his claim as one for which all of the elements are not present. This error would be fatal if Peter were to mischaracterize his claim in his written complaint to the small claims court. Secondly, Peter will deliver a more effective presentation on the hearing date because he will understand the elements of his claims. If the defendant attacks particular components of Peter's claim, Peter will be more prepared to respond.

Common Cases: Negligence and Automobiles

Negligence claims are common in small claims court. Negligence is a type of "tort." A tort is simply a civil wrong like libel, slander, nuisance, fraud, or assault. All automobile cases are usually negligence claims. However, in small claims court, you might not actually hear the word "negligence"—it's just assumed by the judge that negligence is the doctrine under which a plaintiff is proceeding. Negligence comprises the following five elements, each one of which must be proven for a plaintiff to win its case:

- *Duty of care.* The defendant must owe to others a reasonable standard of care when undertaking acts that could foreseeably harm others. In automobile cases, the duty is to simply not harm others with your vehicle, not to exceed the speed limit, not to swerve, etc.
- *Breach of duty.* The defendant must have breached his or her implicit duty of care by not observing the reasonable standard of care imposed upon him or her. In automobile cases, a breach of duty could be proven when a driver fails to drive properly.
- *Factual causation.* Thereafter, a plaintiff must prove that the defendant's breach of duty of care factually caused damage to the plaintiff. Typically, this is a very objective test and its proof is quite simple.
- *Legal causation or remoteness.* This doctrine differs from factual causation, and is more complex. Legal causation examines how remote from a breach of duty to final injury the law will extend a remedy. A famous case, *Palsgraf v. Long Island Railroad*, illustrates the doctrine perfectly. The facts are almost unbelievable: A train conductor ran to help a man into a departing train. The man carried a package that contained fireworks. The conductor's assistance was poor, and the man fell from the moving train. The fireworks slipped and exploded on the ground, causing shockwaves to travel through the train platform. The shockwaves struck some weighing scales causing them to fall, unfortunately, on Ms. Palsgraf. Certainly, there was factual causation between the railroad conductor and Ms. Palsgraf's injuries, but the judge ruled that the injury was too remote, and there was no legal causation.

- *Damage/Injury.* For a negligence claim to be successful there must be provable injury. The damage can be physical (personal injury), economic (financial loss, loss of business opportunities), or both (loss of earnings following a car accident when a plaintiff misses work).

However, the preceding analysis of negligence is somewhat academic. In the real world of small claims cases, you wouldn't get into that detail in your oral presentation. You would however, run the analysis in your research stage—that's what a lawyer would do if analyzing a case. You'd probably need to say little more than "the defendant struck my car while I was at a stop light, and the damages are $1,100, and I have the written receipt right here." A judge, hearing that, would run the negligence analysis: The defendant had a duty to not run into other motorists. The defendant breached that duty by

A Real World Small Claims Case

The following is from an actual California small claims case involving motor vehicles. **The Case:** Michael, the plaintiff and my client, was parked on a narrow wooded street. Michael's driver door was open, as he was gathering up several boxes of books he was bringing to a nearby home where he tutored a student. Mary, the defendant, was driving on the road, and struck Michael's open door, knocking the door off of Michael's car. Michael was not injured, but the repairs to Michael's car would cost about $1,000. In the pre-trail maneuvering, Mary claimed Michael was negligent by parking with his door open and refused to pay for Michael's car repair. Mary (through her insurance company) noted the following from California's vehicle code §22517, "no person shall open the door of a vehicle on the side available to moving traffic... longer than necessary to load or unload passengers." Michael claimed that Mary was negligent for striking his parked car. I recommended to Michael that he proceed with the case anyway, and that his actions were reasonable.

Judgment: Michael won the case. The judge determined that while both parties were partly responsible, Mary bore the far greater responsibility because she was operating a moving vehicle at the time of the accident.

striking the other car. The damages to the vehicle were obviously both the legal and the proximate result of the accident, and there were monetary damages. In this model, all the elements of a negligence case are met, and the plaintiff's case looks quite good.

Where Two Parties Are Negligent

Negligence cases, motor vehicle or otherwise, are rarely clear cut. There is usually some degree of fault between the two parties, either real or imagined. The "real world" automobile case in the sidebar is a fairly typical example. In that case, both parties thought they were in the right, and both had at least arguable claims. As a small claims defendant, if you can prove that the plaintiff was partially, mostly, or wholly responsible for the accident, you might win the case.

Often, negligence and car accident cases devolve into a contest of finger pointing between defendant and plaintiff, with each party attributing blame to the other. These diverging positions can come in two forms. In one type of case, the parties agree to the facts, but don't agree how to apply the law. Again, classic example of this type of case is the real world automobile case example in the sidebar. The parties agreed that Mary struck Michael's open car door; the parties, however, disagreed as to who was negligent. The other type of case is where the plaintiff and defendant have differing versions of the facts. When two parties submit different versions of the facts, the judge must evaluate the credibility of all the parties and witnesses to make his or her best guess as to the actual facts. We discuss witnesses, evidence, and how these are evaluated in Chapter 9: Subpoenas, Witnesses, and Evidence.

Preparing a Negligence Case: The Plaintiff's Guide

Your task as a plaintiff in a negligence case is quite simply to prove all of the elements of your case and to secure all damages to which you are entitled. We have discussed the elements of a negligence case. You must be prepared to prove all the components of negligence. If the facts of a motor vehicle case are disputed, you must present witnesses to support your view of the facts to discredit the opponent's theory of the case and to discredit the opponent's witnesses. But don't bring more than two fact witnesses to court; a small claims judge is not likely to take the time to hear from more than two witnesses, unless the additional witnesses offer further information. If there is damage to your car or other property, have multiple copies of photographs of the damage, and multiple copies of any repair estimates or receipts. If there is personal injury, you should present photographs and medical receipts. Review Chapter 9 to learn more about how to present your evidence and the sorts of evidence that are most effective.

> ### Expert Tip
>
> Don't bring more than two witnesses to a small claims court hearing unless they each have independent information to offer. If you bring too many witnesses, they are not likely to be heard.

Beyond proving liability on the part of your opponent, you must also show damages. As a plaintiff, you want to present the highest amount of damages possible. There may be classes of damages that are available to a negligence plaintiff beyond the simple property damage and medical bills. In a negligence case, a plaintiff is entitled to recover those damages that flowed naturally and proximately from the negligent conduct.

Consider presenting evidence of all of the following classes of damages:

- *Damage to property*. This may seem obvious, but this would include damage to a car in an automobile accident, but also damage to personal property in the car, as well as clothing that was damaged in the accident.
- *Medical expenses*. Again, this may seem obvious, but this would include any doctor's visits (less any insurance benefits that you receive) but would also include prescription medicines, medical supplies such as pain relievers, and other pharmacy products. Just be prepared to show that the expenditures are related to your injury.
- *Lost wages*. This is a class of damages that plaintiffs often miss. If you missed work following an accident due to your injuries, or because you needed to visit the doctor, your lost wages may be recoverable.
- *Pain and suffering*. Damages for pain and suffering are typical components of larger negligence cases. If you feel you are entitled to significant dam-

ages for pain and suffering, you are probably better off with a lawyer in superior court, not in small claims court. However, technically, damages for pain and suffering can be awarded in small claims court.

Damages in negligence cases cannot extend too far, however. In small claims court, a plaintiff is very unlikely to be awarded any of the following:

- Punitive damages of any kind
- Legal fees, unless specifically allowed by a statute
- Damages for emotional distress
- Damages for reputation

Preparing a Negligence Case: The Defendant's Guide

Your task as a defendant in a negligence case is to poke holes in every aspect of the plaintiff's case. You have an advantage as a defendant: The plaintiff bears the "burden of proof." The burden of proof means that a plaintiff bears the responsibility of presenting evidence to prove his or her case. The defendant wins automatically if the plaintiff does not meet his or her burden of proof. You will want to attack the plaintiff on the facts of the case, on the law that applies to those facts, and every component of damages that the plaintiff puts forth. If you've read the section just above on how a plaintiff will put together his or her case, you'll have a good understanding of what you need to do as a defendant.

First, Attack the Facts

Your first line of defense is to effectively present your side of the facts of the event or events. If the case is an auto accident or any other type of physical event or accident, you'll need to testify as to what you witnessed. If one or more witnesses are available, bring at least one witness to court and make sure you know what they are going to say beforehand. Any physical event or accident will nearly always yield two or more differing versions of the facts. Witnesses and parties will nearly always recount differences in say, the speed of a vehicle, or whether a traffic light was yellow or red. Don't be intimidated or shocked when you hear the opponent's witnesses describe facts that differ from yours. Just be prepared to present calm and consistent testimony about what you witnessed.

In negligence cases, you want the fact that you are not responsible for the plaintiff's damages to be one of two very simple truths:

1) it was the plaintiff that was negligent—not you, or

2) the plaintiff's damages were not caused by your actions.

Remember the elements of negligence? You can attack any single element of the plaintiff's negligence claim. For example, you have a duty not to negligently pull out into ongoing traffic. But if the plaintiff was speeding, he breached his duty to travel at a safe speed. You may also attack the plaintiff's case on the issue of causation. Perhaps the plaintiff is claiming damages that are not your fault. There are plenty of automobile accidents and other accidents that are simply the fault of neither party; the accidents may be the result of a damaged or missing road sign, a fallen tree, lightning, a fire truck, a dog in the road, a cyclist, other drivers, etc. If the facts of your case warrant it, point to the fault of another person. Consider the *Palsgraf* case we discussed above. That case is an example of a plaintiff that tried to stretch liability to a defendant that was too remote from the actual injury. Keep in mind that if you plan to attack the facts, you need to have your witnesses lined up and prepared, and you need to have any documentary evidence well prepared.

> ### Why Not Negligence?
>
> Eleven men lost their lives in accidents during the construction of California's famed Golden Gate Bridge. One would assume that the workers' families would have brought negligence claims against the company building the bridge, as well as against the city, county, and state—but no negligence claims were brought. Why not? The answer is that the builders of the bridge followed sound and reasonable safety practices that existed at the time. Injury alone does not create a cause of action for negligence; negligence requires a breach of a reasonable standard of care.

Second, Attack the Damages

The defendant should also be prepared to attack the plaintiff's claim for damages. In a negligence case, the plaintiff will likely be seeking damages for a

The Defendant's Negligence Case Toolkit

A defendant in a negligence case, either automobile accident or other physical accident case, should rely on the following areas of attack:

- Argue that the plaintiff was responsible.
- Argue that one or more third parties was responsible.
- Argue that there is no causation.
- Argue that the damages are inflated or unwarranted.

small collection of individual damage claims. The plaintiff might seek compensation for damage to an automobile or other property, medical bills, pain and suffering, trial expenses, lost wages, and attorney's fees. The plaintiff might even try to extend damages into the area of remote consequential damages—be ready for that. Sometimes a plaintiff will try to argue that "I lost a client because of the accident," or "I missed a job interview, and would have gotten the job."

Your task? Pick each component of the damages sought apart, one at a time. Remote consequential damages are easiest to knock out. You simply argue that the damages are too remote, and subject to other conditions and uncertainties. You'll want to argue that pain and suffering, attorney's fees, and trial expenses are unwarranted and unfair in a small claims case. In fact, in a few states, pain and suffering damages are expressly disallowed in small claims court. As to medical expenses, you'll need to look into the details. You'll want to look for the following weaknesses in the plaintiff's presentation and argue individually against each component of medical expenses:

- The plaintiff may have undergone an unnecessarily long course of treatment with multiple doctor visits over a long period of time for a minor injury.
- Look for delayed treatments. This is a classic plaintiff's maneuver; a plaintiff may not be injured in an accident, but a few days later, the plaintiff starts thinking about building a lawsuit and begins a late course of treatment. Judges and juries are very skeptical of delayed treatments.
- Look for overblown treatments such as a lengthy hospital visit for a minor injury.

- Look for unusual or vanity treatments that have no factual relation to the accident, such as eye exams or plastic surgery. It sounds obvious, but plaintiffs routinely present absurd claims for damage.
- Look for conditions that may have existed before the accident, or may have arisen after the accident.
- If all else fails and it appears if the plaintiff's argument for damages is going very well, demand that the plaintiff testify under oath that he or she does not have health insurance. This is important because many plaintiffs bring medical bills into court when they have a right to reimbursement. Plaintiffs cannot get damages in court for medical expenses covered by insurance.

Common Cases: Contract Disputes

Contract disputes appear frequently in small claims court. Many small businesspersons or consumers find themselves in small claims court over his issue eventually. Let's examine how to pursue and how to defend a contract dispute in small claims court.

It's important to separate contract disputes into two categories. First are contract disputes with a participating plaintiff, and a participating defendant. Second are simple collection matters. Collection matters are very common in small claims court. In a typical collection action, there is an active and participating plaintiff, but the defendant is not participating. The defendant in a collection action has no defense to the dispute, and almost never appears. Collection actions are simply a stepping stone by which a plaintiff advances an overdue bill to a court judgment. We'll cover collection actions first because they are generally simpler, and then we'll discuss contractual disputes. Then we'll talk briefly about collecting on loans, which are really a form of contract.

Collection Actions

As stated, a collection action is initiated by a plaintiff to collect an unpaid bill or invoice. You should think of collection matters more as a pursuit than as a struggle. From that perspective, they differ from regular contract disputes. The plaintiff's goal in such an action is to advance the matter to a judgment. Once the plaintiff has a judgment, he or she (or it, because plaintiffs in collection actions are quite commonly business entities) can use the judgment to collect the debt through garnishment or levy. We discuss collection methods at length in Chapter 12.

In a collection matter, the underlying legal theory is breach of contract. At its core, a collection action is simply one party to a contract seeking to enforce the other party's performance. The collection plaintiff must keep this in mind: He or she must prove that a contract was made, that the plaintiff performed his or her end of the contract, and that the defendant did not pay or live up to his or her end of the contract. Collection actions are filed by parties ranging in size from enormous credit card companies to small mom-and-pop businesses.

Before proceeding with a collection action, you should always attempt to collect the debt through demand letters and other collection techniques. We discuss pre-litigation techniques in Chapter 5.

If all attempts to collect the debt fail, and if you have some certainty that you can recover, then you are ready to bring your collection matter to small claims court. Your case should be lean and simple. You will want to prove the following:

- That you (or your corporate, LLC, or partnership plaintiff) and the defendant entered into a contract. Contract cases are much easier for plaintiffs if a written contract signed by the defendant was made and is brought to court.
- That you, the plaintiff, performed your end of the bargain. Prove this with photographs or copies of work you did, or a delivery receipt, or a statement, or copies of invoices. Be prepared to buttress your documentary evidence with oral testimony to the effect that you held up your end of the bargain by performing on time, and in all other respects in accordance with the contract.
- That the defendant has not paid on the debt.

Beyond that, you might suggest to the judge that the matter is simply a collections matter. If the defendant hasn't responded to your demand letters and bills, point that out to the judge. You want to tell a story of an uninterested and non-participating defendant if you can. If you are lucky, the defendant won't show up and you should easily win your case. If the defendant does show up, he or she will likely make some complaints about the quality of the work the plaintiff did; your collection matter may be a struggle after all.

Defending a Collections Action

Is a defendant's position in a collec-

> ## Think Economically
>
> Do you have more than one deadbeat client from whom you'd like to collect? You can bring economy to your collections by bringing multiple actions against all of them and request a hearing for the same day. If you do, you need to be quite certain that you serve all of the defendants properly and within mandated timelines or those particular defendants will have no obligation to show up on the hearing date. And, you can use this in your demand stage—you can warn your opponent "I already will be at the small claims court at 333 Main Street (casually give the address, it'll make the other side believe you are well-versed and well-prepared) on October 1, so if you don't make good on this debt, I'll include this case on the small claims docket."

tions matter totally hopeless? Even if the defendant's liability is absolutely clear, the defendant can still maneuver. A defendant's goal should not be to avoid the obligation, but should be to get the plaintiff to accept less. Plaintiffs routinely take 20 or 30 percent on completely valid debts. Here's how you can minimize your liability. What a defendant has in his favor is the following:

- *The plaintiff has to undertake a lot of work to collect the full amount of the debt.* But the defendant must act early for this to be an effective strategy. Once the plaintiff has already gone through court, the plaintiff has done most of the work, and the defendant loses this advantage. Also, plaintiffs typically firm up their resolve to collect after they have been through the hassle of going to court.
- *The plaintiff, even after he or she wins his or her case, still must collect the debt.* Most folks don't realize how hard it can be to collect on judgments. In fact, many small claims judgments go uncollected. In many

Definition: Compromise

A plaintiff is said to compromise a claim when he or she reduces the amount of a perfectly valid claim in order to secure the defendant's cooperating in resolving the case.

cases, collecting on the judgment requires more work and expense than winning the judgment at the small claims court hearing!

So as a defendant in a collections matter, you need to act early, in the demand stage of the case. We discuss the demand stage later in Chapter 5: Demand Letters and Settling Your Case. This is the stage where you have a shot at convincing the plaintiff to "compromise" the claim. You'll need to be prepared to pay immediately when the claim is compromised. The plaintiff will only compromise the claim for fast money.

Your goal as a defendant in a collections matter is to communicate clearly to the plaintiff the following:

- That the plaintiff will go through a lot of waiting and work to prepare the claim, serve the complaint, secure a judgment, and then collect on the judgment.
- Any defenses or counterclaims, and point out the financial risk to the plaintiff, all depending on your specific facts.
- That small claims decisions are always unreliable, thereby increasing the risk.

Definition: Judgment Debtor

A judgment debtor is a party against whom a judgment has been entered in a civil case or small claims case. The defendant becomes a judgment debtor when he or she loses the case.

- That the plaintiff will have trouble collecting—the most persuasive point of all. Unless your assets and stability are obvious or well known to the plaintiff, it would be quite easy to convince the plaintiff that collecting on the debt will be a frustrating and fruitless endeavor. You should politely suggest that you won't cooperate with the collection of a judgment (you are not legally required to cooperate, you have rights as a judgment debtor).

Let's try out the preceding points in a sample letter (see Figure 3-1). If the plaintiff later tries to use the letter against you in the small claims hearing, you need to object to the introduction of this evidence. Any statement you make (by letter, fax, in discussions, etc.) during

FIGURE 3-1. **Sample Letter by Defendant to Plaintiff in a Collections Matter**

January 1, 2007

Joe Plaintiff
Ace Collection Agency
1000 Collection Avenue
NY, NY 10001

Dear Joe,

I received your demand letter. While I sympathize with your position, I strongly suggest that you compromise this claim. Otherwise you are likely to receive nothing, even if you go to court. I am making this offer as a good-faith gesture to you.

I hope to spare us both the hassle and time of preparing paperwork, serving each other with papers, serving witnesses with subpoenas, going to court, and then the substantial efforts that you'll need to expend to collect on any judgment you might get.

We have already talked about my defenses and counterclaims. But I wish to remind you that I am steadfast in pursuing my side of the case. Small claims decisions are not reliable, so really neither of us truly knows what is going to happen in court. In light of all this risk, I hope you accept my offer.

But really the main point is that even if you win a judgment for the full amount that you are seeking, you'll still need to expend a lot of effort to collect the debt. Unfortunately, I cannot and will not offer you my cooperation to collect on the judgment if you take me to court, but I do offer my cooperation to settle this case today. While I am now employed, I am considering leaving my job and moving out of state. If I do, you'll need to take the judgment to my new home state to collect. As far as assets, I don't have much, so I can't offer you much.

In order to settle the case, and without admitting any fault or waiving any evidentiary objections, I will agree to settle this case for 25% of what you are seeking, or $250. This is the most I can afford to pay, so this is my final offer.

Please let me know within three days if you accept this offer of settlement.

Yours very truly,

John Debtor

failed settlement negotiations and discussions are not admissible in courts of law. If an opposing party tries to introduce any statement you made during settlement talks, your objection is as follows:

> "Your Honor, I object to the admission of that evidence because it was a statement that I made during talks that we had to settle this case. That evidence is inadmissible."

The letter in Figure 3-1 contains language that you should include in settlement correspondence to shield the statement from being used later in court.

Contractual Disputes

Contractual disputes differ from collection disputes. A collection matter is really all about collecting: The defendant doesn't really have a case, he or she merely seeks to avoid collection of the debt. But a typical contract dispute is, at its core, a disagreement over who breached the contract. So the roles of defendant and plaintiff will be to challenge each other on either the facts of the dispute or the law of contracts. Let's begin with a little background on contract law.

A contract is a legally binding exchange of promises or an agreement between parties to deliver goods, money, services, or other consideration. Contracts can be oral or written. Typically, one party is to receive money, but not always. At its core, a contract requires that one party make an offer, and that the other party accept that offer. Once the two parties reach a "meeting of the minds," the contract is secure. Offer and acceptance does not always need to be expressed orally or in writing. For example, partial performance (such as a down payment) can indicate acceptance without an express communication of intent to accept.

Typically some consideration, or something of value, must be brought to the contract by both parties. If I offer to give you a car and you agree to receive it but later I renege, this is not a contract because you did not give consideration to me. The legal concept of consideration is complex, but at its core, the doctrine of consideration simply requires that something of value be given by both parties to a contract. An exception is "quasi-contract," which I'll discuss in a moment.

An implied contract is one in which some of the terms are not expressed in words. This can take two forms. A contract that is implied in fact is one in which the circumstances imply that parties have reached an agreement even though they have not done so expressly. For example, if you see a dentist, you agree to pay a fair price for the service. If you refuse, you have breached an implied contract to pay for the service, even though you did not sign an agreement to pay a certain sum of money.

A second type of implied contract is a contract that is implied in law, also called a quasi-contract. A quasi-contract doesn't require a meeting of the minds; rather, it is a means for the courts to remedy situations in which one party would be unjustly enriched were she not required to compensate the other. For example, say a company accidentally installs a landscape lighting system in the lawn of the wrong house. The homeowner sees the company installing the lights in her own lawn. Pleased at the mistake, she says nothing, and then refuses to pay when the electrician hands her the bill. Will the homeowner be held liable for payment? Yes, if it could be proven that the homeowner knew that the lighting was being installed mistakenly, the court would make the homeowner pay because of a quasi-contract. Such a claim is also referred to as *quantum meruit*. These claims are rare, but it is good background.

Contracts Made Invalid by the Statute of Frauds

Finally, some contracts require that a contract be committed to writing and signed by the party against whom enforcement is sought in order to be enforceable. Note that only the party against whom enforcement is sought need sign to satisfy the statute, not both parties. This doctrine is known as the "statute of frauds." The term comes from an English law passed in 1677 called the Statute of Frauds and Perjuries. All American states have some form of statute of frauds, but every state's statute of frauds differs. Historically, the statute of frauds required a written contract and signature in the following types of cases:

- Contracts in consideration of marriage.
- Contracts that cannot be performed within one year.
- Contracts for the sale of an interest in land.
- Contracts to pay the debt of another.
- Contracts for the sale of goods above a certain value.
- Contracts in which one party becomes a surety (acts as guarantor) for another party's debt or other obligation.

Of course, each state differs slightly. For example, California's statute of frauds (Civil Code §1624) generally falls in line with the historical guidelines above. However, California's statute of frauds has no provision for contracts for the sale of goods above a certain value, but does carry a provision requiring a written contract, or other signed writing to enforce a promise to lend money in an amount greater than $100,000.

Preparing a Contract Case: The Litigant's Guide

First, is the contract in writing? If the contract is written, the plaintiff enjoys the upper hand and is halfway home. With a written contract, the defendant cannot impose the statute of frauds against the plaintiff. Furthermore, the defendant cannot alter the terms of the contract in his testimony (e.g., "I was only supposed to build a wall three feet high, not five feet high"). The defendant cannot deny acceptance (e.g., "we were still negotiating that agreement, and never came to final terms"). Also, a written contract indicates formality on the part of both parties, and a willingness to be legally bound.

If there is no written contract, the plaintiff will need to begin by establishing that a contract exists. The plaintiff will need to point very clearly to the moment the agreement was reached—state the time and place, and what both parties said (e.g., "we were in the defendant's front yard on a Friday afternoon. He said 'I agree to that price,' and then we both shook hands. I remember the defendant had his golf bag over his shoulder").

For the defendant, the opposite is true. Without a written contract, the defendant begins with the upper hand. The defendant can dispute the very heart of the case: the terms of the contract. Or, the defendant may argue that an agreement was never reached. Keep in mind that it is impossible to argue that an agreement was never reached if you partially performed the contract. For example, if a defendant made a partial delivery on a contract for the sale of goods, no judge in America will believe that the defendant did not agree to be bound to a contract.

The next stage in a contract dispute is where the meat is: the argument of who breached the contract, and to what degree. When a contract is breached by one party, generally the opposing party has no further obligation to perform under the contract. Contract disputes generally devolve into a he said-she said argument over how the opposing parties failed to perform. I worked on a case where the plaintiff, a home decorator, was seeking a refund of money spent to a defendant (my client) who had manufactured some custom roman blinds. The plaintiff was dissatisfied with the blinds. The plaintiff was also seeking some consequential damages to her reputation for the allegedly botched job (we'll discuss consequential damages in contracts cases in a moment). The defendant argued that the blinds were acceptable and that the plaintiff's objection was to the style of the blinds, not the quality. Most of the discussion focused on whether the blinds were up to the standards required by the contract. Ultimately, the judge ruled that the plaintiff was entitled to a partial refund, but not a total refund, since she received something of value, just a lesser value than what she wanted.

Plaintiffs sometimes seek consequential damages in small claims cases. The home decorator sought consequential damages because some real estate agents had seen the blinds and related the poor workmanship to her skills as a designer. We disputed that charge as factually improbable and outside of the range of damages typically allowed in contract disputes. The judge agreed. The only time that consequential damages are allowed in contract disputes is if it is determined that such damages were reasonably foreseeable or "within the contemplation of the parties" at the time of the contract. As a defendant, you always want to limit consequential damages by arguing that such damages

> **Expert Tip: Corroborate Your Testimony**
>
> When you state corroborating facts like the time, place, date, what people were wearing, etc., you buttress your testimony about statements that an opposing party or witness made. Thereby, you reveal and demonstrate that your memory is complete and clear.

were not contemplated and never discussed. And, as a preventative measure, you should never agree to clauses in contracts that allow the recovery of consequential damages.

Collecting on Loans

A loan is simply a contract to repay money. The most important points for plaintiffs to focus on is to demonstrate the loan either with a written document (written contracts or loan documents are always the strongest) or with proof that the loan was delivered to the defendant and that partial payments were made on the loan. Always be prepared to show a detailed statement of the payments the defendant made, if any. The small claims judge will be looking very carefully to make sure that you have credited the defendant for any sums he may have paid on the debt. As a defendant, you will want to show any and all payments that you made on the debt.

Common Cases: Landlord-Tenant Disputes

Landlord-tenant disputes arise from the relationship between a landlord and a tenant, either in a commercial or residential setting. Leases are a special manner of contract that are governed by special rules. Our legal system views tenancy and rental security deposits as specially protected rights. Keep in mind that in some states, landlord-tenant disputes are not heard in small claims court. Check Table A-3: Small Claims Court Summaries for All 50 States in the appendix and then call the court to see if landlord-tenant disputes are heard in small claims court. In most states, evictions are not heard because an eviction is the termination of a valuable right: the right to possess real property. It's more likely though, that the small claims court will hear a dispute over a security deposit, damage to a rental unit, or for back rent following the abandonment by a tenant of a rental property.

Security Deposits

Disputes over security deposits are common in small claims courts. Generally, the amount in dispute is less than the jurisdictional limit, so these cases are a good fit. Tenants have the advantage here. Remember that a security deposit never really belongs to the landlord. In a sense, the deposit is held in trust for the tenant by the landlord, and can only be retained in very specific instances. I have seen a lot of landlords lose very badly in small claims court. A good example is a recent Massachusetts case involved the withholding of $500 from a $1,000 deposit. The landlord claimed that the unit was left in terrible condition, and that the tenants had taken two bar stools. The tenant (a colleague of mine) in the settlement phase, offered to accept $200 to settle the $500 claim. The landlord was stubborn, and probably figured that the former tenant would not pursue the matter. The tenant brought his case in small claims court. The landlord's evidence was weak; he had almost no receipts to substantiate the $500 in cleaning costs and furniture replacement. The tenant made clear that the unit was spotless and that the bar stools were at least 25 years old and probably worth $5. The tenant won the full return of his security deposit. In addition, the Massachusetts statute allows triple damages and attorney's fees, so the total judgment was nearly $3,500. The landlord appealed and lost the appeal as well.

> **Alert: Rent-Controlled Jurisdictions**
>
> If you are a landlord in a rent-controlled jurisdiction like San Francisco or New York, you should never take any action against your tenants without speaking to a qualified attorney first—the local laws in those jurisdictions provide hefty punitive damages for failing to observe a tenant's legal rights.

Some important points to remember in a security deposit dispute:

- The law is on the side of tenants.
- The judge likely has a bias in favor of tenants. They tend to be less well off than landlords, and are commonly abused by landlords.
- A security deposit is property that belongs to tenants, not to landlords.
- The handling of security deposits requires that rules and laws be carefully followed.
- Victorious tenants in security deposit cases can generally bump up the damages by using statutory provisions that favor tenants.
- Make sure the small claims court will hear your dispute.

Cases to Recover Back Rent

Actions to recover overdue rent following the end of a lease are common in small claims court. These cases arise at either the end of the term of a lease, or when the tenant abandons the property before the end of the lease. Cases brought at the natural end of a lease are simpler. A plaintiff landlord should be prepared to introduce the lease into evidence, and to provide some sort of statement showing what rent was paid, and what rent was not paid. If any security deposit was withheld, the landlord should be prepared to offer substantial and meaningful proof that the withholding of the deposit was warranted. Defendants can use a withheld security deposit to counterclaim against a landlord.

Cases concerning the abandonment of a rental property are more complex. When a tenant abandons a rental property, the tenant may leave six months or more on a lease term. As a landlord, you will be tempted to sue for the entire remaining term of the lease. However, the law may not afford a landlord such a generous remedy. Landlord-tenant law generally requires landlords to actively and meaningfully "mitigate their damages" by seeking out a new tenant. So as a landlord, you need to show that you actively advertised the property, and showed it to potential renters. If the landlord does not demonstrate an active attempt to mitigate his or her damages, the defendant can keep his or her damages very low, despite the defendant's breach of the rental agreement.

Common Cases: Suing on a Bad Check

By one estimate, Americans write one million bad checks a year. A check is a form of promise. A check is a promise that a stated amount of money will be available for delivery to the holder of the check. Few people realize that a bad check can be the basis for a lawsuit. Lawyers call it "suing on the check," or "suing on the draft." Suing on a check is a slam-dunk case for a plaintiff. In addition, some states allow doubled or tripled damages in lawsuits on bad checks. California allows plaintiffs in bad check cases to collect the amount of the check, plus three times the amount of the check, up to an additional $1,500. That law is found in California's Civil Code section 1719. Other states have similar provisions. If you are a plaintiff suing on a draft, you should research additional damages. And, if you're defendant being sued on a draft, you would be wise to make good on the check very promptly.

Common Cases: Dog Bite Cases

Each year aggressive dogs bite over 500,000 Americans, killing an average of twelve. The majority of dog bite victims are children. Most dogs do not exhibit aggressive tendencies; nevertheless, sufficient provocation may tempt even the gentlest dog to bite.

Obviously, one cannot sue a dog. Lawsuits in dog bite cases are brought against dog owners. The first place to start is to research the "bite rule" in your state. About a third of the states follow the traditional English "one-bite" rule. This means that a dog owner is shielded from liability for her animal's first violent episode. After the first bite, however, the owner can be held responsible for all subsequent episodes. However, the dog owner may not be able to shield herself with the one-bite rule if the animal is a breed with natural aggressive tendencies. If you are an owner of an animal with repeated violent tendencies, you may find yourself losing badly in court.

Most states, however, have abandoned the one-bite rule and simply hold an animal's owner responsible for harm. Plaintiffs: before court, determine the breed, and research that breed. If you can, try to determine if the animal has been violent in the past by asking the dog owner's neighbors. Other facts that would be relevant would be if the dog were clearly maintained as a guard dog, or is mistreated or lives outside. These circumstances make dogs more aggressive, and these facts would help a defendant and hurt a plaintiff if they could

be established. Defendants should be prepared to prove that the victim pro-
voked the attack, or was trespassing.

When establishing or attacking claims for medical treatment in a dog bite
case, follow the guidelines outlined earlier in the subsection Common Cases:
Negligence and Automobiles.

Not-So-Common Cases: Libel, Slander, and Defamation

Far less common in small claims court are the family of cases that fall under
the umbrella of reputational damage. These cases are libel, slander, and
defamation of character, also simply called "defamation." Libel is the making
of defamatory statements in a fixed medium, such as a magazine, newspaper,
or on the internet. Slander is the making of defamatory statements by a spoken representation. Defamation is the issuance of a false statement about
another person, which causes that person to suffer harm. The typical elements
of a cause of action for defamation are:

- A false and defamatory statement of fact concerning another. Opinions
  are not statements of fact.
- The unprivileged distribution or expression of the statement to a third
  party.
- If the defamatory matter is of public concern, fault amounting at least
  to negligence on the part of the publisher.
- Some sort of damage to the plaintiff.

First off, some small claims courts do not hear reputational damage cases.
This is a wise policy. You'll need to check Table A-3: Small Claims Court
Summaries for All 50 States in the appendix and research your state's law to
see if your state allows the small claims court to hear cases of this type. If you
are a plaintiff, you might think twice about bringing a defamation case in small
claims court. Determining damage to the plaintiff can be a subjective affair.
There is no receipt to wave in the air and say "this is what this matter has cost
me." The damages tend to be intangible. Remember, small claims courts are
courts that offer "easy liability, low damages." If you've really been harmed,
you should strongly consider taking your case to an upper court.

CHAPTER 4

Procedural Matters

The Statute of Limitations, Jurisdiction, and More

American courts have are procedures for everything. There are procedures for objecting to evidence, there are procedures for where you can sue, when you can sue, who you can sue, who can sue you, and whether you can sue at all. There are procedures for motions, orders, judgments, pleadings (papers filed in the court), service of process, memorandums, executions of judgments, levying property, etc. Our courts are so procedure-intensive that our legal system requires hundreds of thousands of lawyers just to operate.

However, all things are relative, and small claims courts operate according to a simplified set of procedural rules. The procedure in a small claims court will be the minimum necessary to ensure justice. In this chapter, you'll learn about the procedural principles that you must observe if you participate in a small claims case. There are opportunities and responsibilities for both plaintiff and defendant here. Plaintiffs must observe procedural formalities in pursuing their claims, and defendants have the opportunity to point to errors in the plaintiff's observance of procedure to defeat a plaintiff's case.

The Statute of Limitations

All civil claims that arise in small claims court will be subject to some statute of limitations. A statute of limitations is a law that dictates the number of years within which a claim must be brought for liability to attach to a defendant. If a plaintiff waits beyond the expiration of the statute of limitations to bring his claim, the claim is lost forever. Consider also that statutes of limitation will differ from claim to claim. For example, in California, an action for personal injury must be brought within two years of the incident, while an action for damage to personal property must be brought within three years of the incident. If you are involved in a car accident case that is two and a half years old, the plaintiff in the case cannot sue for personal injury damages, only for damages to property. Similarly, in California, actions on contracts must be brought within two years for oral contracts, and four years for written contracts.

Example: Multi-State Claims

John of New York State enters a contract with Julie of California for the immediate sale of valuable baseball cards. The contract is oral, and is entered on January 1, 2005. Julie immediately pays John, but John never delivers the baseball cards. Julie puts the matter off until February 1, 2007. The statute of limitations on oral contracts is two years in California, and six years in New York. Because two years have passed since the breach of contract, Julie can no longer bring her claim in California—she must bring her claim in New York. Now John enjoys a geographical advantage, because in order for Julie to pursue the case, she will have to travel across the country. In addition, John can now argue in New York court that the case should have been brought in California.

Also, statutes of limitation will differ by state. (See Table A-2 in the appendix for a list of the statutes of limitations for every state.) In New York State, actions on contracts must be brought within six years. Most states have a shorter statute of limitations on contracts. If your claim (or a claim against you) is a few years old, you may wish to employ some strategic maneuvers to ensure that your case is heard in a particular state.

When Does the Statute of Limitations Begin to Run?

Generally speaking, the statute of limitations for a particular claim will begin from the time the plaintiff learned of the claim. A plaintiff must file his claim with the court before the expiration of the statute. In negligence and personal injury actions, the statute begins to run from the time the plaintiff learned of the injury. Imagine for a moment a case where a doctor leaves a sponge inside a patient during an operation. The patient may not know the sponge is there for years after the operation. Would it be fair to the patient to have her medical malpractice claims expire before she even knew that a claim existed? Of course not, and that is why the plaintiff must know of the claim before the statute of limitations can begin to run. In contract actions, that means from the time the contract is breached, not from the time the contract is signed. As you might imagine, claims that fall very close to the expiration of the statute of limitations can wind up being argued solely on the fact of when the statute began to run.

The statute of limitations "clock" can sometime be frozen temporarily to protect worthy plaintiffs. This principle is called a "tolling" of the statute of limitations. Tolling statutes, like most laws, differ from state to state. Some general rules have emerged, though. Statutes of limitations will generally be tolled when a plaintiff is serving in the military, is a minor, is declared incompetent, is the subject of a bankruptcy proceeding, etc. When the circumstances that caused the tolling of the statute no longer exist, the statute of limitations starts to run again.

The statute of limitations is a powerful and effective weapon in the defendant's toolbox. As a defendant, you want to scour the facts of your case to determine if you can knock out any of the plaintiff's claims under the statute of limitations.

Subject-Matter Jurisdiction

Subject-matter jurisdiction refers to the authority of a court to hear cases dealing with a particular subject matter. All courts are bound to hear only those cases within their subject-matter jurisdiction. For our purposes, let's begin with the notion that small claims courts are courts of limited subject-matter jurisdiction. First, we've already discussed that small claims courts have jurisdictional monetary limits and cannot grant award in excess of their jurisdictional limits. But small claims courts are also restricted as to the types of claims they can hear.

Subject matter jurisdiction is an area where small claims courts differ greatly from state to state. Some small claims courts cannot hear libel or slander cases. Almost no small claims courts will hear eviction cases. Another common type of case that small claims courts cannot hear are those involving real estate or title to real estate. Some of the limitations on what types of cases small claims courts can hear were covered in Chapter 3.

When evaluating your case, you must make a preliminary determination of whether your case falls within the small claims court's subject-matter jurisdiction. And you'll have to check your local laws, because every state is different. If the small claims court cannot hear your case, you'll need to take your case to an upper court.

Personal Jurisdiction

Personal jurisdiction refers to the ability and authority of a court in a state to have jurisdiction over the parties to a dispute. Personal jurisdiction operates on a state-by-state basis. So if a court in a state has personal jurisdiction over you, the courts in the same state have personal jurisdiction over you. A small claims court, like any court, must have personal jurisdiction over the parties in order to render a decision. The most important concept in understanding personal jurisdiction is that the parties must have some connection to a state in order for a court in that state to have jurisdiction—the legal authority to adjudicate the dispute—over them. In other words, a defendant can't necessarily be sued in Alaska because of a case that happened in Florida. If the parties have never been to Alaska or never done business in Alaska, Alaska courts do not have personal jurisdiction over them.

Issues of personal jurisdiction will always arise when the litigants reside in different states. If you reside in California and you get into a car accident while traveling in Nevada and then return to your home state, you can't assume that you can bring an action in a California court based on that accident. You can, however, bring your action in Nevada because that's where the accident took place. The driver of the car in Nevada that struck your car doesn't necessarily have any connection with California. He or she may never have been to California. As such, the Nevada driver cannot be sued in California because California courts, small claims or otherwise, do not have personal jurisdiction over the Nevada driver.

A court will have personal jurisdiction over the parties to the dispute if any of the following is true:

- if any party resides in the jurisdiction
- the person did business in the jurisdiction because that person is said to have availed themselves of the benefits and protections of the laws of that jurisdiction
- the person owns property in that jurisdiction
- if one or more the parties waive the objections to personal jurisdiction.

In small claims court, if all the parties to the dispute reside in the same state, then personal jurisdiction will never come up as an issue. If, however, the parties to the dispute reside in different states, then personal jurisdiction may arise as an issue. Plaintiffs must consider carefully a defendant's connection to the state before blindly charging ahead. Defendants, on the other hand, have an opportunity to avoid liability if they can successfully argue that personal jurisdiction does not attach to them.

But how does one object to the imposition of personal jurisdiction over them—wouldn't an appearance at court be an admission that the court has authority over the person? The legal device used to contest personal jurisdiction is the "special appearance." A special appearance is an appearance, typically made by one's attorney, to appear in court *solely* for the special purpose of arguing personal jurisdiction.

Venue

Venue is a doctrine that may at first seem closely related to personal jurisdiction. The doctrine of venue asks the question "Is this the proper place to have this case heard?" While personal jurisdiction is a statewide concept, venue is a concept that applies on a county or district basis. Generally, small claims courts will hear cases in the county where an accident happened, where a contract was to be performed, or where one or more of the parties resides. In the appendix, we have included quick summaries of each state's venue rules in Table A-3: Small Claims Court Summaries for All 50 States. If your case is more complex and you think you have a venue issue, you may need to do a little research to make sure the court you have selected is in the proper venue. For defendants, again, here lies an opportunity for you to harness a procedural error that a plaintiff might make.

Attorneys in Small Claims Court

An important procedural consideration is whether attorneys are allowed to represent you in small claims court. Every state differs. Some states allow attorneys to represent anyone, and some states allow attorneys to represent only entities like corporations and limited liability companies. Some states don't allow any attorney representation. California, for example, does not allow attorney representation in small claims court. Understand, however, that a prohibition on attorney representation will not prevent an attorney from representing him or herself. The prohibition is only against attorneys representing others in a traditional attorney-client relationship. Similarly, an attorney who was the sole owner of a corporation or limited liability company would be allowed to appear at a small claims court hearing in California. Understand also that attorneys can appear and serve as witnesses as long as their appearance does not involve any advocacy on behalf of a party.

You may not need an attorney to assist you with your case. Your instincts on this point will probably be correct. For example, if your matter is a collections matter, perhaps you are less likely to need an attorney. However, if your case is a negligence case and you expect fierce opposition on the facts and law, you'll likely benefit from having an attorney present in court. Keep in mind that if you appear in small claims court without an attorney, you are not going to be totally helpless. The judge is not going to let the legal process overwhelm you. The judge's main concern is finding the proper result. If you leave out an important fact the judge will likely ask you about it. We have included a brief description of the attorney representation rule for each state in Table A-3 in the appendix. If in doubt, simply ask the clerk of the court, and they will tell you the local rule.

CHAPTER 5

Demand Letters and Settling Your Case

Some of you may be wondering we when will stop talking about all this procedure and background and get to the meat of the case. The previous four chapters have focused on the analysis, evaluation, and procedure of your case. Such an analysis is indispensable. However, in this chapter, you will begin to go head-to-head with your opponent. You'll learn how to achieve a favorable settlement in your case. Think of settlement as a phase in your litigation. This will be the final phase that you will undertake before taking your case to trial.

There are three primary rules you need to remember when trying to settle your case.

1. Attempting a settlement is always worthwhile.
2. Fruitless settlement discussions should be abandoned immediately.
3. Be prepared to compromise in order to settle.

Strong cases garner the strongest settlements. The same case that would be a slam-dunk trial should be a slam-dunk in the settlement phase. That's why evaluating your case is so important. If your case is well researched and if your evaluation is sound, you will enter the settlement phase with a distinct advantage. Now you may find your opponent to be completely unreasonable at this stage of the litigation. There may be two reasons for this. One, your opponent may simply have an unrealistic assessment of their own case. Or, your opponent may be bluffing or stalling. Many defendants just bluff their way through this stage.

Your goals in this stage are to articulate your case to your opponent, make an offer to your opponent that is favorable to you, and to make your opponent accept the offer.

A Note on Insurance

One or more potential parties to a lawsuit may be insured for damages. It's important not to overlook insurance. For defendants, insurance will pay for a lawyer to defend the claim, as well as pay any liability that a defendant may ultimately owe. Insurance is good news for plaintiffs, too. A plaintiff always wants to reach insured defendants because an insurer will generally pay a successful claim immediately, while an uninsured defendant might be judgment proof, or may not cooperate with judgment collections.

Insurance is, quite simply, a contract that binds an insurance company to indemnify (a fancy word for "protect") a defendant from a specified loss. The most familiar type of insurance to most Americans is automobile insurance. And while nearly every state requires drivers to maintain automobile insurance, a driver must pay his or her insurance premiums in order to maintain insurance coverage. Obviously, some drivers fail to maintain coverage. And so, in automobile cases, defendants should always reach out to their insurance companies when an automobile accident occurs. If the defendant has paid his or her insurance premiums, the insurance company will provide a defense to the claim.

There are other types of insurance that may provide coverage to defendants. One common type of coverage is "commercial general liability," commonly known as "CGL." A commercial general liability policy protects business owners from a wide range of liability, from slip-and-fall cases, to instances to alleged trademark infringement. And some homeowner's insurance policies will protect defendants in residential slip-and-fall cases, and dog bite cases. The insurance policies differ, of course, but as a defendant, you should always take a hard look at your coverage—you may be surprised to find that you are covered.

As a plaintiff, you always want to find out if the defendants have insurance coverage for the underlying claim. Insurance companies have unlimited amounts of money to pay claims and almost never declare bankruptcy, while individual defendants and small businesses can easily present tremendous obstacles during collections. Uninsured defendants might be judgment proof, might declare bankruptcy, or may move away.

How can a plaintiff find out if a defendant is insured? Well, in automobile accident cases, the defendant is obligated to present his or her insurance information to the other parties to the accident. But even if this were not the case, it is in the defendant's interest to present proof of coverage. The plaintiff should simply ask the defendant if he or she is insured for the loss.

In the event the defendant is insured, a plaintiff will simply pursue his claim against the defendant's insurance company. The insurance company will assign an insurance adjuster to manage your claim, and work out a resolution. When dealing with an insurance company, bear in mind that the insurance company may try to reduce the amount of damages that the insurance company has to pay to a plaintiff. In nearly all cases though, a plaintiff will get a better settlement offer from an insurance company than from an uninsured defendant.

Insurance companies are generally required by law to pay fair and reasonable claims that are presented by claimants. Insurance companies are bound by "bad faith" laws that prevent them from making low-ball offers to desperate claimants. Therefore, an insurance company cannot offer a paltry $1,000 to a plaintiff that has just had a $20,000 car destroyed by the act of a defendant.

The Psychology of Litigation

Recall that earlier we discussed the role of litigants. A plaintiff's task is to push a case forward and ultimately bring the defendant to bear. A defendant's job is somewhat easier. All a defendant really needs to do is to evade the plaintiff. Bearing that in mind, it is the plaintiff's task to begin and to pursue a settlement in the case. A plaintiff has to know when his or her case is strong and he or she has to know what a favorable settlement in the case would be. But a plaintiff must also know when a defendant is being unreasonable and when settlement discussions should be abandoned. It's true; some defendants will never settle and must be brought into court.

As a young lawyer, I learned a very important lesson from my interactions with other lawyers. I noticed very quickly that young lawyers argue and shout much more than senior lawyers. I also noticed how utterly ineffective arguing and shouting can be. And then I wondered what all these senior lawyers know that the younger lawyers do not. The answer is simple. Experienced lawyers don't shout and argue because there is no profit in it. As your own lawyer—as you will likely be in your small claims case—you are more likely to be financially successful in the pursuit of your case if you stay calm and polite. On the other hand, if you're rude and threatening, all you will do is strengthen your opponent's resolve. Your task in the pursuit of your case is to achieve the most financially beneficial deal for you. You'll achieve that by making your opponent want to give you that deal. If you force your opponent to make his or her case into a crusade, your opponent will behave much differently. You want your opponent to think, "It's only money." You don't want your opponent to think, "This is the fight of my life." In a sense, it might be helpful to think of a settlement as an event that takes place only after all discord is resolved between plaintiff and defendant.

There was another lesson I learned from interacting with other lawyers: The best lawyers are the lawyers that understand the mind of their opponent.

Understanding the expectations, the motivations, and the resolve of your opponent may be more important than having a slam-dunk case. Let's examine some ways to get into the mind of your opponent.

Finances

You should always consider the financial circumstances of your opponent. This will have a strong impact on how your opponents will behave. Is your opponent wealthy? Is your opponent broke? Wealthy people tend to shrug off small losses. Wealthy people tend not to bother with court. They figure their time is more valuable and they would rather do something else. Some well-off people may actually think small claims court is beneath them. They may feel that it is pedestrian to be in a court arguing over $1,500 in front of a group of strangers. That may be an advantage to you in some circumstances if your opponent is wealthy. On the other hand, a wealthy opponent may simply turn the entire matter over to a lawyer.

Consider the amount in dispute. Wealthy or not, it is easier to make an opponent part with a smaller sum than a larger sum. Consider what will go through an opponent's mind based on the amount that they stand to gain or lose. An opponent may say that he or she is going all the way to court, but beware—your opponent may be bluffing.

If your opponent is not wealthy, the amount in dispute may be significant to them. In that case, they are more likely to give you a fight.

Time

Another significant factor you should always examine when analyzing your opponent is how much free time they have. Opponents with more free time are more likely to be enthusiastic and effective litigants. These opponents will have time to research the case, analyze the case, and appear at hearings. If you don't know your opponent that well it may be hard for you to determine how much free time he or she has. However, you may be able to make some educated guesses based on your observations of your opponent. Look for signs of the overburdened opponent. Does your opponent travel a lot for work? Does your opponent have young children? Is your opponent a single parent? These are all signs of someone who is overburdened. These are the sorts of litigants for whom a trip to court will be an almost insurmountable inconvenience. If your opponent falls into this category, your case may be a good candidate for a very favorable settlement. The opponent you don't want, however, is the opponent with tons of free time. Retired folks tend to fall into this category. People who run small businesses are busy but they often have the flexibility in their schedules to make court appearances.

Education

Another background factor you should analyze if it's possible to do so is the education of your opponent. Educated litigants are more effective. Pursuing any legal claim, either as a plaintiff or defendant, requires research skills, analytical skills, advocacy skills, and public speaking skills. These skills come more easily to a person with a higher level of education.

You must analyze your case as a whole, and try to get within the mind of your opponent. If you can truly understand your opponent, you can better predict what he or she will do.

Drafting the Demand Letter

The device that plaintiffs typically use to begin settlement discussions is what's called a demand letter. A demand letter is just like it sounds; it's a written letter directed to the defendant or defendants outlining the strength of the plaintiff's case and making a demand for the payment of a specific sum of money in exchange for settlement. Lawyers use demand letters all the time.

A plaintiff needs to convey several ideas in a demand letter. One of the most important is to convince the defendant that settling the case is better than going to trial. There are some things you will always say in a demand letter. For example, you will always make a general statement that it is better to settle a case than to spend the expense and time of going to trial. Even if everyone knows it, you should say it anyway; it conveys good faith and a cooperative attitude. A good demand letter should be threatening without being combative—there is a difference—and it should be persuasive.

Drafting a demand letter is a good idea for another reason. Some cases in some courts require that a demand be made before a case is filed with the court. But researching whether a demand is required isn't even worth the effort; it's easier just to send a demand and save a copy of it. Even if the demand isn't required by law, sometimes judges will ask informally if the demand has been made. Judges always like to see that some effort at settlement has been made before coming to court.

Drafting a demand letter is very simple. A demand letter states the following:

- Introduce yourself and outline the parties to the dispute in the opening paragraph.
- Provide a brief summary of the underlying dispute. For example, if the case is a contract case, you should outline the basic terms of the contract. Or if the case is a negligence case, you should outline the basic facts of the incident.
- State your monetary demand in clear terms. You must also state a time frame for the acceptance of the offer.
- Advise your opponent of the actions you'll take if the demand is not accepted.

Now let's put these ideas into to practice and examine and analyze a sample demand letter. The demand letter in Figure 5-1 is very close to an actual demand letter from a contract dispute that I used in my practice. The plaintiff in a contract dispute had performed some software development and the defendant had not paid.

Let's take a look at a few key points from this demand letter. First of all, notice that the person drafting a letter is not the plaintiff; he's the president of a company that is the plaintiff. The letter begins with an introduction and proceeds very quickly to describe the basic facts of the dispute. Here, the con-

> ## Expert Tip
>
> When communicating with an opponent, never say "you might want to get a lawyer to help you with your case" or "you need to get help with this down at the court, they have free help" or anything to that effect. An experienced lawyer would never say such a thing—it amounts to giving good advice to your opponent. You don't want your opponent to have a lawyer; they are more likely to make a mistake if they represent themselves.

FIGURE 5-1. **Sample Demand Letter**

Michael Samuels
731 9th Avenue, Suite E
San Diego, CA 92101
619.501.3825 fax: 419.735.2386

January 15, 2008

Kevin R. Baker
Big Bob's International Inc.
Royal Bank Building, Suite 2000
335 8th Ave. S.W.
New York, New York 10001

VIA U.S. MAIL
RE: Demand for Payment under Professional Services Agreement

Dear Mr. Baker,

As you know, I am president of I-Storm, Inc. ("I-Storm"), and I am writing to you about claims that I-Storm has against your company, Big Bob's International Inc. ("Big Bob's") under the Professional Services Agreement ("Agreement") dated March 17, 2006.

This letter shall serve as our final demand for payments under the Agreement.

Under the terms of the Agreement, I-Storm is entitled to $13,000. Our records show that we have received $8,500. This leaves a remaining balance of $4,500.

Furthermore, I-Storm performed extra work beyond the terms of the Agreement in the form of additional software modules and changes from the specifications outlined in the Agreement ("Overages"). Our invoices show $2,800 in Overages.

With the preceding in mind, we therefore submit the following demand:

1. The remaining balance of $4,500 must be paid within five days of the date of this letter in the name of I-Storm, Inc.

2. With respect to the balance for Overages of $2,800, we will accept $500, also to be paid within five days of the date of this letter in the name of I-Storm, Inc.

3. Upon receiving the full balances due under the Agreement, I-Storm will grant a full license to Big Bob's of all work product under the Agreement.

FIGURE 5-1. **Sample Demand Letter** (continued)

4. You must agree in principle to the terms outlined herein within two days of the date of this letter. Thereafter, I will draft a settlement agreement formalizing these terms before the five-day deadline for payment of the outstanding balances.

This offer is not subject to negotiation, including any arguments that Big Bob's might impose with respect to issues of performance under the Agreement. If you do not accept the offer outlined in this demand in writing within two days of the date of this letter, this offer will be automatically and permanently withdrawn.

Upon the withdrawal of this offer due to your non-acceptance, you are instructed (i) to return to I-Storm all work product under the Agreement, including, but not limited to, all software code, files, documentation, and other materials; (ii) that I-Storm shall terminate the Agreement pursuant to the "Breach and Termination" clause, and pursuant to such clause, all sums under the Agreement shall become due and payable and shall bear 1% interest per month from the date of invoice; and (iii) that I-Storm shall take immediate and permanent steps to ensure that Big Bob's never receive a license to the work product under the Agreement.

Thereafter, we will pursue the case through the court system. It is only fair to warn you that we may report this matter to the credit reporting bureau, and in that event, your credit rating may suffer. You can avoid the time and expense of court by resolving this matter. Our offer is generous, and we sincerely hope you accept it.

I await your response, and sincerely hope that you accept the terms of our demand on behalf of Big Bob's.

Yours truly,

Michael Samuels

President, I-Storm, Inc.

tract is for $13,000 and the defendant has only paid $8,500. In the actual case, the defendant disputed the quality of the work. We don't mention that here. Whether to get into the details of an underlying case is up to you. If you do, keep in mind that you may simply be inviting a response instead of an acceptance. Your goal with a demand letter is to get paid, not to enter a push-pull with your opponent regarding who's at fault. Accusatory statements such as "you breached the contract" or "you messed up this transaction" should never be offered. Even if such statements are true, they aren't going to help you get paid; they'll only inflame the other party.

Another thing to notice about this demand is that it clearly states the amount that must be paid and it clearly states the amount of time the defendant has to accept the offer and to make payment on the settlement.

The demand letter then continues by stating that the offer is not subject to negotiation and will be withdrawn if it is not accepted. This was a clause that I started using in demand letters because I found that quite often defendants would use the settlement phase to simply buy more time. Of course, that wasn't consistent with my goals as a plaintiff's lawyer. My goal was to progress the case as quickly as possible. And so in my demand letters, I tend to use very short timelines for compliance and acceptance. If you are mushy in a demand letter, your defendant will take advantage of it. And if you give a defendant 30 days to consider an offer, he will use all 30 days.

The next paragraph may not be applicable to your case. You might want to include in your demand some statement that interest will accrue on the demand amount. The law may not grant you interest on your claim but the other side may not know that. Finally, you should make some statement to the effect that you'll take the matter to court if it isn't resolved, and an indication that you *may* report the matter to credit reporting agencies. The threat of credit reporting can be a powerful tool. Use this threat wisely; you should never actually make a report to a credit reporting agency without carefully checking the law first. There are serious legal consequences that arise from improper reporting to credit agencies.

Note that this letter doesn't threaten legal action in small claims court although the $5,000 the letter demands is within the jurisdictional limit of most small claims courts. The letter simply says that the case will be pursued through the legal system. Small claims court is not always your greatest threat as a plaintiff. From a defendant's perspective, being sued in an upper court is far more expensive and unpleasant than being sued in small claims court. Small claims court is an advantage to plaintiffs when a plaintiff wants a speedy recovery. So I would tend not to show that card right away; I would keep the defendant guessing about what I was going to do.

The Value Calculation

Settling your case requires you to apply a numerical value your case. Cases have a value to both the plaintiff and the defendant. Of course, the value of a case to a defendant is a negative number. The plaintiff wants to fetch the highest figure possible, while the defendant wants to part with the smallest figure possible to make the case go away. The value of your case will change over time, and will change as circumstances change.

The true value of a legal case is rarely the full amount of the claim—claims are subject to a "litigation discount"—a natural devaluation that erodes the value of a claim that has not yet been brought through the legal system. Even a judgment that is secured following a trial is rarely worth as much as its face value. In fact, judgments are bought and sold in a secondary market and almost never trade for their full face value. Let's use an example to illustrate. Let's say you have a promissory note for $5,000—a slam-dunk case. But in order to win a small claims trial, you'll have to spend five or six hours preparing for the case and appearing at the hearing. Plus, you'll have to wait two or three months to have the case heard. Then you may have difficulty collecting on the judgment. The defendant may move out of state or out of the country. Or if the defendant declares bankruptcy, the full amount of the judgment can be discharged by the bankruptcy court. All these factors work together to devalue even the strongest case. A slam-dunk case for $5,000 even with a defendant that possesses a clear ability to pay might really be worth only $3,500.

Now, if your case is subject to possible defenses or counterclaims, then the value of your case drops even more. And so it's the true value of your case and not the full amount of your claim that should be your settlement value. It might seem frustrating to have to accept a smaller amount than you are due, but cases are compromised all the time. Plaintiffs need to be realistic about what their case is really worth. And defendants have an opportunity to discount their exposure and liability in the settlement phase. Before proceeding with the settlement of your dispute, you need to establish your value calculation. Even though the value calculation may be difficult and subjective, you must attempt to reduce your claim to a numerical value.

Negotiating the Settlement of Your Dispute

Now that you have sent the demand, you may find yourself in the position of evaluating a counter offer. It's fairly rare that a defendant accepts the offer made in a demand letter. It's far more likely that the defendant will make some sort of counter offer. Even if the counter offer is fairly poor, you still have an opportunity to negotiate a better deal.

What If Your Opponent Will Not Negotiate?

In 13 years of law practice, I've seen everything. I've seen opposing litigants fight like cats and dogs and I've also seen opposing litigants completely abandon a worthwhile case and just walk away. I've seen several instances of opposing litigants not bothering to show up for trial. I've also seen opposing litigants simply disappear. You really need to be ready for anything.

In some cases, your opponent will not negotiate. There are usually a few reasons for this. One reason is that your opponent is deluded as to the strength of their case. That's fairly common. When this happens, you should abandon the negotiations. No amount of effort or persuasion will ever sway a deluded opponent; such an opponent you simply need to drag in front of the judge.

Another reason some litigants don't negotiate is because they abandon their cases—the ostrich syndrome. Some folks just give up. If your opponent is the plaintiff and they give up, that means you've won your case. However, it's far more likely that a defendant will abandon a case. Remember that it is the plaintiff's role to pursue the defendant and it is the defendant's role to evade the plaintiff. It's actually quite natural for some defendants to completely ignore the entire case. A defendant that avoids negotiation is an indication of trouble down the road.

Plaintiffs should note that such a defendant is not likely to cooperate with the collection of any judgment a plaintiff might win at trial. We talk about the difficulties and challenges of judgment collection later in this book. When you are facing a defendant that refuses to negotiate, you should cease all negotiations immediately. You are wasting your time; you will never persuade such a defendant to participate in negotiation. You will be forced to pursue this kind of defendant through trial and through judgment collection.

Occasionally, there are plaintiffs that refuse to negotiate. This tends to occur when the plaintiff is outraged by the defendant's conduct. This sense of outrage may be real or perceived. To such litigants, their cases become crusades. Either way, these plaintiffs can be fairly unpleasant to deal with. If you are facing such a plaintiff and you cannot bring them to the negotiating table, you may simply be forced to go to trial. At trial, you might consider mentioning to the judge in your presentation that your opponent refused to negotiate. That fact alone won't win your case but it might color your case more favorably in what is, as we've learned, typically a plaintiff-based court.

Negotiating the Settlement

Negotiating a settlement is like negotiating any other transaction. You have your goals and your opponent has her goals. You need to remember those goals. You need to consider strongly the factors that we ran through in the section on the psychology of litigation. What does your opponent want? You want to get your opponent to a place where he or she will part with their money to make you go away—it's really no more complicated than that. Always remember that discord between litigants yields no monetary benefit. You must dispel any anger your opponent feels. With these things in mind, let's proceed with the steps necessary to negotiate your settlement.

A few days after you've delivered your demand letter, call or visit the defendant and ask if they would consider discussing the case. Ease your opponent into a discussion. Don't jump right in and ask for money; be slow and

Expert Tip: Listen

The best negotiators listen more than they talk. Listening to your opponent lets your opponent blow off steam. Furthermore, you'll learn more about your opponent's position, and you can harness that knowledge to gain the upper hand.

polite and simply offer discussion. If the defendant agrees, you've just taken a step. From there, briefly outline your case and then ask the defendant what he or she thinks. Always give your opponent an opportunity to speak. Ideally, you should let your opponent speak 60 percent of the time. Allowing your opponent to speak should give you several benefits. First, it allows your opponent to simply vent some anger. Let them vent. Don't disagree with each individual point your opponent makes in the discussion. Let your opponent's discussion pass from topic to topic. If your opponent mentions a topic and passes over it, it will then likely be forgotten. By interjecting an argument, you'll only ensure that your opponent remembers and focuses on that point.

When your opponent finishes, ask for permission to address some of the points raised. By asking for permission, you show that you have respect for your opponent, you put them at ease, and you make them feel as if they are in a dominant position. Address your points calmly and without emotion. You should put forth not only the underlying facts of your claim but also ancillary matters such as the inconvenience and expense of going to court. When the conversation progresses naturally to a comfortable and calm juncture, you should then proceed to the nuts and bolts of negotiating.

At no point in your initial discussions should you unilaterally agree to sweeten your offer. You want to nudge your offer up methodically, not impulsively. Try not to use terms like the following: payment, compensation, and money. Use agreeable terms such as resolution, compromise, and agreement. If you have previously submitted a demand letter, you should invite your opponent to counter when the time is right. You can suggest this gently by saying, "if you don't agree with my demand, do you have a suggestion for resolution?" Professional negotiators always try to invite the other side to offer rather than submit an offer themselves. You might be surprised by the offer your opponent makes. If your opponent surprises you with a very appealing offer, do not let on that you expected something less favorable. Say something to the effect of, "well, I was hoping for something more favorable but I am interested in resolution." If it's an offer you want to accept, tell the other party that you accept and shake their hand. Tell them that you will draft a settlement document and send it over in the next day or two. Once you and your opponent shake hands on a settlement, you are about 80 or 90 percent sure to close the deal. Sometimes though, either you or your opponent will back out of the settlement before settlement papers are signed. A settlement is a contract that waives important rights. As such, a settlement is not final until committed to writing.

It's possible that your opponent will initially make a weak offer. If that happens, you have two choices. First, you can negotiate right there on the spot. Always begin by saying that you appreciate the offer. But continue that you can't accept the offer because your losses were substantially more. Then express your interest in resolution and cooperation. Finally, submit a counteroffer. You can repeat this a few times and you'll likely get a sense of whether things are moving in your favor or in the other party's favor. If things are not moving in your direction or if your opponent's offer is completely unreasonable, then you should suspend the negotiations.

You can politely suspend the negotiation by saying, "I'm not sure I can do that. Why don't we talk in a week or so?" Then, after five or seven days, make another offer, sweeter than your first, and submit it to your opponent either on the telephone or in writing. Then begin the negotiation discussion again. Generally, settlement offers improve over time. However, settlements will never go back and forth more than three or four times. In other words, if you don't reach a settlement in the first three or four times, you probably never will.

A settlement is worth pursuing but not at all costs. Never give away everything. You always have your chance in court if you need to take it. If you can't fetch a figure close to the value calculation for your claim you may simply need to take your case to court.

The Settlement Agreement

If you reached a preliminary settlement with your opponent, your next step is to draft and present a settlement agreement. A settlement agreement is a written contract of three pages or so in which the parties agree to waive all claims against each other now and forever in exchange for a monetary payment from one party to another. A settlement agreement is absolutely final—that's the entire point. You must never expect to revive your claim later or have a claim revived against you once the settlement is reached.

The sample settlement in Figure 5-2 is the final memorialization of a settlement agreement between a furniture store and a graphic design service. The party that owes the obligation is called the debtor and the party to whom the obligation is owed is called the creditor.

Let's take a closer look at the settlement agreement and break it down by parts. The first paragraph is called the *recital*. In the recital, the parties reference the underlying agreement and state their names. If you modify this settlement agreement, you will obviously change the names and the date. In the next paragraph, titled "background," the nature of the underlying claim is set forth. In our sample case, the services were graphic design, marketing, and other creative services. In your case, your description will likely be different. For example, if your dispute is regarding a traffic accident you to simply enter, "debtor and creditor were involved in an automobile accident."

Paragraph number one deserves mention. Subparagraph "a." sets forth the settlement compensation, and also requires that the payment be made within 72 hours following the execution of the agreement. If the payment is not made according to the terms of the settlement agreement, the settlement agreement will be invalid even if it is signed by both parties.

The remainder of the settlement agreement is fairly self-explanatory. It makes clear that no further payments are required by any party and that the settlement is absolutely final with respect to all claims now and forever. It sets out that no party is admitting fault and that no party can later make a claim against the other for someone unforeseen or unknown claim. Finally, note that in paragraph 10 the agreement is to be governed according to California law and that any dispute over the settlement will be heard solely by arbitration in Marin County California. Naturally, you'll want to change those locations to your home county and state.

FIGURE 5-2. **Sample Settlement and Compromise Agreement**

MUTUAL RELEASE AND WAIVER AGREEMENT

THIS MUTUAL WAIVER AGREEMENT AND MUTUAL RELEASE ("Agreement") is entered into as of March ____, 2008, by and between Muirfield Furniture Company, Inc. ("Debtor") and Elizabeth Berkey, d/b/a Berkey Design ("Creditor") (collectively "Parties or Party"). For the purposes of the Agreement, "Party" includes subsidiaries and parents of a Party and includes owners as well as individuals serving as directors, officers, employees, agents, consultants, and advisors to or of a Party.

A. BACKGROUND

1. Debtor and Creditor entered into an agreement or series of agreements (the "Contract") whereby creditor provided graphic design, marketing, and other creative services to debtor.

2. Since the time of entering into the Contract, the Parties have determined that a settlement of the mutual obligations between them is appropriate and would best serve the interests of all of the Parties, and this Agreement is intended to express the Parties' intent to equitably settle the obligations arising from or related to the Contract.

B. AGREEMENT

NOW, THEREFORE, IN CONSIDERATION OF THE FOLLOWING, THE FOREGOING, THE MUTUAL COVENANTS, PROMISES, AGREEMENTS, REPRESENTATIONS, AND RELEASES CONTAINED HEREIN, AND IN EXCHANGE FOR OTHER GOOD AND VALUABLE CONSIDERATION, THE RECEIPT, SUFFICIENCY, AND ADEQUACY OF WHICH IS HEREBY ACKNOWLEDGED, THE PARTIES HEREBY AGREE AS FOLLOWS:

1. Payment to Creditor.

a. Debtor shall pay $4,000.00 to Creditor, such payment to be made no later than 72 hours following the execution of this Agreement. Payment under this paragraph is a precondition to the effectiveness of this Agreement.

b. Debtor shall owe no further liability or obligation to Creditor in connection with any services.

2. No other Payments. No additional funds shall be required to be paid or transferred by Creditor to Debtor, or by Debtor to Creditor.

3. Nature and Effect of Agreement and Conditions Thereon. By executing this Agreement, the Parties intend to and do hereby extinguish the obligations heretofore existing between them and arising from the Contract.

4. Admissions. This Agreement is not, and shall not be treated as, an admission of liability by either Party for any purpose, and shall not be admissible as evidence before any tribunal or court.

5. Release and Discharge. The Parties hereby compromise and settle any and all past, present, or future claims, demands, obligations, or causes of action for compensatory or punitive damages, costs, losses, expenses, and compensation whether based on tort, contract, or other theories of recovery, which the Parties have or which may later accrue to or be acquired by one Party against the other, the other's predecessors and successor in interest, heirs, and assigns, past, present, and future officers, directors, shareholders, agents, employees, parent and subsidiary organizations, affiliates, and partners, arising from the subject matter of the Contract.

6. Unknown Claims. The Parties acknowledge and agree that upon execution of the release, this Agreement applies to all claims for damages or losses either Party may have against the other whether those damages or losses are known or unknown, foreseen or unforeseen.

[Note: the remainder of Paragraph 6 is only for use in the State of California]

In the event that this Agreement is deemed executed in California, the Parties thereby waive application of California Civil Code Section 1542.

The Parties certify that each has read the following provisions of California Civil Code Section 1542:

"A general release does not extend to claims which the Debtor does not know or suspect to exist in his favor at the time of executing the release, which if known by him must have materially affected his settlement with the debtor."

The Parties understand and acknowledge that the significance and consequence of this waiver of California Civil Code Section 1542 is that even if one Party should eventually suffer additional damages arising out of the facts referred to in Section A, above, it will not be able to make any claim for these damages. Furthermore, the Parties acknowledge that they intend these consequences even as to claims for damages that may exist as of the date of this release but which the damaged or harmed Party does not know exists, and which, if known, would materially affect that Party's decision to execute this release, regardless of whether the damaged Party's lack of knowledge is the result of ignorance, oversight, error, negligence, or any other cause.

7. Conditions of Execution. Each Party acknowledges and warrants that its execution of this compromise agreement and release is free and voluntary. All Parties and signatories to this Agreement acknowledge and agree that the terms of this Agreement are contractual and not mere recital, and all Parties and signatories represent and warrant that they have carefully read this Agreement, have fully reviewed its provisions with their attorneys, and know and understand its contents. It is understood and agreed by all Parties and signatories to this Agreement that execution of this Agreement may affect rights and liabilities of substantial extent and degree and with the full understanding of that fact, they represent that the covenants and releases provided for in this Agreement are in their respective best interests.

8. Entire Agreement. This Agreement constitutes the entire agreement between the Parties and signatories and all prior and contemporaneous conversation, negotiations, possible and alleged agreements, and representations, covenants, and warranties, express or implied, or written, with respect to the subject matter hereof, are waived, merged herein, and superseded hereby. There are no other agreements, representations, covenants, or warranties not set forth herein. The terms of this Agreement may not be contradicted by evidence of any prior or contemporaneous agreement. The Parties further intend and agree that this Agreement constitutes the complete and exclusive statement of its terms and that no extrinsic evidence whatsoever may be introduced in any judicial or arbitration proceeding, if any, involving this Agreement. No part of this Agreement may be amended or modified in any way unless such amendment or modification is expressed in writing signed by all Parties to this Agreement.

9. Counterparts. This Agreement may be executed in multiple counterparts, each of which shall be deemed an original but all of which together shall constitute one and the same instrument. When all of the Parties and signatories have executed any copy hereof, such execution shall constitute the execution of this Agreement, whereupon it shall become effective.

10. Governing Law. THIS AGREEMENT WILL BE GOVERNED AND CONSTRUED IN ACCORDANCE WITH THE LAW OF THE STATE OF CALIFORNIA AND THE UNITED STATES OF AMERICA, WITHOUT REGARD TO CONFLICT OF LAW PRINCIPLES. This Agreement shall not be strictly construed against any Party to this Agreement. Any controversy or claim arising out of or relating to this Agreement, or the breach thereof, shall be resolved by arbitration administered under the rules of the American Arbitration Association in accordance with its applicable rules. Such arbitration shall take place within Marin County, California, and shall be binding upon all Parties, and any judgment upon or any an award rendered by the arbitrator may be entered in any court having jurisdiction thereof.

IN WITNESS WHEREOF, the Parties and signatories execute this Agreement on the dates indicated.

Muirfield Furniture Company, Inc., Debtor:

_____

Donald LeBuhn, President

Elizabeth Berkey/Berkey Design, Creditor:

_____

Elizabeth Berkey

When the time comes to sign the settlement papers, present them to your opponent with your signature already affixed. Your opponent is more likely to sign the papers if you have already affixed your signature. Both parties should retain one original, so you should prepare two copies. If you are the plaintiff in the settlement, it's good idea to have pre-arranged payment to be delivered at the time the appointment was set for the execution of the agreement. Although the settlement papers are drafted to be conditional on payment, you still would not want to sign unless you have received payment.

Once you have payment, or have given payment, and both parties have executed the settlement agreement, your dispute is resolved and final. Unless one or more parties reached a settlement agreement, you should file a settlement agreement away and forget about the matter.

Figure 5-3 shows a demand letter for an amount due following a bounced check.

FIGURE 5-3. **Sample Demand Letter For Bad Check**

Michael Samuels
731 9th Avenue, Suite E
San Diego, CA 92101
619.501.3825
fax: 419.735.2386

January 15, 2008

Kevin R. Baker
Big Bob's International Inc.
Royal Bank Building, Suite 2000
335 8th Ave. S.W.
New York, New York 10001

VIA U.S. MAIL
RE: Demand for Payment on Check No. 1102

Dear Mr. Baker,

As you know, I am president of I-Storm, Inc. ("I-Storm"), and I am writing to you about claims that I-Storm has against your company, Big Bob's International Inc. ("Big Bob's") for a bad check that Big Bob's made payable to I-Storm (the "Draft") dated March 17, 2006 in the amount of $450.

Unless full payment of the check is received by cash within 30 days after the date this demand letter was mailed, together with $____ in bank fees [write amount charged by your bank to process the bad check], and $_____, the cost of mailing this demand letter by certified mail, we will file a court case against you.

The claim will also request damages for the amount of the check, $450, plus $1,350 damages assessed at three times the amount of the check [calculated by starting with a minimum penalty of $100 up to a maximum penalty of $1,500, under California Civil Code section 1719], for a total claim of $1,800 against you.

It is only fair to warn you that we may report this matter to the credit reporting bureau, and that that event, your credit rating may suffer. You can avoid the time and expense of court by resolving this matter now. Our offer is generous, and we sincerely hope you accept it.

I await your response, and sincerely hope that you accept the terms of our demand on behalf of Big Bob's.

Yours truly,

Michael Samuels

President, I-Storm, Inc.

Who Can Sue and Who Can Be Sued

At the beginning of Chapter 5, we learned that settlement is a phase in litigation. Chapter 6 will begin the next phase, which is the preparation of a case for small claims trial. We will begin at the very beginning: Who is the proper party to a lawsuit? The proper party is one of the most slippery concepts in litigation. The concept is deceptively complex.

A proper party analysis is complex because of statutes regarding the proper party and because of complexity in the law of business organizations.

When a Business Organization Sues or Is Sued

A business organization such as a corporation, limited liability company, or partnership is a separate legal entity in the eyes of law. If you are wronged by a business entity, you cannot simply bring a lawsuit against the shareholders or the officers or directors of that entity. Similarly, if you are wrong by an individual, you can't simply bring a lawsuit against a corporation that that individual owns. The shareholder didn't necessarily wrong you and the shareholder is legally separate from the entity. Corporations and limited liability companies shield their shareholders from liability for the acts of the entity. Partnerships, on the other hand, do not shield their shareholders from liability for the act of the partnership. Now, you may have a claim against one or more shareholders, you may have a claim against the entity itself, or you may have a claim against both. Whom you can sue depends on the facts of your case and upon the nature of the entity involved.

To determine who the proper party to a lawsuit is you must ask, "Who was the actor?" For example, in a breach of contract case, the actor is the person or entity who undertook the contract. If you have a written contract the actor will be the person who executed the contract. If your dispute follows an automobile accident, the actor can be more than one person. The actor can be the driver of the car or the owner of a car who negligently entrusted the car to the driver. It could be a person who negligently served alcohol to the driver of the car. It can even be a policeman who negligently ignored the erratic driving that the driver displayed. In lawsuits, there are always obvious actors and then there are less obvious actors. To extend a lawsuit to a larger class of parties, you may be forced to research your claim.

There are a couple general principles you want to follow as a plaintiff in a proper party analysis to make your case as strong as possible.

First, when you bring a lawsuit, you want to have as many defendants as possible. The more defendants you have, the greater the likelihood that you'll collect on a judgment. If one defendant is insolvent, you'll simply pursue the judgment against another defendant. Also, you have a greater likelihood of making your argument for liability "stick" to someone if you have more defendants in the courtroom.

Secondly, when you bring a lawsuit, you want to have as many individual defendants (individual persons, not corporations or LLCs) as possible. From a plaintiff's perspective, judgments against individuals are far more preferable to judgments against corporations and limited liability companies. It is more difficult to enforce a judgment against a corporation or a limited liability company. Corporations and limited liability companies tend not to accumulate large amounts of assets such as savings accounts and real estate. And because these entities shield their owners from personal liability, a judgment against a corporation or limited liability company has very little consequence to its owners. Also, a corporation or limited liability company does not necessarily have or care about its credit rating. However, all individuals care about their credit rating to some degree. For these reasons, you always want to find and pursue individual defendants if you can.

If the Plaintiff Sues the Wrong Party

In the section just above, we discussed adding additional defendants to your complaint if possible. But you need to be careful not to include wholly innocent parties as defendants. The judge will not look favorably upon you if you include innocent parties as defendants without any basis whatsoever. And if you sue the wrong party, you will not obtain a judgment against that party. You want to be aggressive about including additional defendants without being reckless. Let's examine some guidelines to follow.

First, recall that you learned to frame a lawsuit in terms of a specific legal claim. A specific legal claim can only extend to specific legal parties. Examine your claim or claims in that light. For example, a claim for breach of contract is a claim against a contracting party. If ABC Construction Company contracted to build you a fence but its workers performed poorly, the workers did not breach the contract, ABC Construction Company breached the contract, and they are your sole defendant.

If we change the facts slightly though, you may find it possible to include additional defendants. If ABC is a corporation whose charter has been revoked at the state level for failure to pay taxes, then ABC can hardly enjoy the right to shield its owners and managers from liability. In that case, you could include

ABC's owners as defendants. If ABC is a partnership, then ABC cannot shield its owners from personal liability for ABC's actions. In that case, you can and should include ABC's owners as defendants.

The following checklist will help you determine when it's acceptable to include additional defendants in your claim, and how to bring suit against the proper party:

- When a defendant is a partnership, you can include as defendants all owners of the partnership.
- In a contract case, you can include as defendants any party that contracted with you.
- In order to sue a subcontractor or other party with whom you do not have a direct contractual relationship, it may be possible to sue that party under a *quantum meruit*, or unjust enrichment, theory. Under this theory, a subcontractor who was paid but did not perform services can be forced to disgorge the sum they received because they would be otherwise unjustly enriched.
- Negligence cases generally allow for the inclusion of a wider class of defendants. For example, in a car accident, the driver may be guilty of negligence as well as anyone who negligently entrusted the driver with the car.
- In a dog bite case, you would include as defendants all adult members of the household where the dog resides.
- In a case where the defendant is a minor, you would name the minor as a defendant as well as the minor's parents.

The following checklist will help you determine when it is not acceptable to include additional defendants in your claim:

- When a defendant is a corporation or limited liability company, you cannot include as defendants owners of the company when the company is the principal actor in your claim.
- You cannot bring a breach of contract claim against a subcontractor, except as described above.

- You cannot sue the spouse or other family members of a principal actor simply because of the family relationship.
- Don't include a party as a defendant simply because you want that party to appear at the trial to testify. You will compel that party to testify at the trial by subpoena, which we will cover later.

Minors, Estates of the Deceased, and Government Agencies

Minors can be parties to lawsuits, both as plaintiffs and as defendants. However, because of their age, a *guardian ad litem* may be required to represent the minor's interests. A parent can serve as a *guardian ad litem* for a child.

A suit can be brought on behalf of or against a deceased person. Such suits are brought by or against the estate of the deceased person. Suing the estate of a deceased person can be tricky; you'll need to research the issue.

Some small claims courts will have very specific rules about how to sue a government agency or entity. In fact, some small claims courts will not allow lawsuits to be brought against a government agency. Furthermore, in California, an administrative claim must be filed against a government agency before being filed in any court. If your case involves a claim against a government agency or entity, will need to research the issue carefully.

CHAPTER 7

Filing (and Answering) the Complaint

Your lawsuit officially begins when you prepare and deliver to the small claims clerk a small claims complaint. A complaint is a legal document in which you state the names of the parties, the nature of the claim, and a request for relief. All lawsuits begin with the filing of the complaint, from small claims cases to cases in America's highest courts. A small claims complaint is far more informal and far more forgiving than a complaint in an upper court civil action. A lawsuit is officially begun when the clerk of the small claims court accepts a complaint for filing. These days most complaints are available in fill-in-the-blank forms. You can obtain these forms either by visiting the court or in some cases online.

Defendants, you should always keep in mind that your property, your house, your wages, and your bank accounts cannot be taken by a plaintiff until legal process is followed. Generally, a plaintiff must proceed through a lawsuit, and bring that lawsuit to a judgment—a final resolution and determination of a court—before a defendant's property can be taken.

Drafting the Complaint

Drafting a complaint is actually one of the easier tasks you'll undertake as a plaintiff in your small claims case. If you are a defendant, you would obviously not prepare a complaint; you would be the person upon whom the complaint would be served. Because you have already researched your case, analyzed your parties and venue, and framed your case in terms of specific causes of action, the drafting of the complaint is simply committing what you already know to writing.

Small claims forms are generally pre-prepared and nearly complete; you simply need to fill in a few blanks with some basic facts about your action. Let's examine Figure 7-1, which is a California small claims complaint. This is the document that a plaintiff would file with a small claims court to begin a case. Note that in California, the complaint is titled "claim and order to go to small claims court." California recently revised its form for 2007. The California form (Figure 7-1) is a model of simplicity and clarity and will serve as an excellent illustration of how to complete a small claims complaint. Let's break it down step-by-step.

The California small claims form is divided into numbered sections. In Section 1, the plaintiff simply inserts his or her name and contact information. Note that there is a second line for additional plaintiffs. Any legal case can have more than one plaintiff. For example, if you and three family members were traveling in a car and were struck by a reckless driver, all four of you would be potential plaintiffs. A plaintiff should also be sure to list the names of all plaintiffs on the line at the top left. Leave the box in the upper right that

FIGURE 7-1. **Sample Small Claims Complaint Form, California**

		Case Number:

Plaintiff *(list names)*: _____

(1) **The Plaintiff (the person, business, or public entity that is suing) is:**

Name: _____ Phone: (___) _____

Street address: _____
                  Street   *City*   *State*   *Zip*

Mailing address *(if different):* _____
                           Street   *City*   *State*   *Zip*

If more than one Plaintiff, list next Plaintiff here:

Name: _____ Phone: (___) _____

Street address: _____
                  Street   *City*   *State*   *Zip*

Mailing address *(if different):* _____
                           Street   *City*   *State*   *Zip*

☐ *Check here if more than 2 Plaintiffs and attach Form SC-100A.*

☐ *Check here if either Plaintiff listed above is doing business under a fictitious name. If so, attach Form SC-103.*

(2) **The Defendant (the person, business, or public entity being sued) is:**

Name: _____ Phone: (___) _____

Street address: _____
                  Street   *City*   *State*   *Zip*

Mailing address *(if different):* _____
                           Street   *City*   *State*   *Zip*

If more than one Defendant, list next Defendant here:

Name: _____ Phone: (___) _____

Street address: _____
                  Street   *City*   *State*   *Zip*

Mailing address *(if different):* _____
                           Street   *City*   *State*   *Zip*

☐ *Check here if more than 2 Defendants and attach Form SC-100A.*

☐ *Check here if any Defendant is on active military duty, and write his or her name here:* _____

(3) **The Plaintiff claims the Defendant owes $ _____. *(Explain below):***

a. Why does the Defendant owe the Plaintiff money? _____

_____

_____

b. When did this happen? *(Date):* _____

If no specific date, give the time period: *Date started:* _____ *Through:* _____

c. How did you calculate the money owed to you? *(Do not include court costs or fees for service.)* _____

_____

☐ *Check here if you need more space. Attach one sheet of paper or Form MC-031 and write "SC-100, Item 3" at the top.*

FIGURE 7-1. **Sample Small Claims Complaint Form, California** (continued)

Case Number: _____

Plaintiff *(list names):* _____

④ **You must ask the Defendant (in person, in writing, or by phone) to pay you before you sue. Have you done this?** ☐ Yes ☐ No
If no, explain why not: _____
_____

⑤ **Why are you filing your claim at this courthouse?**
This courthouse covers the area *(check the one that applies):*

a. ☐ (1) Where the Defendant lives or does business.   (4) Where a contract (written or spoken) was made,
(2) Where the Plaintiff's property was damaged.   signed, performed, or broken by the Defendant *or*
(3) Where the Plaintiff was injured.   where the Defendant lived or did business when
                                                                        the Defendant made the contract.

b. ☐ Where the buyer or lessee signed the contract, lives now, or lived when the contract was made, if this claim is about an offer or contract for personal, family, or household goods, services, or loans. *(Code Civ. Proc., § 395(b).)*

c. ☐ Where the buyer signed the contract, lives now, or lived when the contract was made, if this claim is about a retail installment contract (like a credit card). *(Civil Code, § 1812.10.)*

d. ☐ Where the buyer signed the contract, lives now, or lived when the contract was made, or where the vehicle is permanently garaged, if this claim is about a vehicle finance sale. *(Civil Code, § 2984.4.)*

e. ☐ Other *(specify):* _____

⑥ **List the zip code of the place checked in ⑤ above** *(if you know):* _____

⑦ **Is your claim about an attorney-client fee dispute?** ☐ Yes ☐ No
If yes, and if you have had arbitration, fill out Form SC-101, attach it to this form, and check here: ☐

⑧ **Are you suing a public entity?** ☐ Yes ☐ No
If yes, you must file a written claim with the entity first. ☐ A claim was filed on *(date):* _____
If the public entity denies your claim or does not answer within the time allowed by law, you can file this form.

⑨ **Have you filed more than 12 other small claims within the last 12 months in California?**
☐ Yes ☐ No   *If yes, the filing fee for this case will be higher.*

⑩ I understand that by filing a claim in small claims court, I have no right to appeal this claim.

⑪ I have not filed, and understand that I cannot file, more than two small claims cases for more than $2,500 in California during this calendar year.

I declare, under penalty of perjury under California State law, that the information above and on any attachments to this form is true and correct.

Date: _____   ▶ _____
   Plaintiff types or prints name here   *Plaintiff signs here*

Date: _____   ▶ _____
   Second Plaintiff types or prints name here   *Second Plaintiff signs here*

Requests for Accommodations
Assistive listening systems, computer-assisted, real-time captioning, or sign language interpreter services are available if you ask at least 5 days before the trial. Contact the clerk's office for Form MC-410, *Request for Accommodations by Persons With Disabilities and Order. (Civil Code, § 54.8.)*

Revised January 1, 2007

**Plaintiff's Claim and ORDER
to Go to Small Claims Court**
(Small Claims)

SC-100, Page 3 of 5
→

indicates the case number blank; the clerk of the court will assign a case number upon the filing of the case.

In Section 2 of the small claims form the plaintiff inserts the name and contact information of the defendants. This form contains room to include two defendants. If you wish to include additional defendants, you would need to attach form SC-100A (not shown) and list the additional defendants on that form.

In Section 3, the plaintiff will outline the specific claim for which he or she seeks relief. California makes it very easy. The plaintiff simply includes the amount of the debt and why the defendant owes a debt to the plaintiff. On the line corresponding to "Why does the defendant owe the plaintiff money?" you would simply describe your claim. For example, "the defendant borrowed money and did not pay it back." Or, "the defendant struck my car while I was stopped at a stop light. I suffered damage to my car and back injuries." You need not include any information beyond that. Since pleading in small claims court is very informal, you do not need to use the terms "negligence" or "breach of contract." A plaintiff merely needs to state the basic facts of his or her claim and the judge will determine which specific cause of action is applicable to the case. In some higher courts, legal pleadings must be made with far greater specificity.

Section 4 highlights an idea that we discussed earlier. This section inquires whether the plaintiff has made a demand upon the defendant for the amount due. In California, and in some other states, plaintiffs are legally required to make a demand before dragging a defendant into court. Regardless of whether a demand is legally required, it is always a good idea to make a demand before going to court. A plaintiff that does not make a demand before filing the complaint creates an opportunity for the defendant to either knock out the plaintiff's claim or to curry favor with the judge.

Section 5 requires the plaintiff to designate the proper venue for the case. We discussed venue at length earlier. The choices available in "a" through "d" mirror California's venue law. The venue choices in paragraph "a" are the most common: A plaintiff can bring a case where the defendant lives or does business, where the plaintiff's property was damaged, where the plaintiff was injured, or were a contract was made, signed, performed, or breached. Paragraphs "b" through "d" are venue rules for specific transactions such as household goods and loans, retail installment contracts, or vehicle finance sales. Paragraph "e" lets a plaintiff specify an independent basis for venue. That's risky. Without research, a plaintiff would never know if the venue choice was proper. Without a proper basis for venue, the defendant can have the case dismissed. The plaintiff would then be forced to re-file in a county where venue is proper.

Section 6 asks for the zip code of the location set forth in Section 5; the phrase "if you know" indicates that this entry is optional. Generally speaking, I would tend not to give optional information. Offering optional information may simply provide further meat for the defendant to bite into. For example, if the plaintiff were to get the zip code wrong, a defendant could pick at that fact, thereby undermining the plaintiff's chief arguments.

Section 7 is solely for plaintiffs who are attorneys suing their clients. Attorneys that wish to initiate attorney-client fee disputes must first take their cases to arbitration. California passed this law to protect clients from aggressive attorney collection practices. If you're not an attorney, simply check the "no" box.

Section 8 is intended for plaintiffs to bring claims against public entities such as police departments, schools, and public hospitals, and city, county, and state governments. In California, claims against public entities must be made directly to the public entity for administrative resolution first before being brought into court.

Section 9 draws upon a California specific law. California has attempted to curtail abuses of the legal system by slightly penalizing plaintiffs that file more than 12 small claims courts cases in any one-year period. Section 10 is simply a warning to plaintiffs that they do not have the right to appeal a small claims decision. Similarly,

Expert Tip

Claims against government entities in California must be made by filing a written claim with the public entity within six months of the date of the harm to the plaintiff. This rule overrides all other statute of limitations rules. Many plaintiffs have lost their claims due to ignorance of this provision.

Section 11 is a warning to plaintiffs that they cannot file more than two small claims cases for more than $2,500 in a calendar year.

What follows is what lawyers call a "perjury declaration." The perjury declaration deserves discussion. Perjury is a serious crime; perjury is the act of lying or making verifiably false statements on a material matter under oath or affirmation in a court of law or in a written sworn statements. Lying to a friend isn't perjury; to commit perjury, one must be making a statement under the cover of a perjury declaration or perjury oath. President Bill Clinton was charged with perjury because of allegedly false statements that he made under oath during a deposition. He was ultimately acquitted of those charges. More recently, Scooter Libby, former aide to Vice President Dick Cheney and assistant to President George W. Bush, was convicted of two counts of perjury along with other offenses in connection with the Valerie Plame affair. The statements you make in your complaint as well as the statements you make in the small claims hearing are made under oath. As such, false statements can trigger the crime of perjury. You must never make a false statement in a small claims complaint or before the judge in a small claims hearing.

For the sake of comparison, take a look at the small claims form for Michigan (Figure 7-2). We chose this state at random as, obviously, we cannot cover the drafting of the complaint in all 50 states in this book. However, you can find links to small claims court forms by going to the author's web site, LearnAboutLaw.com, and following the links for "research."

If you examine Figure 7-2, you'll notice many similarities between the Michigan complaint form and the California complaint form. For example, the complaint begins with a description of the parties, both plaintiff and defendant. The complaint also requires the plaintiff to set forth the amount of money claimed, as well as the reasons for the claim. As you can see, the drafting of a small claims complaint is not a complicated matter. These two sample small claims complaint forms are fairly representative of what you'll find in any of the 50 states.

FIGURE 7-2. **Sample Small Claims Complaint Form, Michigan**

Approved, SCAO	Original - Court 1st copy - Defendant	2nd copy - Plaintiff 3rd copy - Return
STATE OF MICHIGAN **JUDICIAL DISTRICT**	**AFFIDAVIT AND CLAIM** **Small Claims**	**CASE NO.**

Court address   Court telephone no.

See instructions on the back of plaintiff and defendant copies

1. _____
   Plaintiff

   _____
   Address

   _____
   City, state, zip   Telephone no.

2. _____
   Defendant

   _____
   Address

   _____
   City, state, zip   Telephone no.

NOTICE OF HEARING

For Court Use Only

15. Plaintiff and defendant must be in court on

_____   _____
Day   Date

at _____ at ❑ the court address above
     Time

❑ _____
Location

_____ Fee paid: $ _____
Process server's name

3. I have knowledge or belief about all the facts stated in this affidavit and I am:
   (check one)   ❑ the plaintiff.   ❑ a partner.   ❑ a full-time employee of the plaintiff.
4. The plaintiff is: (check one)   ❑ an individual   ❑ a partnership   ❑ a corporation   ❑ a sole proprietor
5. The defendant is: (check one)   ❑ an individual   ❑ a partnership   ❑ a corporation   ❑ a sole proprietor

6. Date(s) claim arose: _____

7. Amount of money claimed: $_____ (NOTE: Plaintiff's costs are determined by the court and awarded as appropriate. They are not part of the amount claimed.)

❑ 8. A civil action between these parties or other parties arising out of the transaction or occurrence alleged in this complaint

     has been previously filed in _____ Court. The case number, if known, is:_____
     The action   ❑ remains   ❑ is no longer   pending.

9. Reasons for claim: _____

    _____

    _____

10. The plaintiff understands and accepts that the claim is limited to $3,000.00 by law and that the plaintiff gives up the rights to:
    (a) recover more than this limit, (b) an attorney, (c) a jury trial, and (d) appeal the judge's decision.

11. I believe the defendant ❑ is ❑ is not mentally incompetent. I believe the defendant ❑ is ❑ is not 18 years or older.

12. ❑ I do not know whether the defendant is in the military service. ❑ The defendant is not in the military service.
    ❑ The defendant is in the military service.

13. _____
    Signature

Subscribed and sworn to before me on _____ , _____ County, Michigan.

My commission expires: _____   Signature: _____
              Date   Deputy clerk/Notary public

Notary public, State of Michigan, County of _____

14. **Expiration date:** _____

DC 84 (6/05) **AFFIDAVIT AND CLAIM, Small Claims**   MCL 600.8401 et seq., MCR 4.302, MCR 4.303

Filing the Complaint

After you have prepared your complaint, review it for accuracy. Be sure to double check any dates you may have included. An incorrect date can affect the validity of your claim. When you are ready to file the complaint, you'll bring the original complaint to the small claims office in the county where you want to file your case. The court clerk may require that you bring several extra copies. This will differ from state to state, but to be safe, bring four extra copies. The clerk will stamp one copy for you with the date of filing and you'll keep that copy for your files. You'll also need a copy upon which you will serve the defendant, but we'll discuss that further below.

The court will require you to pay a filing fee when you file your complaint. The filing fee will range from $15-$70. We have not included filing fees in the state-by-state reference tables because they change so frequently. As you might imagine, filing fees tend to creep upward from year to year. If necessary, you may be able, in some states, to file an affidavit or motion *in forma pauperis*, which will allow you to proceed without paying a filing fee. Check with the court clerk to see it such a filing is available. Generally, *in forma pauperis* motions and affidavits tend to be rather lengthy and invasive; you will be required to submit very detailed information about your assets and financial condition.

When filing your case, you can go to the court clerk yourself or send someone in your place, such as an employee or a legal filing service. You can find legal filing services in the phone book or in an internet service directory. The legal filing services are convenient because you can generally fax the papers to the legal filing service and they take care of everything. If you've never filed a small claims case before, I recommend you file the case yourself. This gives you the opportunity to learn about the procedure and the opportunity to speak to the court clerks and a small claims advisor if your state has one available.

You have one important choice to make when you file your complaint: the date and time for the hearing. A small number of courts choose these for you, but most courts will allow a plaintiff to select the date and time for the hearing when they file a complaint. There are a few factors to keep in mind. First, you need to make sure that you leave enough time to serve the defendant with notice of the lawsuit; the defendant is entitled to a fair amount of advance notice before the hearing date. Obviously, it would not be fair to serve a defendant on a Tuesday night for a hearing on the following Wednesday or Thursday morning. The amount of notice to which a defendant is entitled will depend on state law. Notice statutes generally give a defendant between 20 and 30 days of notice before appearance at a small claims hearing. Service and notice are serious matters. If either service or notice fails, the defendant can later reverse any judgment that the plaintiff wins at trial.

If you have the opportunity to pick the hearing date and time, you have an opportunity to strategize to your advantage. Ideally, you may wish to pick a hearing date and time that is the least convenient for the defendant. If you are fortunate enough to know the defendant's schedule, you have the option of choosing a hearing date for which the defendant can only attend with some difficulty. Keep in mind though, that court dates can be changed; if the defendant truly can't make the hearing, he or she can change the date.

Once you have filed your complaint, you're now a plaintiff in an active lawsuit. Your next step is to make "service of process" upon the defendant. Service of process, more familiarly known as "service," is a legal term that refers to the procedure employed to give legal notice to a defendant of a court case concerning a person. Service of process is covered in the following chapter.

Drafting the (Usually Optional) Answer

An "answer" is a formal written response to a complaint that is filed in a lawsuit. The complaint, the answer, and the other filings made in the course of a lawsuit are collectively referred to as "pleadings." In upper civil courts, pleadings are naturally more complex. Small claims courts have almost no pleadings; generally, the only pleading that is filed is the complaint. In upper civil courts, a defendant who fails to file an answer will lose his case by default. Only some small claims courts, such as Vermont and Arkansas, require that a written answer be filed.

If you are served with a copy of the complaint in the small claims action, you first must determine if you are required to file an answer. You should read the entire complaint and all the pages attached to it. A written answer is required in a minority of states. You will need to work quickly; the written answer will carry a filing deadline of between 15 and 30 days after you are served. The complaint that is served upon you will most likely describe any requirement that a written answer be filed. If the complaint is not clear about whether a written answer is required or not, you must call the court to resolve the question. The small claims answer will be a preprinted form on which you will enter a few pieces of information. The answer will likely be a single page. The small claims court will have forms available for you, or the form should be available on the internet. You can deliver the form to the court in person or by mail.

> **Warning**
>
> If you are a defendant and you have received notice that you are being sued, you must immediately determine if you're required to file a written answer. A written answer is not required in all states, but if it is required and you fail to file it, you will lose your case.

While a written answer will be required in a minority of states, in most states a written answer is optional. That raises the question of whether it's advisable to submit an answer when it is optional. There are a few advantages to filing an answer. First, it announces your presence in the case, so if something were to happen to you that caused you to miss the hearing, you could possibly point to the answer when asking the judge to forgive your absence and give you a new hearing. Second, it announces to the plaintiff that you are participating and that you're serious about winning. If your case still has a hope of settling, you should absolutely file the answer.

If filing an answer is optional the disadvantage to filing one is that the answer may serve to educate the plaintiff as to your theory of the case. If I were defendant, I would prefer to go into the hearing with my opponent knowing as little as possible about my side of the case. Whether or not to file an optional answer can be a tough call and will depend on the specific facts and circumstances of your case.

The Defendant's Blunt Weapon: The Counterclaim

A defendant has a very powerful tool in his or her arsenal: the counterclaim. A counterclaim is just as it sounds; it is a claim by the defendant against the plaintiff that is filed and served following the plaintiff's original claim. The counterclaim must be written and must be filed with the court and served on the plaintiff—one cannot raise a counterclaim orally at the hearing if no counterclaim filing was made. Once a counterclaim is raised, the plaintiff becomes both plaintiff and defendant, and the defendant becomes both defendant and plaintiff. A counterclaim can also include additional parties that were not defendants in the underlying claim.

> **Definition: Counterclaim**
>
> A counterclaim is just as it sounds: it is a claim by the defendant against the plaintiff that is filed and served following the plaintiff's original claim.

A counterclaim differs from an ordinary claim in several respects. First, a counterclaim is merged with the underlying claim; both claim and counterclaim bear the same case number and are heard at the same hearing. Thus, the cases will be heard by the same judge and according to the same evidence. Second, counterclaims are usually "linked"—they are dependent upon their underlying claims. Such counterclaims are said to be "compulsory" counterclaims. A defendant may lose the right to *ever* bring her compulsory counterclaim unless she brings it as a counterclaim to the specific underlying claim brought by the plaintiff. A counterclaim tends to be compulsory if it involves only the parties currently part of the underlying suit, and arises from the same transaction or event of the underlying suit. In other words, if the counterclaim is closely related to the underlying claim, the counterclaim is compulsory and the two claims *must* be heard together. The reasoning behind making counterclaims compulsory is to conserve judicial resources; the court won't have to hear the same case twice.

There is a third reason why counterclaims differ from ordinary claims. A claim and a counterclaim will be reduced to one judgment. A counterclaim, if successful, will be subtracted from the underlying judgment, thereby reducing the total amount of the underlying judgment. That is fundamentally different from having two independent judgments. Two independent judgments must be collected independently; one judgment might not be collectible due to the insolvency of one of the defendants while the other judgment would be collectible. This would hardly be fair to the litigant with an uncollectible judgment.

Some counterclaims are "permissive." A permissive counterclaim is one that may be brought but yields no waiver of rights if it is not brought. Permissive counterclaims are claims that arise independently from the transaction of the underlying claim. The common example given in law schools to illustrate a permissive counterclaim is the "negligent creditor." Here's how it plays out: John owes Mary $1,000 on a business debt. Mary negligently strikes John's car while driving. John has a claim against Mary for the car accident, and Mary has a claim against John for the debt. The transactions are unrelated, so the counterclaim is permissive and not compulsory. The counterclaim can be brought either as a wholly independent claim or as a counterclaim. This flexibility may help the defendant's legal strategy. The defendant may have the case heard in another court at a different time. In fact, all of the questions of statutes of limitations, personal jurisdiction, venue, parties, and jurisdictional limits are evaluated independently if the permissive counterclaim is brought as a separate action in a separate court.

Counterclaims are common in car accidents and contract disputes. Contract disputes yield counterclaims when both parties can usually make some assertion that the opposing party was first to breach. Car accidents yield counterclaims when both drivers can make a reasonable argument that the accident was the fault of the other driver.

An important warning that plaintiffs must always consider is that once a plaintiff brings a claim, the risk of drawing a claim in the form of a counterclaim goes up tremendously. Consider it for a moment. When a defendant is served with a lawsuit, he or she is already obligated to appear in court, to take time from work, to testify, to

> **A counterclaim is different from an ordinary claim because:**
>
> 1) A counterclaim is merged with the underlying claim
> 2) Counterclaims are usually "linked"—they are dependent upon their underlying claims.
> 3) A claim and a counterclaim will be reduced to one judgment.

bear the risk of paying a judgment, etc. Two dynamics come into play. First, the defendant likely intends to appear in court anyway. Adding a counterclaim is simply a matter of inserting a few lines on a blank counterclaim form and maybe adding some testimony at the hearing. In other words, the convenience threshold for a counterclaim is very low. The second dynamic is the more important one. When a defendant is served with a lawsuit—small claims or otherwise—he or she will experience a range of emotions. Those emotions will likely be a volatile mix of anger, fear, and desire for revenge. The defendant will want to strike back as well as minimize their exposure to liability. A counterclaim is an easy way to answer these concerns.

Of course, a defendant must have a sufficient claim in order to be successful. If you are a defendant and you wish to bring a counterclaim, first you must obtain a blank counterclaim form. You can get this form from the court clerk or sometimes on the internet. When evaluating a counterclaim, you need not consider jurisdiction or venue. If the court has jurisdiction over the underlying claim and venue is proper, than jurisdiction and venue are presumed for the counterclaim. There is another strategic consideration. If a counterclaim exceeds the jurisdictional limit of the small claims court, then the entire matter, both counterclaim and underlying claim, will likely be transferred out of the small claims court and to an upper court. Thus, a counterclaim presents a tactical opportunity to thwart the plaintiff's choice of court.

Finally, always bear in mind that a counterclaim must be properly filed with the court and must be served on all opposing parties to the counterclaim.

CHAPTER 8

Giving Notice to Your Opponent

Serving the Complaint

In civil court cases, litigants have rights. Arguably, the most important right is the right to notice of legal claims being brought against oneself. Notice of legal claims, motions, and other legal pleadings is the responsibility of the party making the claim or motion. A plaintiff has an important responsibility to make service of process upon all defendants to a lawsuit. Similarly, if the defendant files an answer or counterclaim, he or she must make service of process upon all the other litigants. Service of process, sometimes called simply "service," is the procedure by which important court pleadings are delivered to other parties to a lawsuit. Service must be accomplished by delivering written court documents to parties; service cannot be accomplished orally.

Service of process must be accomplished for initial pleadings such as complaints and counterclaims. Once opposing litigants already have received service of process, they are presumed to have notice of the suit, subsequent notice may simply be made by mail. Service of process is a complex legal discipline in itself. There are thousands of cases and millions of hours of litigation that have addressed when service is property accomplished and when it is not. Service must be made properly for a lawsuit to proceed. If service is not made properly, a defendant can attack a judgment months or years after it is entered and have a case thrown out.

Ways to Accomplish Service of Process

There are several means by which service can be accomplished:
- personal service
- substituted service
- service by mail
- voluntary acceptance of service
- by agency
- service by publication

Personal service is most common and is least likely to be challenged by a defendant. Personal service is accomplished by physically placing the legal documents in the possession of the person to be served. Personal service is usually accomplished by a process server that a plaintiff hires for that purpose. Generally, a person to whom personal service is directed cannot refuse service. If a defendant refuses service, or attempts to refuse service, the process server will simply drop the papers on the ground and say "you are served." A process server must be an adult and in most jurisdictions cannot be a party to the litigation. A process server can be, but need not be, a professional process server. Some jurisdictions impose licensing requirements upon professional process servers. If you wish to make personal service upon an opponent, you can hire a neighbor, friend, or relative as long as the person you choose is not a party to the lawsuit. In some jurisdictions, personal service can be made by a court official, such as a sheriff, marshal, constable, or bailiff. You can find a helpful summary of service of process rules in the appendix. You should always check with the court for specific information about service of process.

A variation of personal service is "substituted service." Substituted service is, as it sounds, a way to make personal service upon a party by serving a substitute party, such as a designated agent, another adult in the recipient's home, or the recipient's manager at work. California, Illinois, and many other U.S. jurisdictions require that substituted service be buttressed by mailing a copy of the papers to the target of the service. Substituted service often requires that the process server make some showing that personal service could not be made. Again, you'll need to check with the court to determine the specific rules for substituted service.

Service by mail can be used in some jurisdictions. Service by mail often requires that the process server make some showing that personal service could not be made. Typically, service by mail requires certified mail with return receipt. Service by mail is inexpensive, but also can be ineffective. Service by mail is more easily challenged by a defendant as improper notice. Furthermore, some defendants will simply refuse to accept the service which will delay a plaintiff's case.

Service can also be accomplished by a voluntary acceptance of service. A voluntary acceptance of service is a waiver given by the defendant, and memorialized in a written acceptance of service whereby the defendant agrees to accept service and waive any objections to the manner in which service was made. In order to effect a voluntary acceptance of service, you'll need to have some cooperation with the defendant. You will need to secure from the defendant a written acceptance of service. The form of acceptance of service will vary from state to state. Most defendants tend not to offer their cooperation when they are being sued. As a plaintiff, it might be

> ### Expert Tip
>
> Experienced lawyers choose personal service by professional process servers. Personal service may cost $25-$75, but it is the most reliable manner of service for serving individual defendants. Also, professional process servers will usually file proof of the service with the court as part of their service.

> **Expert Tip:**
> **Never Voluntarily**
> **Accept Service**
>
> Litigation is a tough business. I advise defendants never to voluntarily accept service—the rights involved are too important to just give away. Defendants should always insist that service be made upon them according to law.

worth an attempt to ask a defendant if he or she will accept voluntary service but do not be surprised if he or she refuses.

Service can be accomplished in some circumstances by serving an agent for acceptance of service. An "agent for acceptance of service" or "registered agent" is a person or company pre-authorized to accept service on behalf of a business entity. Most corporations and limited liability companies are required by state law to have an agent for acceptance of service in each jurisdiction in which they are active. The identity of a registered agent can usually be determined from company filings made with the secretary of state. As of the writing of this book, almost every secretary of state's office in the U.S. has made their corporation and limited liability company database available to the public on the internet. Service upon a corporation or limited liability company is thus quite easy. Service upon a registered agent is as simple as sending a process server to the secretary of state's office.

Finally, service of process can be made by publication. This form of service is called "service by publication," and is usually accomplished by printing a notice in the newspaper. You may have seen such legal notices buried in the back of the classified ads in your hometown newspaper. The problem with service by publication is that a defendant is extremely unlikely to ever receive notice of the suit. As such, cases served by publication are routinely overturned by the defendant at a later date. Because service by publication is so often found to be ineffective, it may only be used as a last resort. Furthermore, in states that allow service by publication, a plaintiff will generally need to demonstrate repeated and meaningful failed attempts at personal service, and secure an order from a court allowing service by publication. Essentially, service by publication is only available when the defendant has disappeared. So, a defendant that is served by publication is not likely a defendant from whom a judgment will ever be collected.

After Service: Filing the Return of Service

A "return of service" is a written declaration by a process server, executed under penalty of perjury, in which the process server states the manner in which service was made upon a litigant. The return of service is the "proof" that a defendant was served. The return of service must be filed with the court, because the judge will need to see evidence that the defendant was served properly and with enough advance notice before she or he will enter a judgment against a defendant. If you hire a professional process server to serve your complaint, the drafting and filing of the return of service will likely be included in the process server's tasks. If you hire a friend or relative to perform the service, then you likely need to assist them with the execution and filing of the return of service.

Figure 8-1 shows a fairly representative sample of a return of service. The form is fairly easy to complete. To complete a return of service, do the following:

- Insert the title of the case. Cases are titled "last name v. last name," as in *Smith v. Jones.*
- Fill in the date. The date is the date upon which the return of service is filled out and signed.
- The server must provide their full legal name. A server must be an individual; a server cannot be a corporation or other entity.
- The server must indicate the manner of service, i.e., personal service, substituted service, etc.
- The server must execute the document under penalty of perjury.
- Finally, file the return of service with the court.

Can a Defendant Refuse or Avoid Service?

Defendants often avoid or refuse to accept service of process upon them. The most common example of a defendant avoiding service is the defendant who simply refuses to come to the door of their home. Generally, personal service is not legally effective unless the service is truly "personal"—which means the

FIGURE 8-1. **Sample Small Claims Return of Service**

✎AO 440 (Rev. 10/93) Summons in a Civil Action

RETURN OF SERVICE

Service of the Summons and complaint was made by me[1]	DATE
NAME OF SERVER *(PRINT)*	TITLE

Check one box below to indicate appropriate method of service

☐ Served personally upon the defendant. Place where served: _____

☐ Left copies thereof at the defendant's dwelling house or usual place of abode with a person of suitable age and discretion then residing therein.

Name of person with whom the summons and complaint were left: _____

☐ Returned unexecuted: _____

☐ Other (specify): _____

STATEMENT OF SERVICE FEES

TRAVEL	SERVICES	TOTAL

DECLARATION OF SERVER

I declare under penalty of perjury under the laws of the United States of America that the foregoing information contained in the Return of Service and Statement of Service Fees is true and correct.

Executed on _____   _____
　　　　　　　　　Date　　　　　　　　　　　Signature of Server

_____
Address of Server

(1) As to who may serve a summons see Rule 4 of the Federal Rules of Civil Procedure.

documents must be placed into the hands of the defendant. Process servers have been known to leave legal documents on the front door, or even throw legal documents through a window, if they see a defendant hiding inside a home. Another common way defendants avoid service is by refusing to accept service by mail. In some states, a defendant is presumed to be served even if the defendant refuses to accept the service.

A note to defendants: refusing service works only temporarily. Ultimately, all defendants are served. In fact, a defendant who refuses service risks being served by a less reliable method such as service by mail or service by publication. Thus, a defendant who is dodging service may ultimately be served in a manner that gives him or her no notice of the suit. It is very rare that a defendant succeeds in a case by avoiding service. It is far more likely that a defendant who avoids service will ultimately lose their case by default.

CHAPTER 9

Subpoenas, Witnesses, and Evidence

A fter the small claims case begins with a filing of the complaint, the plaintiff and the defendant must begin to prepare for the small claims hearing. Preparation for the hearing naturally requires the accumulation and preparation of evidence. Evidence can be either written evidence in possession of the parties, or oral testimony by the parties. Evidence will also include written evidence in the possession of outside witnesses, or the oral testimony of outside witnesses. Less likely, but still possible, is demonstrative evidence, such as physical objects, models, videotapes, and audiotapes.

When preparing your evidence, keep in mind the following:

- Your oral presentation must remain brief. If you take a long time to present your case, you are likely to be cut short.
- Evidence is governed by rules. Some evidence is not allowed to be heard in court, such as hearsay statements, highly prejudicial statements, and malicious non-relevant statements (e.g., "the defendant is not even in this country legally").
- If you require an outside witness to testify, you may have to compel that witness to testify.

This chapter outlines the ways to obtain and use various forms of evidence. You must use your evidence (and challenge the evidence of the opposing party) effectively to be effective in court. The evidentiary rules and lessons in this chapter apply equally to the defendant and plaintiff.

What Is Evidence?

Evidence is testimony, documents, material objects, or other tangible objects or things that are legally admissible in court to prove the existence or nonexistence of a fact. Your testimony is evidence; your testimony helps establish the facts surrounding the event or events that are the subject of a lawsuit. Your receipt showing money you spent on car repairs following a fender-bender is evidence that you suffered a financial loss.

The underlying fact must have something to do with your case; the judge will not be happy if you attempt to prove unrelated facts. Your evidence should ultimately tell a complete story. Your story must prove liability in the underlying cause of action, monetary or other damages you have suffered, and your attempts to settle the case. Work with evidence in the following order:

- First, you gather evidence. You will collect your papers and information, and then speak to other witnesses and gather evidence from them.
- Then, you organize and analyze your evidence.
- Then, you must share your documentary evidence with the opposing party. Usually, this occurs just minutes before the small claims hearing.
- Finally, you present your evidence at the trial.

Evidence in Your Possession

You likely already have evidence in your possession. You may have copies of a contract between the opposing party and you. You may have photographs of your car following a car accident. When preparing a case, you should gather all your evidence and determine what is relevant to your case and what is not relevant. You must always endeavor to bring economy to your presentation because the judge will have several cases to hear before and after yours. Remember back to your analysis of claims and how every claim has elements that must be proven; that analysis will serve as an excellent guide to what you will need to show at trial.

You cannot prevent the opposing party from eventually seeing the documentary evidence in your possession. If you wish to present it at trial, the opposing party has a right to see it. Before the small claims trial, the judge or court bailiff will instruct all parties to exchange written evidence with each other. Your oral testimony, however, is a different matter. The opposing party will have no opportunity to know what you and your witnesses will testify to at trial. Obviously, you will not have the opportunity to know what the opposing party and his or her witnesses will testify to either.

The evidence in your possession, supported by your oral testimony, may be all the evidence that you need to present a comprehensive and effective case. You will need to evaluate how complete of a story your evidence will tell. And don't forget, you must not only tell your own story but you must counter the story the opposing parties will tell.

Oral Testimony of Outside Witnesses

Depending on your case, you may find it necessary to seek the testimony of an outside witness. For example, if your case is an automobile accident, you may find it helpful to have witnesses to the accident testifying on your behalf. There are two ways to obtain the testimony of outside witnesses at your trial: You may ask them to voluntarily appear, or you may compel them to appear by subpoena.

Voluntary Witness

In small claims court, many witnesses appear voluntarily. Close friends or employees generally can and do appear voluntarily to testify in small claims hearings. However, a police officer or other government official generally will not appear voluntarily. Asking a witness to appear voluntarily requires no subpoena or other legal process; you are simply asking the witness to appear as a favor.

The problem with voluntary witnesses arises when they don't show up. If a voluntary witness fails to appear at the trial, the judge will likely direct that the case go forward anyway. However, if a subpoenaed witness fails to appear at the trial, the judge will likely postpone the hearing until the subpoenaed witness appears. Now, it may be possible that the judge will postpone the hearing if a voluntary witness fails to appear—but you can't count on it, it'll be up to the judge.

An advantage to a voluntary witness is that they are generally friendlier to your cause then witnesses that are compelled to appear; no one loves getting a subpoena, even for a civil case. But a disadvantage to voluntary witnesses such as employees, family members, and friends is that they tend to be biased in favor of the person known to them. As such, judges tend to weigh such testimony with that in mind.

Subpoenas

A subpoena is a written command to a witness to appear at a time and place to give testimony. It is the device by which a party to a lawsuit compels the appearance of a third party at a small claims trial. A variation of a subpoena is a *subpoena duces tecum*, which is a written command to produce tangible evidence (usually documents) for use at a hearing or trial. We'll discuss *subpoena duces tecum* in the section just following.

A word of warning: The law and the forms used for subpoenas vary greatly from state to state. A subpoena is an ancient concept, one that traces back well into the history of the Roman Empire. The legal doctrines that the states currently employ surrounding subpoenas are as old as the states themselves. As such, many of the states developed quirks and idiosyncrasies about subpoenas over their long histories. So expect to do some research and obtain some assistance if you are going to use a subpoena. But issuing a subpoena is not rocket science; attorneys and parties to lawsuits issue subpoenas every day.

First, we need to clarify to whom subpoenas can be issued. You do not issue a subpoena to an opposing party. The opposing party is already compelled to appear at the hearing because he or she is a named party; they don't need to be compelled twice. A subpoena is used to compel the appearance of third parties. Of course, the target of the subpoena must have information relative to the case. It is not proper or ethical to overuse the subpoena power. If you wish to issue subpoenas to parties that are not relevant to the case or to harass or threaten people, the judge will not be pleased.

How to Issue a Subpoena

Subpoenas are issued in two ways, depending on the state. Typically, subpoenas are issued by a court clerk in the name of the court or of the judge presiding over the case for which the witness will testify. In some states, an attorney for a party can issue a subpoena in his or her capacity as an officer of the court. For our purposes, you may expect that any subpoena you issue must be approved by the court clerk.

Figure 9-1 shows a fairly representative form of subpoena from Connecticut. We'll use this form to illustrate how to prepare, issue, and serve a subpoena effectively.

Note that the Connecticut subpoena form has checkboxes near the top for "judicial district," and "small claims area." This form can be used in small claims as well as in Superior Court. Some states will have a subpoena for all courts, and some states will have a subpoena for use only in small claims court. The court clerk will have blank subpoena forms available to you. Be sure to get the correct form if your state is one that has separate forms for each court.

To prepare the subpoena, enter the name of the case and the docket number on the top line. The court clerk will have issued the docket number when the case was filed. Select the box that says "small claims area," if appropriate, and enter the address of court. On the next line, enter the name of the witness. Then, in the gray box you would enter the time and place where the wit-

FIGURE 9-1. **Sample Subpoena Form, Connecticut**

SUBPOENA/CIVIL
JD-CL-43 Rev. 3-06
C.G.S. § 52-143, 52-144
Pr. Bk. Secs. 7-19, 24-22

STATE OF CONNECTICUT
SUPERIOR COURT
www.jud.ct.gov

INSTRUCTIONS: *Do NOT use this subpoena if the witness is being summoned by the state or by the attorney general or an assistant attorney general or by any public defender or assistant public defender acting in his/her official capacity.*

COURT USE ONLY
SUBISSU

NAME OF CASE	DOCKET NO.

☐ Judicial District ☐ Housing Session ☐ G.A. No. _____ ☐ Small Claims Area | ADDRESS OF COURT *(No., street and town)*

TO: *(Name and address)*

DATE AND TIME YOU ARE TO APPEAR	TIME	. m.	REPORT TO	☐ CLERK'S OFFICE ☐ COURTROOM NO. _____ ☐ PERSON REQUESTING SUBPOENA

BY AUTHORITY OF THE STATE OF CONNECTICUT, you are hereby commanded to appear before the Superior Court in session at the above address on the date indicated above or to such day thereafter and within sixty days hereof on which the action named above is legally to be tried, to testify what you know in said action pending in the court.

YOU ARE FURTHER COMMANDED TO BRING WITH YOU AND PRODUCE:

HEREOF FAIL NOT, UNDER PENALTY OF THE LAW.
To any proper officer or indifferent person to serve and return.

NAME OF PERSON REQUESTING SUBPOENA	TELEPHONE NO.

SIGNED *(Clerk, Commissioner of Superior Court)*	ON *(Date)*	AT

NOTICE TO THE PERSON SUMMONED

You must report to the court at the time and address shown above and remain until this case is disposed of and you are discharged by the court. Present this subpoena when you report.

If you do not appear in court on the day and at the time stated, or on the day and at the time to which your appearance may have been postponed or continued by order of an officer of the court, and one day's attendance and traveling fees have been tendered to you, the court may order that you be arrested. In addition, if the aforementioned fees have been paid to you and you fail to appear and testify, without reasonable excuse, you shall be fined not more than twenty-five dollars and pay all damages to the aggrieved party. **The party requesting the subpoena is responsible for paying the witness fees.**

Any questions regarding this subpoena should be directed to the person who requested it.

RETURN OF SERVICE

JUDICIAL DISTRICT OF	DATE
ss. _____, Connecticut	

Then and there I made service of the within subpoena not less than eighteen hours prior to the time designated for the person summoned to appear, by reading the same in the presence and hearing/leaving a true and attested copy hereof in the hands/at the last usual place of abode of each of the within-named persons, viz:

FEES
COPY
ENDORSEMENT
SERVICE
TRAVEL *(Show miles & amount)*

ATTEST *(Signature of proper officer or indifferent person)*	TITLE *(If applicable)*	TOTAL

DISTRIBUTION: ORIGINAL - Court   COPY1 - Witness   COPY2 - File

RESET   PRINT

ness must appear. Finally, in the bottom section, enter your name as the "name that a person requesting subpoena" and your telephone number.

The next section that begins with "you are further commanded to bring with you and produce" is used only when you are compelling the witness to bring documents and things in their possession. We will discuss the related concept of compelling the production of things (duces tecum) in the next section. For now, we'll focus on compelling on the witness' oral testimony.

When you have completed the subpoena, you must bring it to the court clerk to be signed. Once the court clerk signs the subpoena, it becomes legally effective. The subpoena form in your state will likely bear a very close resemblance to the Connecticut form in Figure 9-1. Once the subpoena is prepared and approved by the court clerk, you are ready to serve the subpoena on the witness.

Serving the Subpoena

Recall our discussion of service of process. Remember that when a person is made a party to a lawsuit, that person has a right to notice of a lawsuit. Similarly, a witness has a right to notice that they are being compelled to appear and give trial testimony. The witness receives notice of the subpoena through service of process. The process of serving a subpoena is much like serving a complaint, but with a few differences.

Don't serve the original of a subpoena unless you are absolutely certain that you are legally required to. Generally, you serve a copy of the subpoena upon the witness. The original subpoena is typically returned to the court along with a proof of service—just like the proof of service of a complaint—and we will discuss proof of service in the next section. Service of a subpoena is generally made by personal service. Recall that personal service is the most reliable and least challengeable method of service available. If possible, use personal service to serve your subpoena.

Who Can Serve a Subpoena

Not everyone can serve a subpoena. First, there are age limits; usually anyone 18 or older can serve a subpoena. Depending on the state, a plaintiff or defendant in the underlying cause of action may be empowered to serve a subpoena. For example, California allows parties to a lawsuit to serve subpoenas. Some states, however, forbid a party to a lawsuit from serving a subpoena on a witness in that lawsuit. There may be alternative methods of service available; the availability of alternative methods, such as certified mail, will depend on the state.

Serving a subpoena is done in the same manner as serving a complaint. The process server simply identifies the witness by visiting them at home or at work, and then presents the witness with the subpoena papers and states "you are served."

Returning the Proof of Service and Witness Fees

The final step is simple: returning the proof of service to the court. The proof of service, sometimes called "return of service," is a simple declaration made by the process server that he or she made effective service of the subpoena upon the witness. The return of service is generally delivered to the court clerk with the original subpoena. If we turn back to the Connecticut subpoena form, we can see that the return of service is a brief section on the bottom of the subpoena form. When the return of service and original subpoena are returned to the court clerk, the clerk will place a copy of the file. Then on the day of your hearing, the judge will have the return of service in his or her possession. This will serve as proof to the judge that the witness was properly subpoenaed.

Witness Fees

You'll need to check with the court clerk about witness fees. Nonparty witnesses are generally entitled to witness fees for their appearance. The fees differ, but generally witnesses are entitled to some flat fee and a mileage calculation based on the travel they must make to the court. The statutes granting witness fees, though, are so hopelessly outdated that the witness fees amount to almost nothing. In some states, the fees are as little as $5 or $10. Don't forget to pay your witness fees; the failure to do so can render the subpoena legally ineffective. Check with the court clerk, they will know the amount of the witness fees. Pay the witness fees directly to the witness, in cash, at the time the subpoena is served, or soon thereafter, but in any case well before the appearance. Make sure you have a record of your witness fee payment.

Written Evidence in the Possession of Outside Witnesses

In the previous section, we discussed how to compel the appearance of a non-party witness at your small claims hearing. In this section, we will discuss a related concept—how to compel the production of documents from a non-party witness. Recall that a subpoena compels a person to personally appear and a subpoena duces tecum compels a person to deliver documents and things. In nearly all cases, the form for subpoena duces tecum will either be an extra section or box within the subpoena form itself, or an attachment to the subpoena form.

As an example, we will again use the Connecticut subpoena form in Figure 9-1. Recall that the Connecticut subpoena form has a section that begins with "you are further commanded to bring with you and produce…" That's the section of the subpoena that gives a party the power to compel the production of documents and things by issuing a subpoena duces tecum. The party preparing the subpoena simply must include on the form a complete and accurate description of the documents and other evidence that he or she is seeking. Of course, the documents and evidence sought should be described with clarity and some degree of precision. Again, the documents must be relevant to the lawsuit, and the subpoena should never be used as a tool of intimidation or harassment.

Enter your description of documents to be produced in the section with the heading "you are further commanded to bring with you and produce." Here are some examples of how to properly phrase a description:

- All written communications, such as letters, notes, faxes, e-mails, etc., between yourself and John Wilson or Wilson enterprises.
- All documents including, invoices, communications, notes, statements, purchase orders, photographs, drawings, etc., related to service you performed on Mr. John Wilson's damaged pickup truck in 2007.

- All records, incident reports, police reports, notes, photographs, etc., in the possession of the San Bernardino police department relevant to the automobile accident that took place at Main Street and Bernardino Avenue on September 7, 2007, at 2:05 p.m. between two automobiles driven by John Wilson and Mark Woodruff.

The preceding examples should give you a fairly clear sense of how to draft a description of documents to be produced. Generally, you want to specify specific dates and specific persons. If you don't deliver your description with a fair degree of certainty and clarity, the witness may fail to produce the documents. The procedure for preparing a subpoena *duces tecum* is the same as for preparing a traditional subpoena. First, you'll need to bring the

---

Objecting to a Subpoena

There are many circumstances under which a party or witness can object to a subpoena. A subpoena is really nothing more than a request for evidence—and evidence is subject to exclusions based on many factors. The most common evidentiary objections to a subpoena are the following:

- that the subpoena is overly broad, burdensome, and oppressive

- that the subpoena is vague, i.e. "the request for information is so vague as to leave the witness unable to determine the relevant information being sought"

- that the information sought is a communication between an attorney and his or her client, and is thus subject to attorney/client privilege

- that the information sought is a communication between a husband and wife, and is thus subject to the marital privilege

- that the information sought requires the formation of a legal conclusion in determining what documents may or may not be required

- if the party being subpoenaed is outside the jurisdiction of the court (in another state), the subpoena has no effect.

---

subpoena *duces tecum* to the court clerk, serve the subpoena, and make a return of service to the court.

After the subpoena *duces tecum* is served on the party, the party is legally bound (subject to the witness' right to object to the subpoena) to produce the documents described. The manner of the delivery of the documents is between you and the witness. For example, if you are seeking documents only but do not require the witness to give any oral testimony, then you shouldn't care whether the witness appears at the trial or not; you simply want the witness to deliver the documents. So even though the subpoena *duces tecum* gives you the right to compel the witness to appear in court with the documents, you may be better off just getting the documents before the trial. To accomplish this, simply contact the witness and ask the witness if he or she would prefer to deliver the documents to you before the trial rather than appearing at the trial. Nine times out of ten, a witness will prefer not to go to court. Most subpoena *duces tecums* are resolved informally and do not result in the witness actually appearing in person to deliver the documents.

When a Witness Disobeys a Subpoena

When a witness disobeys a subpoena, it may require you to take some action to delay your trial and compel the witness to appear or to produce documents. First of all, a subpoena is a demand to a person to appear, but a legal demand does not automatically mean that the witness will comply. Witnesses routinely ignore subpoenas. Furthermore, there may be genuine procedural problems with the manner in which your subpoena is issued or served. For example, a subpoena extends only as far as the state line of the state where the court sits. You can issue a subpoena to an out-of-state person, but the out-of-state person is not legally bound to comply.

Courts use the term "recalcitrant" to describe disobedient witnesses. If you are facing a recalcitrant witness, you have a few choices. Compelling the testimony requires some work; you may wish to consider moving forward without a witness's testimony. The degree to which your case relies upon that witness' testimony will depend on your specific case. If your case can proceed without the witness's testimony, then you need to do nothing. Simply ignore the witness and appear at the hearing. If you choose to proceed without the evidence, tell the judge. During your presentation, say "Your Honor, I issued a subpoena for some documents to Mr. Wilson at Ace Auto Service, but he didn't comply. I believe those documents would help my case, but rather than compel the documents, I'd rather move forward today." The theory behind letting the judge know that you have a recalcitrant witness is that it may sway the judge slightly to your side of the facts.

The other alternative when faced with a recalcitrant witness is to ask the judge to compel the testimony. A subpoena is a demand by court to take some action. In the absence of a valid objection to a subpoena, compliance is mandatory. As such, judges do not look favorably upon disobedient witnesses. First, though, you need to seek a continuance of your hearing. Generally, you won't know whether your witness will comply with the subpoena until the day of the hearing. When any party, plaintiff, or defendant has to face a small claims trial with a handicap of a recalcitrant witness, a judge will almost always allow a continuance in order to obtain the witness' testimony. Typically, when a party to a small claims suit faces this problem, the judge will order a continuance of about 30 to 45 days so that the party who issued the subpoena and the witness can try to work out the dispute. If, ultimately, the recalcitrant witness does not comply, you can ask the judge to compel the witness by court order. Hopefully, your witnesses will honor the subpoenas you issue. Disputes with witnesses are time-consuming, frustrating, and often unproductive.

Analyzing and Organizing Your Evidence

Small claims courts offer speedy proceedings. You may have as little as five minutes to make your presentation. Generally, litigants in small claims actions complain of having too little time to make a presentation. At the very least, all litigants in small claims courts must expect to be pressured to make the leanest presentation possible. To do that, you may need to filter out some evidence that isn't truly relevant. You want to organize your evidence into four categories.

1) *Core evidence.* This is the evidence is absolutely imperative to your claim. An example of core evidence would be the contract at the heart of a contract dispute, or a copy of a check that you made as a down payment.

2) *Supporting evidence.* Supporting evidence is still important to your claim, but is not as important as your core evidence. An example of supporting evidence would be a receipt that the opposing party gave you when you presented a check as a down payment on a contract. Assuming you have a processed check in your core evidence, a receipt for that check is supporting evidence that the check was paid to the opposing party.

3) *Backup evidence.* Backup evidence is evidence that it is only faintly relevant to the case. An example of backup evidence might be evidence of

Real World Case: The Value of Backup Evidence

In 2002, I participated as a litigant in a small claims case. I was a board member of my homeowners' association, and I presented in the association's side of the case. One of the residents was demanding that the homeowners' association pay for a repair of a defective window. I thought the hearing would focus solely on the fact that everyone in the association had the same windows. However, the hearing took a turn toward the discussion of a lawsuit the association had won against the builder of the development several years before. The association had secured about $300,000 in compensation from the builder, and we were using those funds to make repairs to chimneys and decks on the condos—but not to windows. Part of our backup evidence was an architectural report that we had commissioned that prioritized the repairs on several important criteria: safety, structural integrity of the buildings, and building codes. This architectural report—which I thought was mere backup evidence—showed that the association had a very sound basis for prioritizing the repairs and it turned out to be the evidence that clinched our case. If we had left our backup evidence behind, we might have lost the case.

conversations you had with the opposing party well before the contract was signed.

4) Irrelevant material. Irrelevant material should be put aside. This is material that offers no support for your case. You should resist the temptation to introduce irrelevant and ancillary material into your case. You want the judge to focus on the core components of your case.

When organizing your evidence, you want to prepare it so that you present your core evidence first, followed by your supporting evidence. You should not plan on presenting your backup evidence, but do bring it to the hearing. The court hearing may tend to take some twists and turns and the discussion may migrate over to issues covered by your backup evidence.

Sharing Your Evidence

Each opposing party has a right to receive a copy, before the trial, of any evidence the other party intends to present at trial. You will need to bring copies of your core evidence, your supporting evidence, and your backup evidence. An informal evidence exchange will occur just as the court calendar begins. The parties may only have a few minutes to examine the evidence and they do not get the opportunity to quiz the opposing party on the contents of the documents. When you exchange documents, give copies of your core evidence and your supporting evidence to the other party, but do not give a copy of your backup evidence as it is unnecessary and complicates the process at this point. If your backup evidence is required at trial, simply present it to the judge and say "I didn't expect to present this piece of evidence" and be sure to present a copy to the opposing party at the same time.

There is also a question of how to handle evidence in your possession that is damaging to your case. Some ethical issues arise. First of all, you are under no legal obligation to willingly produce damaging evidence to the opposing party unless you are directed to do so. Whether to willingly produce the evidence is your decision. However, your testimony at the hearing will be under penalty of perjury if you are asked at the hearing whether a particular document exists or existed you must answer truthfully.

Organizing Your Presentation

Prepare your presentation before appearing at the hearing. Remember you can never prepare 100 percent of your presentation because you can never guess what the other party's presentation will be, and you can never fully predict the twists and turns a case may take. When organizing your presentation, create an outline and focus first on liability (which party is at fault) and then move on to damages (the amount of compensation).

Figure 9-2 shows a good example of a small claims hearing outline. The outline is well-organized and lean. The subject of the presentation is a contract dispute for the building of fence. Liability is addressed first, followed by damages. The entries on the outline that say "present document to judge" are the points in the presentation were an item of evidence is introduced. Notice

FIGURE 9-2. **Small Claims Hearing Presentation Outline**

I. Liability
    A. Opposing party contracted with me to build a fence in my yard.
        1. PRESENT DOCUMENT TO JUDGE: contract
    B. I paid a deposit of $1,500, 8/1/2007.
        1. PRESENT DOCUMENT TO JUDGE: cancelled check
        2. PRESENT DOCUMENT TO JUDGE: receipt
    C. Defendant breached the contact.
        1. Defendant missed deadline for completion.
        2. Defendant drove his truck in my yard and damaged my lawn.
            a. PRESENT DOCUMENT TO JUDGE: photograph of damaged lawn.
        3. Defendant eventually abandoned the partially built fence.
            a. PRESENT DOCUMENT TO JUDGE: photograph of fence.
II. Damages
    A. Value of fence is nothing in its present condition, so I am entitled to my deposit back of $1,500.
    B. Damage to lawn.
        1. PRESENT DOCUMENT TO JUDGE: photograph of lawn
        2. PRESENT DOCUMENT TO JUDGE: estimate of lawn repair for $250

that in the discussion of the contract breach, there are several independent theories of breach. I call this "layering." You want to have layers to your argument so that if one theory fails, another theory stands just behind it.

No matter how well organized your presentation is, you cannot predict what curveballs the opposing party or the judge will throw at you. It is possible, however, to prepare for the unknown by understanding all facets of your case thoroughly. You can support and improve your understanding of the case by knowing dates and times, and the locations of events. You will also want to be sure that you read all documents thoroughly and know their contents before you are standing before the judge.

The Rules of Evidence

Testimonial facts are subject to the "law of evidence." The law of evidence is the body of laws and rules that governs the admissibility of testimony, documents, and demonstrative evidence in a judicial proceeding. Not all facts are admissible in a court of law. All readers have seen films and television shows where an attorney stands and exclaims, "Objection!" Those attorneys are making objections based upon the evidentiary rules. Certain facts are not admissible because they are considered prejudicial to one or more parties. Facts may not be admissible because the circumstances under which they were made are deemed to render the evidence unreliable. Other classes of facts are not admissible because of privilege—such as the privacy privilege that a husband and wife enjoy. Here is a summary of some of the basic evidentiary rules.

Hearsay

Hearsay is one of the most complex areas of evidentiary law. Almost any television viewer is familiar with the doctrine of hearsay. Hearsay is familiarly known as a secondhand statement offered when the original speaker is not present at trial. An example of hearsay would be, "My cousin told me that he saw the plaintiff, John Wilson, driving too fast." The rule of hearsay would generally require that the cousin offered his own testimony firsthand. An important exception to the hearsay rule is that it does not apply when the original speaker is a party to the lawsuit. So hearsay is admitted for statements made by parties. For example, the following statement, "The plaintiff, John Wilson, told me right after the accident, 'Man, I was flying down that road, it's a good thing I didn't kill someone,'" is not hearsay because John Wilson is a party opponent.

Settlement Discussions

Any evidence of settlement discussions or statements made during settlement discussions is generally not admissible. This evidentiary rule is based on policy, not because the evidence is deemed unreliable. Our courts foster a policy of encouraging settlement discussions. If the evidentiary rules were otherwise, litigants would never enter settlement discussions for fear of having their statements used against them later in court. It would then become impossible to settle a case.

Subsequent Repairs

A subsequent remedial measure is an improvement or repair made to a structure following an injury caused by the condition of that structure. Again, such evidence is generally admissible for a policy reason. Our courts cannot discourage property owners from engaging in repairs and improvements—especially when public safety may be at risk. Evidence of subsequent repairs often comes up in slip and fall cases. For example, suppose a plaintiff slips on the steps to a building. Later, the building owner repairs the steps with non-slip paint. The plaintiff would not be allowed to introduce evidence of the improvement, such as photograph, to prove that the steps were hazardous at the time of the fall.

The Privileges

The privileges refer to several classes of privileged communications. The privileges include the priest-penitent privilege, the doctor-patient privilege, and the husband-wife privilege. These communications enjoying a great degree of privacy and protection in our legal system. These communications are assumed to include a person's most intimate and private secrets; the law endeavors to protect those secrets. Furthermore, our courts do not wish to discourage open and meaningful communications between the parties of these groups. As such, communications made within the confines of these privileges is not allowed into evidence.

Evidence of Prior Convictions or Prior Lawsuits

Evidence of prior criminal convictions or prior lawsuits is generally not admissible to show fault in a civil suit. However, these doctrines are murky and are subject to many exceptions. Judges generally frown upon attempts to admit this sort of evidence. Such evidence is deemed to be prejudicial to litigants.

Relevance

Relevance is a major doctrine in the law of evidence. The doctrine of relevance dictates that evidence must be relevant—that is it must make the truth of the fact at issue in the preceding more or less probable than it would be without the evidence. Evidence that isn't relevant to the dispute is generally inadmissible.

CHAPTER 10

The Hearing and Oral Presentation

F inally we come to the most important chapter, where you will learn how to conduct an effective oral presentation. If you have followed all the instructions in the preceding chapters, you should have a well-documented and well-prepared case. You should have all your evidence gathered and your witnesses prepared to appear and testify. We'll begin with what to expect at the hearing and then we'll examine some techniques to deliver the most effective presentation possible.

The Day of the Hearing—What to Expect

On the day of the hearing, you should arrive about 15 or 30 minutes before the time scheduled for the hearing. When you get to the court, you will need to find the room or department where your hearing is to be held. The hearing will not begin immediately; the court will first address some preliminary matters. And your case will not be the only case heard that day. On the door of the hearing room you may see a printed docket sheet showing all the cases to be heard on the court's calendar (its hearing schedule for that particular session). If you examine the docket sheet, the order in which the cases appear on the docket sheet will usually—but not always—be the order in which the court will call the cases.

Court proceedings tend to be extremely prompt. You should be in the courtroom at your seat before the time scheduled for your hearing. At the beginning of the proceeding, either the judge or the court clerk will address all the litigants with cases on the calendar. The judge or clerk will explain some of the rules of the court, what to expect at the hearing, and any other necessary information. In the proceedings I've attended, the judge or clerk will call roll to see which litigants are absent in which litigants are present. The judge or clerk will then instruct the litigants that they must exchange each other's documentary evidence, and the litigants are given about 5 or 10 minutes to do this right before the cases are called. Sometimes, the judge or clerk will even suggest that the parties attempt to settle their dispute during the brief break. Thereafter, all the litigants in the courtroom are asked to rise together, raise their right hands, and take a perjury oath.

Perjury Oath

We discussed the seriousness of perjury in the preceding chapters. In small claims court, you're an advocate for yourself, but you are also likely to be a witness for yourself. As a witness, you must take an oath before you can present testimony to the court. The oath will be something very similar to the following: "Do you swear to tell the truth, the whole truth, and nothing but the truth before this court in these proceedings today?" Obviously, you'll take the oath because you'll be required to take the oath if you wish to testify. Just remember that the testimony that you will give is subject to penalty of perjury if you give any false statements. You should govern yourself accordingly.

The Mediation Option

In some courts, litigants are encouraged to participate in a mediation program. Mediation is a form of dispute resolution whereby two parties appear before a mediator in an attempt to informally resolve their dispute. Mediation, unlike some forms of arbitration, is not binding upon either party. Mediators often use techniques to improve dialogue between litigants, aiming to help litigants reach an agreement on the disputed matter. Mediation, if offered, might be worth a try. It isn't binding, and the statements you make in mediation are not admissible into evidence. If the mediation fails, you'll simply proceed with your small claims hearing 20 or 40 minutes later. If your mediation is successful, you and the opposing party will appear before the judge and inform her that you've reached a settlement in mediation. Thereafter, the judge will note the settlement, and likely enter it as the judgment.

Meeting With the Opponent Before the Trial

Even if you do not formally participate in mediation, remember that the judge will ask you and the opposing party to exchange evidence. The judge may also suggest in his or her opening remarks that you and the opposing party make one last effort to resolve the dispute. Whether the judge makes a suggestion or not will be a matter of the judge's personal style. There isn't necessarily a danger with discussing settlement with your opponent as long as you follow the rules and principles outlined in Chapter 5. If you get close to settling at the last moment, remember: When calculating the value of your claim, don't consider the time and expense of preparing for, and appearing at, trial—you have already spent those resources because you are minutes away from getting a ruling. Thus, a last-minute settlement should be evaluated solely upon the value of the claim, with an appropriate adjustment for the likelihood of victory at trial and collection following judgment. Let's put that theory into practice.

Assume a plaintiff has a $3,000 claim. The case is a toss up; either side has about a 50 percent chance of winning. If the plaintiff runs a value calculation on the claim, she should be prepared to compromise her claim by 50 percent, simply the statistical chance of losing. Such a plaintiff, while standing in the courtroom moments away from a hearing, should not say to herself, "The time and expertise for the court hearing would cost a few hundred dollars so I can deduct that from what I am willing to accept." Too late—she is there at the courtroom and prepared for the hearing even if it doesn't take place. She should be willing to accept something close to $1,500.

Another thing to consider in last-minute settlement negotiations is that it's a lot harder to bluff when the trial starts in 10 minutes. Similarly, it's far more difficult for a defendant to avoid the claim when the trial is imminent. Remember that a defendant always has a hope—however slim—that the case will not proceed all the way to trial. With an imminent trial looming, those hopes will be dashed. Because most of a litigant's opportunities for maneuvering are gone by the time the trial starts, many cases settle on the eve of trial. Don't let your anger get in the way of your judgment. Remember, your case is merely an asset or a liability that must be managed without emotion and with sound judgment. If you see an opportunity to settle for equal to or better than your value calculation, then take it. This advice applies to both plaintiffs and defendants.

Hearing Before Lower-Tier Official

Fairly often, the regular judge isn't available and a temporary judge (sometimes called a judge *pro tem*) will conduct the hearing. As a litigant, you have a right to have your case heard by a sitting judge, so the judge pro tem cannot hear your case without your written consent. If you are asked to have your case heard by a judge pro tem, you will be presented with a written waiver form. I participated in a hearing before a judge pro tem once, and he was very thorough and thoughtful. Generally, judges pro tem are going to go that extra mile because they may be seeking a full-time judgeship. Should you waive your right to appear before a regular judge and agree to proceed with the judge pro tem? It depends on your goals. If you are a plaintiff, remember that you always want to move your case along, to get to judgment and collection as soon as possible. As a defendant, you'll need to ask yourself about your likelihood of winning. If your cause is lost, you can frustrate the plaintiff and delay the inevitable judgment by delaying the hearing until another time by insisting that your case be heard by a regular sitting judge.

The Small Claims Hearing: How to Handle Defaults

After the preliminary matters are heard, the court will move swiftly to call the first case. The cases are called one-by-one. You may sit through several cases before your case is heard. This may be a good opportunity to size up the judge and learn a bit about how the court operates. Unfortunately, it's an opportunity for your opponent to size up the judge as well.

When your case is first called, the judge will run through a range of preliminary matters—things will slow down for a moment as the judge picks up the next file and orients him- or herself. The judge will ask the litigants to identify themselves on the record, and may ask the identities of witnesses. The judge may confirm that the litigants and witnesses were sworn in. The judge may also delve into a range of other procedural matters depending on the case before the court.

One of the most remarkable things I first noticed in small claims court as a young lawyer was that quite a few people fail to appear for the small claims trial—usually defendants. An observer in small claims court would notice that quite a few of the cases fit into the classes of the "common cases" we discussed

> ### Expert Tip: Addressing the Judge
>
> Never interrupt a judge. If the judge is speaking, do not cut him or her off. Here's a great tip: To indicate that you wish to address a point the judge has just made, raise your index finger slightly to indicate you wish to be heard. Not only will the judge understand that you wish to speak next, but the judge will also know that you waited patiently to speak instead of clumsily interrupting.

earlier. There are always collection cases, contract cases, and small motor vehicle cases. The collection cases are fairly typical of cases in which a defendant is more likely not to appear. If your opponent fails to appear, it is clearly an advantage to you. You might not win your case outright, but you have an improved chance of winning when your opponent fails to appear.

Going For the Default

As mentioned earlier, defendants are far more likely than plaintiffs to fail to appear at the small claims hearing. After all, the plaintiff is the person who initiates the case, and it is the plaintiff that must aggressively pursue the case. If the defendant has little chance of winning, he or she may simply allow the case to proceed against them. There is another reason—far more troubling to plaintiffs—why a defendant might not appear: the defendant may be judgment proof or close to bankruptcy. We discussed judgment-proof defendants earlier in the section "Researching the Likelihood of Recovery." A judgment-proof defendant poses some challenges for a plaintiff, and we'll discuss that topic further in Chapter 12: Collecting (or Avoiding the Collection of) a Judgment.

> ### Courtroom Terminology
>
> In court, you address both a male and female judge as "Your Honor." Your opponent is "the defendant," "the plaintiff," or "my opponent." When you say "the court," you are referring to the judge in the third person.

When the defendant fails to appear, your goal as a plaintiff is to get the judge to grant a default against the defendant. A default actually has two components: an "entry of default" and a "default judgment." The entry of default is a finding by the court that a defendant against whom proper service of process was made has failed to appear and participate in the action. The entry of default "freezes" the defendant's case—he or she may no longer make appearances in the action or be heard, except to motion to "vacate," or undo, the default. Immediately following the entry of default, the court will proceed to enter a default judgment.

But what amount of damages does the judge award in a default judgment? The judge has a few choices. Typically, the judge will ask the plaintiff a few questions about the underlying claim to discern the actual amount of damages due. Sometimes the judge will award the full amount of the written complaint, or sometimes a bit less. This process of court inquiry into the specifics of damages is called a "prove-up." The judge may say something like "Please break down for me why you are entitled to $2,800." The plaintiff must prove-up his or her damages—the judge just wants to make sure that the amount awarded to the plaintiff is fair, has a factual basis,

Expert Tip

When your case is called, stand immediately, move to the front of the room, and stand—don't sit unless the judge tells you to sit—at the table designated for plaintiff or defendant. You want to be up front, at attention, in front of the judge at the very beginning. If there are any preliminary procedural matters such as a party's failure to appear, or a problem with service, or a technical problem with the pleading/complaint, you'll need to speak quickly so you want to be up front where the judge can hear and see you.

and is well grounded in law. Once the judge is satisfied by the amount of the prove-up, the court will enter a judgment against the defendant in the amount that the judge awards.

The plaintiff who has the potential to win a default judgment has a preliminary challenge though. The judge may not wish to make an entry of default on the *first* missed appearance by the defendant—the judge may be inclined to give the defendant a second chance to appear. The first thing the judge will do when faced with an absent defendant is look to the proof of service. The judge knows that a default is a powerful remedy with serious consequences for the defendant. The judge will be looking to make certain that before the court enters a default judgment against the defendant, that the defendant was properly served. The judge will look in the file for a copy of the proof of service, and he or she will confirm with the plaintiff the conditions under which service was made. If the service was flawed in even the slightest way, such as a missing check box, or a line or word left blank, the court will not enter a default. A default requires that the underlying service be impeccable. If the service is faulty, the judge will point out the error set a new trial for a few weeks in the future, and instruct the plaintiff to re-serve the defendant.

If the service is legally sound (remember my admonition to use professional process servers—judges almost never question their means of service) then the judge still may be wary of entering default. In this case, the judge will set a new trial for a few weeks in the future and give the defendant one more chance to show up. This procedure is called a "continuance." If the judge orders a continuance, the plaintiff does not re-serve the defendant—a defendant is entitled to formal service of process only once. The defendant will be notified of the continuance by mail. As such, there is a likelihood that the defendant will never receive the notice of the continuance—he or she may, for instance, have moved. So at the continued hearing, there is always a substantial risk that the defendant will again fail to appear. After two failed appearances, the judge will almost certainly proceed with default against the defendant.

A plaintiff has the opportunity to influence the judge's decision of whether to enter a default. If the judge gives some hint that he or she is wavering between considering a continuance or considering entering default, it's time for the plaintiff to speak up. The following are some arguments that a plaintiff can put forth to a judge to entice the judge to act—and enter default against the defendant:

- Always mention that the defendant was properly served. Effective service is always a key component in cases of default.
- In collections cases, advise the judge that the case is a simple collections case, and that the defendant has no meaningful defense to the case.
- If you have had settlement negotiations with the defendant or any sort of ongoing dealings with the defendant, advise the judge of this and point out, "the defendant knew we would be here today; he's quite aware of the case."
- Offer to submit evidence: Advise the judge that the case is simple, that the defendant has no defense, and outline the case in a few sentences for the judge.
- Offer an immediate prove-up: "Your Honor, I am prepared to prove-up damages right now."

- Finally, remind the judge that a default defendant has remedies available to him or her. Note that the defaulting defendant can later move to have the judgment vacated.

Going for the Dismissal

There may some rare cases where the plaintiff—the party initiating the suit—fails to appear at the hearing. If you are a defendant, don't pin too much hope on it but it does happen. A non-appearing plaintiff is a great opportunity for the defendant. In this section, we will discuss how to harness this rare opportunity and make the most of it. Potentially, the defendant can ask the judge to dismiss the plaintiff's case. If the judge orders a dismissal of the case, the case is over, and the defendant owes the plaintiff nothing.

There are two types of dismissals, though, and the difference is crucial to a defendant. The first type of dismissal is "with prejudice." A dismissal with prejudice is a dismissal whereby the underlying case is finally and forever dismissed and the plaintiff is barred from ever bringing that cause of action again. The other type of dismissal is a dismissal "without prejudice." A dismissal without prejudice is a dismissal whereby the underlying case is dismissed, but the plaintiff is free to re-file the claim and resume the suit at a later time. A dismissal with prejudice is generally rare, and is typically only used when the lawsuit is finally settled. If you are a

---

**Expert Tip:
The Supernatural Interjection—"If I May..."**

There will be moments in the trial where the opposing party is speaking, or the judge is speaking—do not interrupt at that time, but you may wish to use the "Expert Tip" provided earlier and raise your finger to indicate that you'd like to follow up. There will, however, be times where the back and forth dialogue reaches a lull; this presents an opportunity to speak up even if it isn't necessarily your turn to speak. To interject during a lull and regain control of the dialogue, raise your index finger and use the phrase "if I may, Your Honor...." This phrase has almost supernatural power over most judges. You are accomplishing a few very valuable objectives with this phrase: You break the flow of dialogue without disrupting the court, you are expressing politeness, and you are asking—not demanding—to address the court. The judge will, in most cases, turn to you and allow you to speak.

defendant and the plaintiff fails to appear, the best you can hope for is a dismissal without prejudice. When a case against a defendant is dismissed without prejudice, the defendant remains vulnerable because the plaintiff is free to re-file the same case against the defendant. Some cases that are dismissed without prejudice are ultimately re-filed, and some are not. Despite the chances that a defendant faces of having a dismissed case resumed against him or her following dismissal, it is still to the defendant's benefit for the case to be dismissed if possible.

When a plaintiff fails to appear at the small claims hearing, the defendant should move into action to persuade the judge to dismiss the case. Whether or not the judge will be receptive to dismissing a case following a plaintiff's failure to appear will depend on the judge's individual style. Some judges will not even ask the defendant—they will simply dismiss the plaintiff's case immediately. Other judges will not dismiss the case under any circumstances; they will order a continuance of a few weeks and give the plaintiff another chance to appear.

If the judge dismisses the plaintiff's case, you're done—unless the plaintiff comes back in a few weeks or months and re-files the complaint against you. However, the judge may hesitate to dismiss, or make some indication that he or she is unwilling to dismiss, or express some indication to order a continuance of the case—this is the moment that the defendant should speak up and try to convince the judge to dismiss the case. The following are some arguments that a defendant can and should put forth to a judge to entice the judge to dismiss the complaint brought by a non-appearing plaintiff:

- Point out that the plaintiff initiated the suit, and it is the plaintiff's responsibility to move the case forward.
- Point out that it is unfair for you to have to attend multiple hearings because the plaintiff fails to appear at the trial.
- If you have any specific knowledge as to why the plaintiff did not appear, offer that information to the judge. Of course, never offer any false statement. For example, perhaps your opponent was a neighbor who moved away.

- You might offer the following (if you have a legitimate basis for saying so): "Your Honor, I was going to ask the court to allow me to initiate a counterclaim, but if you dismiss the case, I won't need to bring my counterclaim."
- The final argument is always the following: "Your honor, your dismissal would be without prejudice, so the plaintiff would be free to re-file if she chooses." The judge knows this, of course, but to hear it repeated may help.

However the judge chooses to handle the non-appearing plaintiff, the defendant is in a more favorable position when a plaintiff fails to appear. Either the defendant has the case dismissed, or he or she faces a second hearing—and the plaintiff will almost never get a third chance if he or she fails to appear at the second hearing.

The Case in Chief

The court will begin to hear the case in chief after all of the preliminary matters are heard. There are some absolute truths in small claims court, some generalized guidelines that all litigants and witnesses should always follow. Most of these guidelines are universal in any court: from small claims court all the way up to U.S. federal court. Of course, these are guidelines from whose dictates you may have to stray when it becomes necessary.

- Follow the "flow" that the judge puts forth. The judge will say things like "let's hear from the plaintiff first, and then the defendant can tell her side." That is the judge giving you a roadmap of what she wants to hear, and the order in which she wants to hear it. Follow the flow and the judge is more likely to follow your presentation closely.
- Don't interrupt the judge or the other witnesses or litigants. I know this warning appears about five times in this book, but it is so often disregarded. Even more specifically, don't interrupt *no matter what the opposing side says or does.*
- Brevity wins cases. Your presentation should be as brief as possible without omitting anything.

- Documents speak louder than words. Consider the following fact: Defendant John Wilson signed a contract on September 1, 2008. What is the stronger evidence to support that fact: your oral testimony that John Wilson signed the contract, or a contract with John Wilson's signature on it? Obviously, it's the written evidence itself. Use documents whenever possible.

- Legal jargon won't help you. Fancy legal jargon will not impress the judge—a solid well-delivered presentation with strong evidentiary support will.

- Don't "lawyer" people. When working with a witness, let their story develop naturally. You shouldn't need to draw out any testimony from witnesses unless they leave something out.

- Begin with a "theme sentence," such as, "Your Honor, I am bringing this breach of contract case because I paid the defendant $550 to repair my car; I paid the money, but the defendant did no work and my car is still broken." Then launch into the full bulk of your presentation.

- Use your presentation outline as a guide, but don't just read from it.

- The judge will likely ask you questions. If she does, answer the questions directly. This is a good opportunity to get a sense of what the judge is thinking. By answering the questions directly, it is a good opportunity to help your case along.

- There may be a whiteboard in the courtroom. Drawings and diagrams can be helpful in accident cases or any case involving any physical motion or event.

- Don't bother with undisputed facts. For example, if the case is a contract case, and the written contract has already been presented to court, you don't need to bother pointing out, "well, we both signed the contract and it is legally binding." The presentation of your case should focus on those areas that are disputed.

- Practice your presentation beforehand with someone you respect and trust. Ask them to poke holes or raise questions about the presentation; this will help guide you to more fully develop the weak points of your presentation.

- Don't hesitate to ask for a continuance if necessary. If one of your witnesses doesn't show up, or fails to comply with a valid request for documents, you should as for a continuance. In other words, you don't have to proceed with the case at that time with your hands tied. If you lack evidence that you need for a full presentation through no fault of your own, the judge is quite likely to grant the continuance.

The Plaintiff's Case

Your "case in chief" is the main bulk of your case. For a plaintiff, it is the facts that underlie your claim, your legal theory, and your damages. For a defendant, your case in chief is your defenses, and your legal arguments. The court will begin to hear the case in chief after all of the preliminary matters are heard.

A plaintiff should, above all else, deliver a logically organized presentation. In Chapter 9, we covered how to develop a hearing presentation outline. We examined and discussed a sample outline in Figure 9-1. Your preparation for the hearing begins with your research and your evidence gathering. If you have prepared an organized and effective presentation outline, all you really need to do during the presentation is move chronologically through your outline, beginning with your theory of liability and proceeding with damages. Along the way, you'll introduce documents and offer bits of evidence from yourself or other witnesses.

The plaintiff is the party that is putting forth their theory of liability; it is only natural that the plaintiff presents his or her argument first. The defendant must generally wait patiently through the plaintiff's presentation. The plaintiff's presentation of his or her case in chief is the "heart" of the entire case, and it is the portion of the oral presentation where interruption is least helpful, effective, or welcome. After the plaintiff's presentation, the courtroom "opens up" and the dialogue can be more "back and forth."

The Defendant's Case

A defendant's case is comprised of challenges to the plaintiff's facts, specific defenses, challenges to the plaintiff's damages, and specific legal arguments. A mistake that most defendants make is that they squirm, sigh, gesture, and try to speak out while the plaintiff is addressing the judge during the plaintiff's case in chief. First of all, judges appreciate order above all else, and judges don't like it when litigants speak out of turn or disrupt either party's presentation. Probably the greater danger, though, is that a frustrated litigant isn't paying attention, and isn't taking notes of exactly what the plaintiff is saying.

Judges have heard it all. They are quite used to hearing two wildly different versions of the facts, absurd legal arguments, and unwarranted requests for damages. The judge *wants* to hear the defendant's side of the story, and the defendant always gets a chance to speak after the plaintiff. The defendant's best move when the plaintiff is speaking (and vice versa) is to listen intently and take notes.

A defendant can challenge the plaintiff's factual case. For example, in a contract case where the plaintiff has alleged that the defendant failed to perform work adequately on an automobile, the defendant could offer evidence that he or she replaced parts, tested the vehicle after the work was done, and the vehicle worked fine. The defendant can offer specific defenses such as the expiration of the statute of limitations. The defendant should always endeavor to pick apart each individual component of the plaintiff's damages.

Finally, the defendant can use legal arguments to defeat otherwise uncontested facts. For example, a defendant might say,

"Your Honor, I worked on the plaintiff's car and he paid me $550 for the work. That much is true. But the car worked fine when I delivered it, and the plaintiff drove away in it. I don't know why the car broke down this time, but the plaintiff can't say that the breakdown is my fault. We guarantee our work for 30 days; that's what the law requires. We received no notice within the 30 days, and in fact, we received notice about 90 days after the repair. So our shop is under no obligation to refund this money. I want to be sympathetic, but the law is the law."

The defendant, much more than the plaintiff, must be able to think on his or her feet. The plaintiff's presentation is more regimented and formalized; the plaintiff must conform his presentation to a legal theory and then must prove liability and then move on to damages. Thus, the plaintiff's case is fairly straightforward. The defendant, however, needs to do more "bobbing and weaving," so to speak. The defendant may be surprised by a witness or a document, or some outrageous claim for damages. That's why a defendant has a tougher time preparing for the case because the defendant never knows exactly what the plaintiff will say.

A Sample Small Claims Hearing Transcript

One of my colleagues participated in this small claims case in Massachusetts. At the heart of this dispute was a security deposit—a common type of case in small claims court. The plaintiff had rented a small house on a month-to-month basis, and lived there for about seven months. Ultimately, the plaintiff's family gave notice and moved out and requested the return of their security deposit. The landlord returned $480 of a total security deposit of $1,000. The plaintiff felt entitled to a full return of the deposit and sued for the $520 that the landlord withheld. Let's examine how the case progressed, and then we'll discuss the outcome.

Clerk: The next case is Kleinman v. Graham. Will the parties come up to the tables here, the plaintiff at the left table there.

Judge: Well, I had a moment to review the complaint—and you are both lucky because I don't always have time to do that. So maybe we can save some time. Are all parties and witnesses here?

Plaintiff: Yes.

Defendant: Yes.

Judge: Well, you must be Mr. Kleinman. Why don't you start and then we'll hear from the defendant.

Plaintiff: I am Bob Kleinman, and this case is about a house my family and I rented from the defendant at 145 Minnesota Street right here in town. I am seeking my deposit back and the triple damages that I believe are allowed in Massachusetts. But I don't know the statute number for that provision.

Judge: That's ok, I know the statute number.

Plaintiff: Oh, thank you. I rented the house from January of '07 to August of '07. I gave notice in early August of '07 that I'd be moving out at the end of August. I wrote this letter to the defendant on August 5 and personally delivered it, and I'll give a copy to you now.

Judge: Thank you.

Plaintiff: Then my family and I moved to Texas—and I had to fly here to appear at this hearing. On October 1, 30 days after I moved out, I wrote letter number two, which I'll hand to you now, Your Honor, where I inquired why I hadn't received my deposit. My understanding at the time was that I was entitled to the return of my deposit in 30 days. Finally, here is letter number three that I wrote in late October, which is basically a demand for the return of my security deposit. About two weeks later, I got the following a letter from the defendant with a check for $480. As you can see, the letter explains that we had left the house in an unclean condition and that $520 was being withheld.

Judge: What was the condition of the house when you moved out, Mr. Kleinman? And don't worry, Mr. Graham, I am going to ask you the same question in about two minutes.

Plaintiff: My wife and I cleaned the house thoroughly, and took three pictures that I'll show you now. And even though we cleaned the house thoroughly, I don't think that is the issue because I was supposed to get my deposit back in 30 days with a written explanation of all amounts withheld. What I got was a letter about 70 days later and it says little more than the house was dirty and money was withheld. The letter doesn't say how much was spent, to whom, and there are no receipts. So, I guess my theory is that the notice did not meet the legal standard, so I get my deposit back anyway. But I don't mean to suggest that we didn't leave the place clean, because we did and the pictures show that.

Judge: Mr. Graham, I can see you over there dying to speak up. Well, it's your turn now.

Defendant: First of all, I am not a professional landlord. This house is a little cottage out in the back of our property. We never intended to do anything wrong or late. I have a high school diploma and then went into the service, and I really don't see why all these rules need to be so complicated. We gave back what was fair. The house was not clean. You can't tell from a picture whether a house is clean or not.

Judge: Well, do you agree that you received the three letters from the plaintiff, and that you sent the October letter to the plaintiff? I am concerned about how long it took to return the deposit. Landlords need to be mindful that a security deposit isn't their property; it's really the property of the tenant. Whether the rules are complicated or not—and don't worry, I still want to hear your whole story—it's still fair that a tenant get his deposit back in a reasonable time.

Defendant: Yes, the letters are all fine, we wrote those to each other. As for the cleaning, I spent $210 on the cleaning and I have a receipt here. I did not know that I was supposed to give a copy of that receipt to the tenants, because I am not a lawyer. And, I want to counterclaim for damages for rent because the tenant was supposed to give 30 days notice, but they gave notice on August 5 and moved out August 30. So, I feel we are owed 5 days of rent, or $310.

Plaintiff: Your Honor, the defendant hasn't filed any counterclaim papers and has never shown any papers to me, so I have no notice of that claim, I don't think he has a right to bring that claim today.

Judge: Just a moment. Thank you for the receipt for the cleaning, Mr. Graham. I am not going to penalize you for not showing this receipt to the plaintiff earlier. The receipt looks genuine. Now, the question of whether the cleaning was necessary is still my decision, but I accept the receipt. Now, your request for a counterclaim is a problem. In small claims things are very simple, but we still have some rules that need to be followed. And one rule is that a counterclaim needs to be in writing. There's a clear indication on the complaint form we use in this court that says in bold type, "all counterclaims must be made in writing at least 15 days before the hearing." I am sorry, but that rule couldn't be clearer. Without papers before me, I can't hear a counterclaim. I am sorry, but that's the way it is.

Defendant: Then I have a witness, another neighbor who saw the condition of the property after the tenant moved out.

Witness: My name is Trisha Gold, and I came over to Mr. Graham's house after the Kleinmans moved out. I saw the place, it was ok, but it wasn't sparkling clean. The bathroom looked a little dirty to me.

Judge: OK, thank you.

Plaintiff: Your Honor, I wasn't finished with my presentation of damages.

Judge: OK, but let's see if Mr. Graham has another witness, or anything to add.

Defendant: No, Your Honor, I have said what I came to say.

Plaintiff: Yes, Your Honor, I wanted to talk just for a second about damages. My damages were $520, but our state statute says that if a security deposit isn't returned on time, that I am entitled to three times the actual damages in addition to my refund. I also would like my costs.

Judge: OK, if no one has anything more to add, you will receive my decision in a few days.

This is a real life case that is loosely paraphrased here. Obviously, the plaintiff had the upper hand. The plaintiff is an attorney friend of mine, and he won a judgment for $310 (the $520 less the $210 receipt that the defendant produced) and tripled damages, an additional $930. Of course, my friend had to travel from Texas to Massachusetts to pursue the case. Interestingly enough, the defendants appealed the case and lost again in a superior court trial.

There are several lessons in this sample transcript. First of all, the plaintiff laid out his presentation fairly well. He was prepared and presented written evidence in chronological order. He didn't dwell on unnecessary points, but snuck in the "I live in Texas and had to travel" remark, which was good thinking. The defendant had a tougher case, but spoke up when necessary and produced a receipt that lessened his liability. The defendant also produced a witness that was likely helpful to his case. What killed the defendant in this case was the triple damages provision.

If You Absolutely, Positively, Cannot Attend the Hearing

If you face a sudden emergency and cannot attend the hearing, you must request a continuance from the court well before the hearing date—5 to 10 days before is usually sufficient. This procedure will vary from state to state and quite possibly from court to court. You must check with the court clerk to learn what form to use. Some courts will have a fill-in-the-blank form (see Figure 10-1 for a sample from California), and some courts will require you to write a letter. You are not automatically entitled to a continuance; you must make a "showing," a demonstration of the reason why you deserve a continuance. An acceptable reason would be an event or obligation outside of your control such as "I am a doctor and I am scheduled to deliver a baby that day and time," or "I have a vacation scheduled for that week and can't change it." Always note that the other event cannot be changed. An unacceptable reason would be, "I don't like getting up that early," or "I don't have time to prepare." Continuances are routinely granted when a litigant is detained with some other responsibility or obligation.

FIGURE 10-1. **Sample Small Claims Continuance Request Form**

SC-110

| PARTY (Name and address): | To keep other people from seeing what you entered on your form, please press the Clear This Form button at the end of the form when finished. |

TELEPHONE NO. (Optional):
E-MAIL ADDRESS (Optional):
FAX NO. (Optional):

SUPERIOR COURT OF CALIFORNIA, COUNTY OF
STREET ADDRESS:
MAILING ADDRESS:
CITY AND ZIP CODE:
BRANCH NAME:

PLAINTIFF:

DEFENDANT:

| **REQUEST TO POSTPONE SMALL CLAIMS HEARING** | CASE NUMBER: |

IMPORTANT NOTICES

A copy of this request must be mailed or personally delivered to each of the other parties in this case. File the original request with the court and keep a copy. (Code Civ. Proc., § 116.570(a)(3).)

If the request is not filed with the court at least *10 days* before the hearing, the requesting party must give the court a good reason why the request is being filed later. (*Explain under item 2b below.*) The court will decide whether good cause was shown. (Code Civ. Proc., § 116.570(a)(2).) If the court denies your request to postpone, your case will remain set on the original date.

If the plaintiff's claim was timely served on the defendant, there is a non-refundable $10 fee for filing a request to postpone the hearing. (Code Civ. Proc., § 116.570(d).) Submit the fee with this request.

REQUEST

1. I am the ☐ plaintiff ☐ defendant in this case.

2. a. I request that my small claims hearing *(date):* be postponed for the following reason *(be specific):*

   b. ☐ This request is being made less than 10 days before hearing for the following reason *(be specific):*

3. a. A copy of this request was ☐ mailed ☐ personally delivered to each of the other parties in this case on *(date):* at the following address as required by Code of Civil Procedure section 116.570(a)(3)
   (specify name and address):

   b. ☐ *(Optional)* In addition to the requirement above, each of the other parties was also notified of this request by ☐ telephone ☐ e-mail ☐ fax on *(date):*

I declare under penalty of perjury under the laws of the State of California that the foregoing is true and correct.

Date: ▶

_____
(TYPE OR PRINT NAME)

_____
(SIGNATURE)

Page 1 of 1

Form Approved for Optional Use
Judicial Council of California
SC-110 [New January 1, 2004]

REQUEST TO POSTPONE SMALL CLAIMS HEARING
For your protection and privacy, please press the Clear This Form button after you have printed the form.

Code of Civil Procedure § 116.570
American LegalNet, Inc. | www.USCourtForms.com

[Print This Form] [Clear This Form]

Final Thoughts on the Small Claims Hearing

It should be obvious that strong research and thorough preparation pay big on the day of the hearing. It's always good, if possible, to "layer" your arguments. In other words, in a breach of contract case, don't just point to one breach of the contract—point to three different ways that your opponent breached the contract. Attorneys call this "giving the judge something to hang her hat on." The judge may like only one or two of your arguments. With respect to the oral presentation, you want to control the dialogue, to the extent you can, without being dictatorial or interrupting.

If you get confused or the pace is moving too fast for you, put the brakes on by saying, "Your Honor, I am not a frequent visitor to this court"—that's a trick that lawyer's use when they get into trouble. Or, you can simply say to the judge, "Your Honor, I am not trained as a lawyer, and this is moving too fast for me."

Don't be afraid of the hearing. It's your chance to get justice. All in all, courts have a funny way of finding the truth.

CHAPTER 11

Appealing the Judgment

There is a great degree of inconsistency between the states with respect to whether appeals are allowed from small claims decisions. In my home state of California, the plaintiff cannot appeal, but the defendant can. Some states do not allow appeals at all. And if you lost your case by default because you failed to appear at the hearing, you are most likely not entitled to an appeal unless you first "set aside" the default.

If you are the defendant who lost your case, do not pay any money to the plaintiff if you plan to appeal. You may not be able to easily get that money back if you win your appeal, and the opposing side may use the fact that you paid the judgment against you in the appeal.

There is usually a fee associated with filing an appeal, and this fee will vary from court to court. If you win your appeal, you'll likely be able to add your filing fee to the judgment, and later collect it from the opposing party. In many states, the party filing an appeal must post a cash bond to cover the amount of the judgment if he or she loses. See the court clerk about filing fee requirements, and the procedure to secure a cash bond.

The Standard for Appeal

Appeals can be heard from lower courts according to different standards. For example, an appellate court can review a case for "obvious error"—that means that the lower decision will not be overturned unless the lower court made an obvious error in the application of law in the case. Appeals from small claims decisions will generally be heard by *trial de novo*—meaning "new trial." This means the entire case is heard again without any regard for what degree of care the lower court judge exercised.

There is a slightly different standard used in some states for small claims appeals: appeal on questions of law only. This standard is used in Alaska, Colorado, Wisconsin, and Vermont. The "question of law" standard of review imposes on an upper court the obligation to follow the factual findings of the lower court, and charges the upper court with the responsibility of reviewing only the rules of law applied to the facts. Here's how such a case might work: An employee sues his former employer for $2,500 in overdue wages. The employee wins the case and also secures a supplemental $2,000 in punitive damages. State law allows up to a $1,000 penalty as punitive damages on a claim for wages. In this case, the amount of the overdue wages is a question of fact because it depends upon the employee's hourly rate, and how much time that employee worked. The punitive damage award, however, is statute-based, and the amount of the

> ### Definition: Appellate Court
>
> A higher court that reviews the decision of a lower court when a losing party files for an appeal.

punitive damage award is a clear question of law. So only the question of the amount of punitive damages could be heard in an appeal that is adjudicated by the "question of law" standard.

Deadlines for Filing an Appeal

An appeal, if available, is initiated by filing a Notice of Appeal with the clerk of the court. Summaries of each state's appeal requirements appear in the Appendix. You should, however, always check with the court clerk for filing requirements in your state and local court. If you wish to appeal, you must file your appeal within the time period imposed by the court—and these deadlines are extremely strict. If you miss the deadline, you will not get your appeal.

> **Definition: De Novo**
>
> To newly consider a case, the same as if it had not been heard before and as if no decision previously had been rendered.

The time for filing a notice of appeal varies from state to state, but generally the time falls between 10 and 30 days. But be warned: You only have two days to file your appeal in Rhode Island and three days in the District of Columbia. Check with the court clerk if you aren't sure: the clerk will likely know the rule off the top of his or her head. Typically, you file your appeal at the small claims court. The small claims court clerk then compiles the entire file of the case and transfers the case to an upper court. The upper court then hears the appeal.

What to Expect at the Appeal Hearing

Small claims court appeals differ by state, and may even differ by county. In some localities, the appeals are heard in informal hearings much like a small claims court. In other localities, the appeals are heard in a regular civil trial format, with rules of evidence, opening and closing statements, and formal examination (questions and answers) of witnesses. In some instances, the judge hearing the case will decide the format—I have seen both informal and formal formats used in the San Francisco courts. It is wise to get some idea of the likely format for the hearing so that you can prepare. If, indeed, the format is a full trial, you might consider getting a lawyer to assist with your case.

Most likely, your case will be heard *de novo*, so all the preparation and evidence that you prepared for your original hearing can be re-used at the appeal. You should always tweak your presentation based upon the arguments and evidence that the opposing side offered in the underlying case. Keep in mind, that if you need witnesses for a *de novo* hearing on appeal, you will need to subpoena those witnesses to appear—the prior subpoena does not compel an appearance at the appellate hearing.

CHAPTER 12

Collecting (or Avoiding the Collection of) a Judgment

If you are a plaintiff who just won a judgment, you still have to collect the judgment. Neither the court nor the police will help you collect. You are on your own, with a little help from the sheriff's office—but you'll need to initiate the collection efforts and pay the sheriff's office for their help. Most people are shocked when they first learn how difficult judgments are to collect. Of course, we discussed the importance of predicting the likelihood of collecting a judgment in the section "Researching the Likelihood of Recovery" in Chapter 1. If you followed the dictates of that chapter and you can be reasonably assured that the defendant has some resources available to satisfy the claim, you stand a good chance of collecting.

> ### Warning: Don't Harass the Debtor
>
> When you become a judgment creditor, you become subject to the laws that protect debtors from abusive or unfair conduct. Generally, laws require that you don't make repetitive or late-night phone calls to the debtor or libel him or her to others.

Judgment collection is time-consuming and often fruitless. There is a lawyer's adage that says "collecting the judgment is half the battle." And of course, some judgments are never collected.

A defendant's property is protected from a plaintiff until judgment. Before the plaintiff secures a judgment, the defendant's property cannot be taken, liened, or seized. Once the case reaches a final judgment, however, the plaintiff becomes a judgment creditor and can begin the process of taking a defendant's property.

In this chapter, we'll take a slightly different approach than in previous chapters. We will address judgment collection step by step, beginning with the moment you step out of the courthouse and ending when your judgment is fully paid or abandoned. This chapter is drafted as an instruction to plaintiffs, but the lessons here are valuable and informative to defendants as well.

Themes in Judgment Collection

There are a few guiding themes by which you should abide during the process of collecting a judgment. These themes also apply if you are the judgment debtor, the target of the judgment collection process. The themes are as follows:

- *Acrimony makes judgment collections more difficult and less effective.* If you are a plaintiff and you harass and annoy the debtor, the debtor will simply fight you harder. If you are the judgment debtor, annoying and insulting the plaintiff will only make him or her pursue you harder. If you keep a cool head and behave politely, you'll get further.
- *The easiest judgment collection is a voluntary collection.* This is a corollary to the previous theme. Judgment collection is unpleasant work, so always attempt voluntary collections first. Only when voluntary collections fail should you move onto the involuntary methods such as garnishments and levies.

- *Timing is important: Don't attempt collections too early.* Creditors should not pursue judgments during a period where an appeal is available (or risk triggering the debtor to appeal).
- *Timing is important: Don't attempt collections too late.* Conversely, judgments get "stale"—they are harder to pursue as time goes on. The best time to collect a judgment is when the judgment is fresh. As time passes, the debtor may move to another state (this makes collection more difficult), may die, or may declare bankruptcy (thereby wiping out the judgment). As a result, the success ratio of judgments decreases as time passes. The only exception to this rule is the specific technique of placing a lien on real property: the lien attaches until the property is sold. We cover real property liens later in this chapter.
- *Don't ever outline your collection plans to a judgment debtor.* If you tell a judgment debtor, "I am coming for your bank account," the debtor can close the account that day and open a new one. A debtor who moves from bank to bank can avoid a judgment creditor for months or years. Your collection plans must remain secret to be effective.
- *As a general rule, don't hold out for one lump sum payment.* The partial payment of $200 that the defendant is offering you today may be the only $200 you will ever receive. Take what you can get at any time.

Keep these themes in mind as you work to collect your judgment. Now let's move on to the step-by-step process of collecting a judgment. The audience for the following steps is obviously judgment creditors, but judgment debtors are advised to review these steps as well—they are a fairly good indication of the steps a well-organized judgment creditor will take against you.

Step 1: Let the Defendant Cool Down

This step is half psychology, half strategy. When the losing defendant first walks out of the court, he or she is angry and disappointed. Defendants react in different ways, but they are never happy after losing a case. You should leave the defendant alone for at least a week. If you make a demand on the courthouse steps, you will further infuriate the defendant. Remember, you always want to appeal to the defendant's reason, without triggering the defendant's emotion. The defendant is under no legal obligation to pay you immediately, but the defendant may not know this. Judgment collection is a complex area of law and a discipline unto itself. The judgment creditor (the party that won a money judgment at trial) has rights and the judgment debtor (the party that lost at trial) has rights. Also, as we will see, a defendant can easily frustrate a plaintiff's judgment collection efforts by imposing legal objections, hiding money, making transfers of assets, etc. A good attorney or determined defendant can delay the collection of a judgment by months or years.

There is another very good reason not to immediately pounce upon the defendant—you never want to do anything that would induce the defendant to file an appeal. If the defendant feels cornered by aggressive judgment collections, he or she is far more likely to file an appeal. Of course, the availability of an appeal varies from state to state. Once the judgment is final, the period for filing an appeal begins to run. Your appeal, if available, must be within 2 or 30 days depending on the jurisdiction. (The court clerk will know this figure by heart.) As a plaintiff, you want to let the appeal period pass quietly.

The easiest way to collect a judgment is to ask the defendant to pay it. Some defendants promptly pay their judgments, and others do not. A cooperative defendant is the easiest way to collect a judgment. A defendant is most likely to voluntarily pay a judgment after they have been given a chance to cool down and let their anger and frustration subside. Ideally, after a few weeks the defendant will have calmed down and hopefully has not filed his or her notice of appeal. While you are waiting for the notice of appeal deadline to pass, you can work on step two, below, in preparation for step three. Once the deadline for the notice of appeal passes, the plaintiff should then move on to step three, and make a formal written demand to the judgment debtor.

Step 2: Locate the Judgment Debtor

Your collection efforts are going to be much easier if you make contact with the judgment debtor. Remember, the easiest way to collect on a judgment is to ask to be paid. If you can't locate the judgment debtor, you'll need to do a bit of legwork to make contact. There are several steps you can take to track a judgment debtor down:

- If the debtor has moved, neighbors usually know to where the defendant moved. Mutual acquaintances are also a good source of information.

- If the judgment debtor has moved, here's a great trick that will only cost the price of a stamp. Send a letter to the defendant's last address. Under your return address, write "Return Service Requested. Do Not Forward." If the person filed an address change with the post office, you'll get the letter back with a sticker showing the new address. This works in about 50% of cases.

- If the debtor owns property, the tax assessor's office or county clerk in the jurisdiction where the property is situated can search the tax rolls for you. Some counties have this public information available for free on the internet.

- If you only know the person's phone number, try to get the address from a reverse telephone directory. Some public libraries have such a directory. There are also several reverse phone directories available on the internet. To find them, search for "reverse phone directory" with any of the major internet search engines. The address will not be in the reverse directory if the phone number is unlisted.

- If all else fails, you can use one of the many internet-based "people finder" searches. Start with a general search engine such as Google, but in addition, there are dozens, maybe hundreds of lost person search services available on the internet. Two of the largest and most successful are zabasearch.com and intelius.com. Both work effectively, but you'll need to pay for the service, generally around $20 for a basic address search. Full asset searches cost up to $80. As an added benefit, you'll also discover any other judgments against the judgment debtor. A

> ## Expert Tip: The Debtor's Cancelled Check
>
> If a debtor writes you a check, either in settlement or in partial payment, keep a copy of the check. This check will have the debtor's address, bank name and branch, and bank account number. This is valuable information that may help a judgment creditor to levy the funds in that bank account.

debtor with too many outstanding judgments may be judgment proof. You won't collect a judgment from a judgment-proof debtor, but at least you won't waste time and money trying to collect.

Step 3: Write to the Debtor/Defendant with Demand for Payment

Once the time for appeal has passed, and you have the address of the judgment debtor (an e-mail address should work fine, too), you should write to the judgment debtor. Your post-judgment demand is the opening salvo in your collection efforts. How the defendant responds will give you a fairly reliable idea of whether the defendant will cooperate with the collections process or not.

In a sense, the demand letter has two purposes. One, it might just get you paid. The less obvious purpose is that it "flushes out" the debtor and forces him to either respond or ignore the demand. If the debtor ignores the letter (certified mail will help confirm that the debtor received the letter), don't bother sending multiple copies. The debtor has shown his colors, and is obviously not going to cooperate by paying the judgment or agreeing to a payment plan. If a judgment debtor does not respond meaningfully to your demand, it's time to move on to levies and garnishments.

Figure 12-1 shows a post-judgment demand in a case concerning a software development contract. You may wish to compare this letter to the sample demand letter in Chapter 5.

Step 4: Consider Accepting a Payment Plan

The judgment debtor may request a payment plan. You should consider accepting it because anything you can get is better than nothing. Some judgment debtors will never complete their payment plan—but those judgment debtors would not be the ones to pay their judgment in full anyway. As a general rule, as a judgment creditor, you want to take whatever you can get, whenever you can get it.

In some states, a judgment debtor can request that the court order a payment plan. A judgment debtor can make this request during the court proceedings,

FIGURE 12-1. **Sample Post-Judgment Demand Letter**

Michael Samuels
731 9th Avenue, Suite E
San Diego, CA 92101
619.501.3825   fax: 419.735.2386

January 15, 2008

Kevin R. Baker
Big Bob's International Inc.
Royal Bank Building, Suite 2000
335 8th Ave. S.W.
New York, New York 10001

VIA U.S. MAIL
RE: Demand for Post-Judgment Payment, Case No. 07-0245

Dear Mr. Baker,
As you know, I am president of I-Storm, Inc. ("I-Storm"), and I am writing to you to demand payment of the Judgment (Case No. 07-0245) against your company, Big Bob's International Inc. ("Big Bob's") in the amount of $4,500.

Yours truly,
Michael Samuels
President, I-Storm, Inc.

and sometimes following the entry of judgment. If a judgment debtor gets such an order, then the payment plan is mandatory, and you'll have to go along with it. You cannot proceed with collection devices such as garnishments and levies when a payment plan is in place. Only if the judgment debtor defaults on the payment plan can you then act to enforce the judgment with legal means.

You shouldn't agree to a payment plan for longer than two years or less than about $80 a month as a general rule. This rule is mostly a rule of convenience—

Debt Collection Do's and Don'ts

There are federal and state laws that protect judgment debtors from unfair debt collection practices. State laws vary, but certain general principles are universal. You should abide by the following rules when contacting the judgment debtor:

- You should call only at a reasonable time (e.g., 9 a.m. to 8 p.m.).
- You should identify yourself truthfully.
- Use professional business language when you speak and write.
- Don't use obscene language, call collect, harass the debtor by contacting them too often, or pretend to be a lawyer, a consumer credit reporting agency, or someone associated with the government.
- Don't threaten to harm the debtor or the debtor's family, property, or reputation.
- Don't suggest the debtor will face criminal charges (if no crime was committed) or that the debtor's property will be taken (unless the law permits it and you intend to do this).
- Don't contact the judgment debtor's friends, relatives, business associates, or employer.

If you fail to follow these guidelines, the judgment debtor may sue you for abuse of process, a violation of the Fair Debt Collection Practices Act, defamation, invasion of privacy, or interference with employment relations or potential economic relations.

you don't want to be cashing and recording tiny checks forever. And the longer a payment plan extends, the more likely the judgment debtor is to default on the payment plan.

If the payment plan is court-awarded, the plaintiff has very little work to do. The defendant is the one who must request a payment plan from the court. In some states, the court has a form to make such a request. Ask the court clerk for the court's approved form for requesting a payment plan. Or, in states without a payment plan request form, a simple letter will do the trick. As a defendant, you can always make the request at the court hearing. Of course, you don't want to admit liability. The way to request a payment plan in court without giving up your case is to say, "Your Honor, I do not feel that

I am liable in this case, but in the event that you make an award against me, I ask that you order a payment plan of no more than $200 per month." If the defendant requests the payment plan properly, it will usually be awarded. The judge will draft the judgment that sets forth a payment plan. A judgment creditor merely needs to wait for the judgment debtor to meet the payments.

What if the Judgment Debtor Defaults on the Payment Plan?

Many payment plans fail. If the debtor misses install payments, the judgment creditor can be in a tough spot. The judgment creditor has an immediate right to collect the *missed* payments, but has no right to collect the *future* payments. The future payments have not come due, so the judgment debtor has no obligation to pay them yet.

For an example of a payment plan gone wrong, say Big Company, Inc., won a judgment against Sally for (we'll use nice round numbers) $1,200 to be paid in $100 installments on the first of each month in 2008. Sally pays $100 on January 1, and makes no other payments. On May 2, Big Company has a right to collect $400—the payments for February 1, March 1, April 1, and May 1. However, Big Company has no right to collect payments for June 1 through December 1.

In such an instance, the judgment creditor has a few options. First, the creditor can wait for all the payments under the installment plan to come due. By waiting, the creditor stands the chance that the debtor will catch up with the payment plan. At the end of the payment plan, all unpaid payments are due and owning, and the creditor can then either demand payment of the entire judgment, or act to levy property or garnish wages. But waiting, as we know,

> ### Expert Tip: Don't Get Fooled Twice
>
> You need to follow the signs that a debtor gives to you. If a debtor ignores you or misses appointments and payments, they are a simply a bad debtor and will continue to cause collection problems for you. Such a debtor is extremely unlikely to ever turn over a new leaf and later honor their obligations willingly. Don't give debtors multiple chances to make good on their obligation. If a debtor doesn't cooperate, move on to involuntary methods of collection.

> ### Expert Tip:
> ### When the Debtor Pays by Check
>
> When you are collecting a judgment (especially with a payment plan), a check written to you by a judgment debtor is pure gold. A check has a bounty of valuable information. A check has the debtor's bank and bank account number. The debtor's bank account, as we'll learn in later chapters, is a prime target for levy. The check might have extra addresses or phone numbers. The check might also have a business name or address on it. And, if the check bounces, you have a new cause of action (in addition to your original case) that may entitle you to the face amount of the check, plus additional damages. Such a suit is called "suing on the draft." State laws vary widely, so you'll need to research before bringing such a claim.

carries the risk that the judgment debtor will fall further into debt, move away, or declare bankruptcy.

The creditor has a second option: He or she can "pick away" at the judgment by acting on the overdue portions of the installment plan as they become due. This would mean several individual garnishments every two or three months or so. The problem with this approach is that once a debtor has had his or her wages garnished or bank account levied, they will cease to cooperate with any payment plan. Furthermore, a judgment debtor that has had his or her bank account levied will simply open a different bank account at a new bank—then the judgment creditor will need to discover the new bank account. As we will learn later in this chapter, a lien on a bank account is usually only effective once—after the account has been discovered and levied by a judgment creditor, the judgment debtor nearly always abandons the account.

The creditor has a third option: The creditor can apply to the court to have the payment plan set aside. Some courts have a form for this; a simple check with the clerk's office can establish if there is a form to modify a judgment or to set aside a payment plan judgment. If the court has no specific judgment modification form, ask the court clerk for a "motion" form. A motion is a request made by a litigant of the judge to enter or modify an order. Judge's can also make motions themselves. A motion is not a full court case—it's just a request for a court to enter an order. In full-blown civil trials, lawyers file motions for all sorts of things, from asking a court to compel another party to produce documents to asking for a continuance. In a motion hearing, the person making the motion is the "movant," the person answering or opposing the motion is the "respondent." Motions are rare in small claims court simply because the small claims procedures are streamlined—there is often no need to file motions. But motions are allowed in small claims court if the litigants require an order.

With the motion form, you can ask the court to modify the judgment. Specifically, you'll argue that because the judgment debtor did not make the installment payments, the installment payment judgment should be modified so that the full amount is payable. Such a motion is very likely to succeed, unless the judgment debtor has an extremely good excuse, such as a brief period of incarceration or a medical emergency.

Step 5: Consider Compromising the Claim

In the early chapters of this book, we advocated the notion that it might some-times be best to compromise the claim in order to settle. A plaintiff is said to compromise a claim when he or she reduces the amount of a perfectly valid claim in order to secure the defendant's cooperation in resolving the case. Unfortunately, some plaintiffs may find that it is necessary to compromise their claim during the collection stage (defendants, take note as well, this is a good opportunity).

If a judgment creditor is facing a long, time-consuming and potentially unproductive collection process, he or she may be forced to consider reducing the amount due in exchange for immediate satisfaction of the judgment. The value calculation that we undertook in the early chapters of this book applies at this stage as well: Is the amount of the judgment going to be difficult or impos-sible to collect in full? If yes, then the present value of the judgment is reduced.

As a judgment creditor, you don't want to announce to the judgment debtor that you'll consider compromising the claim—the judgment debtor may not know the option is available. As a judgment creditor, you should (initially, at least) present the impression that you intend to collect the full amount of the judgment. Let the judgment debtor bring up the issue, if possible.

Judgment debtors have a good last opportunity to reduce their liability at this stage. In fact, I believe that about 9 out of 10 judgments can be reduced from their face amount by simple negotiation. The judgment creditor, if he or she is smart, will compromise their claim for immediate collection. So, as a judgment debtor, if you have the present ability to pay part of the judgment, you can work to get the judgment creditor to accept a reduced amount. You want to communicate the following to the judgment creditor:

- You would like to pay the entire judgment, but cannot.
- You do not have the money to pay the entire judgment, and your wages are not high enough to pay the judgment any time soon.
- If you pay child support, note that, because amounts paid in child support are not available to creditors.
- Remind the judgment creditor that much of your wages are exempt from garnishment.
- If supportable by fact, tell the judgment creditor that you intend to move to another state, and that the judgment creditor will have to pursue the judgment there.
- Finally, offer a reduced sum for immediate payment.

One key to this process is to be absolutely sure that the judgment creditor files the satisfaction of judgment form when the agreed-upon amount is paid (we discuss satisfaction of judgment later in Step 8). In fact, if you do settle the matter, insist on a copy of the satisfaction of judgment form to be exchanged for the final payment; then, file the form at the courthouse yourself.

Step 6: Discover the Judgment Debtor's Assets

It is at this stage that the collection phase goes from cooperative (working with the judgment debtor, negotiating, etc.) to investigative (finding property that can be taken from the judgment debtor). This investigative phase is the beginning of the compulsory collections phase—where a judgment creditor takes property from the judgment debtor through process of law. But first, a judgment creditor must find out what assets a debtor owns. The process of searching out a debtor's assets is called "asset discovery." And as you will see, the person that will help you the most with the asset discovery endeavor is the judgment debtor himself. A judgment debtor can be forced to answer questions about their finances and property—and must answer under oath, under penalty of perjury.

There are two ways of conducting asset discovery. The first is through the legal process of formal asset discovery, which includes submitting written questions to the judgment debtor, and, at the judgment creditor's option, conducting a court-supervised examination of the debtor. The second way of asset discovery is informal asset discovery: the use of publicly available information without any input from the debtor.

I usually begin my asset discovery with informal asset discovery

> ### Expert Tip:
> ### Dealing with Collection Agencies
>
> Some judgment creditors sell their judgments to firms that specialize in purchasing court judgments. The judgment purchase firms then pursue the judgments against the judgment creditors. Believe it or not, buying and trading judgments is a thriving industry in America. Some judgments are even sold more than once. Or some judgment creditors hire standard collection agencies. If you are a judgment debtor and you are contacted by either a judgment purchase firm or a collection agency, you should absolutely negotiate the claim to a lower amount. These firms always buy the judgments at a 40 to 60 percent discount to face value; thus, all collection firms routinely compromise their claims to substantially reduced levels. You might be able to reduce your liability up to 40 or 50 percent. Best approach: Take your time—the longer you hold out, the better deal you will get.

first as these informal methods are done quietly and without tipping off the debtor that you are looking for assets. Conversely, the formal asset discovery process announces to the debtor that you are searching aggressively for assets. Remember that a common theme in collections is that as a judgment creditor you never want to outline your collection plans to a judgment debtor. Stealthy judgment collections are more effective.

An Introduction to Judgment Debtor's Asset Protection

The judgment creditor's goal in the both the informal and formal asset discovery phase is to discover reachable assets owned by the judgment debtor, preferably without alerting the judgment debtor that you are sniffing around. Note that assets must be "reachable." This means that a judgment creditor want to find assets that can be attached or levied—and not all assets are available to satisfy civil judgments. Some assets are subject to asset protection rules and can't be touched by a judgment creditor.

Asset protection refers to a set of legal techniques that protect a person's property from creditors and judgments. Asset protection planning ranges from simple devices such as transferring assets to a retirement account, to more complex arrangements such as offshore trusts.

In 1997, a civil judgment entered against celebrity O.J. Simpson in the amount of roughly $33,500,000 in a civil case brought by the family of his former wife and the family of Ron Goldman following their alleged murders by Mr. Simpson. One might think Mr. Simpson's property would have to be relinquished to satisfy this enormous judgment. Yet Mr. Simpson lives in a lavish Florida mansion, and enjoys a steady pension. Sure, some assets have been seized, but the bulk of Mr. Simpson's property remains out of reach of his creditors. In fact, Mr. Simpson has never declared bankruptcy or taken other action to extinguish the liability.

How is this possible? The answer is that Mr. Simpson arranged his financial affairs in a completely legal manner that left his assets out of the reach of his creditors. Florida, his new home state, just so happens to be one of the most advantageous states for asset protection. When asked about his choice of domicile, Mr. Simpson responded in an interview that while he intended to move to Florida anyway, "...an added benefit is some of the laws here in Florida." To be sure, the states differ widely in what assets are available to creditors and what assets are protected from creditors.

Asset protection planning can be effected in essentially three ways. The first is divestiture, by which a judgment debtor transfers his property to another, either by outright transfer or by having liens or mortgages placed upon the asset. This method relies on the simple truth that a creditor cannot have what a debtor does not own. The second way is through exemption planning, where an individual transfers assets to a statutorily protected class of property, such as residential homestead, life insurance, pensions, or an IRA.

These classes of protected property vary widely by state, but all states offer some protection. The third way is through the use of liability shielding entities such as corporations and LLCs. Hiding one's assets is not part of responsible or effective asset protection planning; it may be against the law, and it doesn't work well.

Several general themes apply in asset protection:

- No asset protection plan can ever give anyone 100% protection from creditors; asset protection planning can only shield most of a person's assets from creditors. Some assets will always be exposed.

- The proper goal of an asset protection plan is to frustrate creditors by altering the creditor's economic analysis of a lawsuit (by making it more expensive and uncertain for the creditor). In other words, the plan itself doesn't give the protection; how the creditor perceives the plan gives the protection.

- Timing is important. An asset protection plan must be put in place well before a creditor or plaintiff emerges. Otherwise, the plan will be exposed as a transparent last-minute effort to thwart creditors.

- An effective asset protection plan can be made even more effective by "layering" applying different legal protections over the same assets.

- Compartmentalization is an effective asset protection planning tool. For example, an owner of rental properties (rental properties generally carry a high risk of liability) can place each separate rental property in a separate LLC or corporation. If one property results in liability, a creditor will be forced to pursue liability against only one entity, and will not reach either the owner and her other properties.

- A simple asset protection plan is generally more effective than a complex plan.

Asset Shielding the Family Home: Homestead and Liens

For most Americans, the most valuable asset they own is their personal residence. The home offers some of the simplest and most effective asset protection planning. The first device is the homestead. A homestead is, quite simply, a legal device that protects a person's residence (or a portion of it) from creditors. A judgment creditor cannot levy on the homestead portion of a person's residence. The amount of homestead protection differs widely by state. Texas and Florida offer unlimited homestead protection (unlimited in value, but limited by acreage), while Alabama offers a meager $5,000 homestead exemption for single persons and $10,000 for a married couple. In practice, a creditor attempting to levy on an Alabama residence can reach all the equity (after mortgages and liens) except for the homestead-protected amount. In the event of a forced sale of the residence, the ousted creditors would receive the homestead exemption in cash. Homestead protection is afforded automatically in most states, but it's always a good idea to file appropriate papers to claim the homestead.

In states with low homestead protection, mortgages and liens provide a very effective means of protecting the personal residence—and serve as a constant frustration to judgment creditors. This process is sometimes referred to as "equity stripping." A residence with liens on it is essentially owned by the bank. The home's lienholders have priority over subsequent creditors. Any creditors who levy a home with one or more existing liens take a disadvantaged position behind the lienholders. In the event of a sale, the creditor is less likely to get a recovery. A property owner can lien up his or her own property by increasing the size of an existing mortgage, or by getting a home equity line of credit (HELOC).

If the judgment debtor is a homeowner, you may be able to place a lien on the property, but your judgment will likely have to wait for the ultimate sale of the property.

Asset Protection Through Property Exemptions

Every state protects certain classes of assets through property exemption statutes. The property exemption statutes serve a dual purpose. First, they denote types and amounts of property that are unreachable by judgment creditors. Second, these statutes also denote types and amounts of property that cannot be lost by a debtor in bankruptcy. A bankruptcy court is a *de facto* creditor, so a bankruptcy court can only reach what a creditor can reach. This principle applies to homestead laws as well, except for some recent erosion built into the 2005 bankruptcy law revisions. So good asset protection planning is also effective pre-bankruptcy planning.

The property exemptions are plainly valuable to judgment debtors. Again, property exemptions differ widely by state. Texas places the full amount of all IRAs beyond the reach of creditors, while California exempts retirement accounts "only to the extent necessary to provide for the support of the judgment debtor when the judgment debtor retires and for the support of the spouse and dependents

> ## Expert Tip:
> ## Debtors, Don't Pay with a Check
>
> We advise judgment creditors to save copies of checks because checks contain valuable information that can help identify debtor's bank accounts. As a debtor, you should never pay with a check. If you do, you'll be identifying your bank account, and some address and phone number information. The better route is to pay with a money order. A money order is drawn on the bank itself and does not pass any of your personal information. However, a money order from "State Bank" may indicate to the judgment creditor that you maintain an account at State Bank. So get a money order from the post office, or from a bank where you do not maintain an account.

of the judgment debtor." I have found California courts to be extremely reluctant to allow attachment of an IRA account. California's subjective test for retirement account exemption results in frequent disputes. Florida exempts an automobile of up to only $1,000 in value, while Texas exempts one automobile of unlimited value per spouse. Florida and Texas exempt wages from garnishment, while most states do not. You'll have to navigate your state's exemption rules to some degree.

Asset Protection Through Liability Shielding Entities

Nearly all business owners can protect their personal assets by conducting their business operations through a liability shielding entity, a corporation or LLC. Both forms of entity serve the same liability shielding purpose. LLCs and corporations serve the specific purpose of isolating the liabilities of a business enterprise with the entity. A liability arising out of the corporation's operation attaches to the corporation only, and cannot reach the owner's or owners' property. Of course, extreme misuse of the corporate or LLC form can erode that liability protection. If your judgment debtor is a corporation or LLC, you may be forced to seek satisfaction from the entity alone, without reaching any personal assets.

Judgment Debtor Protection from Wage Garnishment

Wage garnishment is the process whereby a judgment creditor obtains, directly from an employer, part of the salary of an employee who has failed to fully satisfy a judgment. The wages of American workers are partially protected from garnishment by both federal and state laws. In general, federal wage garnishment protection limits the amount of garnishment to either 25 percent of the disposable earnings of an employee, or 30 times the minimum wage per week, whichever is less. In general terms, personal tax and non-tax payments are about 15 percent of personal income, which makes disposable personal income about 85 percent of personal income. The federal protections extend to all American citizens.

However, some states restrict garnishment to a lower percentage of income than the federal law (Delaware, Hawaii, Illinois, Missouri) and some states do not allow *any* garnishment of wages by any court (except for special circumstances such as taxes and child support). For example, the states of Texas, Florida, South Carolina, and Pennsylvania severely restrict creditors from attaching the wages of judgment creditors.

So where does this leave a judgment creditor? Certainly much of a judgment debtor's assets may be exempt from attachment. Nevertheless, a judgment debtor will usually have some assets available for attachment. Generally, the most productive assets for collection are real estate (despite existing liens and homestead protection), cash bank accounts, and wages. In the steps that follow, we'll closely examine the procedures for attaching a judgment debtor's property.

Informal Asset Discovery

A sound background in asset protection will help a judgment creditor identify and pursue reachable assets. Now we will turn to several ways to discover a judgment debtor's assets through informal asset discovery. Generally speaking, the tools a judgment creditor will utilize in informal asset discovery are public databases, the internet, investigative services, and—as you will see—the judgment debtor himself.

We will begin with what can be learned from the judgment debtor herself. Go through all your records of communications, e-mails, checks, and other documents concerning the judgment debtor. As a judgment creditor, here are some things you want to look for:

- *Look for addresses on correspondence and checks.* Each one of these addresses may be the address of a business or home that the judgment debtor owns. You can use these addresses to search county records to see if the judgment debtor, or one of his or her businesses, is on the deed to any properties.

- *Search for the judgment debtor through the major internet search engines.* Such a search may turn up additional phone numbers and addresses that can be pursued.

- *Does the judgment debtor operate a web site?* A judgment debtor's e-mail address may contain a web site name. You can do what's called a "whois lookup" using the web site address. A whois lookup is a search conducted over the internet to determine who the registered owner of a web site is. To find a web site that conducts free whois lookups (there are several), simply go to a search engine and search for "whois lookup." The whois lookup may show a company name, or another address. Again, that new information can be pursued.

- *Search with the secretary of state's office in the state where the judgment entered for the judgment debtor's name.* Most secretary of state offices have an online searchable database of company officers. Such a search will reveal if the judgment debtor has an officer position with a corporation or LLC—and this may mean that the judgment debtor is an owner of that entity.

Checks are pure gold. Did the debtor ever write you a check? If so, you have the debtor's bank, bank account branch, and bank account number.

Expert Tip: Prior Bankruptcies

In your investigation of the debtor's financial history, you may find evidence of a prior bankruptcy. This may actually be good news for judgment creditors: a debtor cannot file bankruptcy within six years of receiving a prior bankruptcy discharge. Thus, a prior bankruptcy means that a debtor must wait before seeking bankruptcy protection. In the intervening time, a judgment creditor is free to pursue collections.

If you want to conduct a very thorough search of the debtor's assets, you can use one of the online "asset search" services. We don't recommend a particular one, but a couple of the larger and more successful ones are knowx.com and ussearch.com.

All of these search methods can be conducted without the debtor's knowledge. The obvious advantage to searching for assets without the debtor's knowledge is that the debtor won't necessarily have time to scramble to move assets around. A debtor can't change jobs easily, but a debtor can certainly move a bank account to a new branch. Debtors that are hounded by creditors often open and close bank accounts frequently.

The judgment debtor's everyday bank account is the cornerstone of a creditor's collection efforts. Unlike wage garnishment, a bank account is more likely to yield the entire amount of the judgment in one lump sum. Garnishments are effective, but take a long time. See the sidebar for an expert tip on how to obtain a debtor's bank account information.

Formal Asset Discovery: Before You Start

As we have noted, there is a fundamental difference between informal and formal asset discovery; formal asset discovery alerts the judgment debtor that her assets are being hunted. And so, a judgment creditor is wise to use the information garnered in the informal asset discovery and attempt collections before proceeding to formal asset discovery. Of course, it may depend on the circumstances. As a judgment creditor, you may know your judgment debtor very well; you may already be aware of their financial condition and the range of their assets. The key is that formal asset discovery may trigger the judgment debtor to start hiding assets, so you may want to attach whatever assets you can before the judgment debtor has a chance to hide assets.

Formal Asset Discovery: The Process and Procedure

The formal asset discovery process involves compelling the judgment debtor to answer questions about their assets, and compelling the judgment debtor to appear at a court-supervised examination of the debtor. At the debtor examination, the judgment creditor, or her lawyer, gets to ask detailed questions about the judgment debtor's finances. The written answers to questions and the testimony given at the debtor examination are given under oath, under penalty of perjury.

Before proceeding with the formal asset discovery process, it is a good idea to give the judgment debtor one last chance to pay. Debtor examinations are extremely unpleasant for debtors, and most debtors will avoid examinations at all costs. A judgment creditor might consider writing the letter to a debtor found in Figure 12-2.

> ### Expert Tip:
> ### How to Get the Debtor's
> ### Bank Account Information
>
> If you don't have the debtor's bank account information, here's a time-tested lawyer's trick. The crux of this device is to have someone you know write a check to the debtor. When the debtor cashes the check, it will be returned to the person who wrote the check with a bank name and numerical codes on the back of the check; that printed information on the back of the check is the debtor's bank account information. You, the judgment creditor, can then use that bank account information to levy the account. This trick will work if the debtor runs any sort of day-to-day business like a retail shop. Otherwise, you can issue a fake refund check to the debtor, or a fake survey with a $5 check. Or any other person you know that ever paid the judgment debtor with a check may have a copy of the check with the debtor's bank account information.

Such a letter will carry a lot of weight with debtors. Many debtors finally submit to full satisfaction of a judgment when they are facing a debtor's examination. However, some debtors will resist, and it may be necessary to proceed with the formal asset discovery process.

How to Compel Written Answers Regarding a Debtor's Assets

Judgment creditors have powerful tools on their side. In the eyes of the law, a judgment creditor has won her case, and the judgment debtor has lost his case. As such, judgment debtors enjoy only limited rights. One right the judgment

FIGURE 12-2. **Sample Letter to a Debtor**

Dear Mr. Baker,

As you know, I am president of I-Storm, Inc. ("I-Storm"), and I am writing to you to demand payment of the Judgment (Case No. 07-0245) against you in the amount of $4,500.

I just wanted to let you know that if we don't receive full satisfaction of the judgment, we will compel your appearance at a judgment debtor's examination. At that examination, which will be at the Kern County courthouse, our lawyer will be asking some very detailed questions about your financial circumstances, your employment, and assets that you own. As you probably know, your must answer all questions under oath, and under penalty of perjury.

Yours truly,
Michael Samuels
President, I-Storm, Inc.

creditor enjoys is the right to question the judgment debtor about her assets. All states have some procedure by which a judgment creditor can obtain written answers from a judgment debtor regarding their finances. In fact, in several states, including California, a judgment debtor is required by law to submit a "Judgment Debtor's Statement of Assets" to the judgment creditor within 30 days after the entry of judgment; the requirement is mandatory and the judgment creditor does not even need to request the statement from the judgment debtor.

But, as often happens, judgment debtors do not submit their statement of assets as required. When a judgment debtor fails to complete the statement of assets, the judgment creditor can ask the court to hold the debtor in contempt, or issue a bench warrant for the debtor's arrest. These actions, however, do not necessarily get the judgment paid. If the judgment debtor fails to submit the statement of assets, a simple reminder letter should usually force the debtor to act.

Figure 12-3 is a sample of the Judgment Debtor's Statement of Assets form used in California following a small claims judgment. See the clerk of the court in your state for the equivalent form. You'll also need to know your state's rules about serving a statement of assets on a debtor. In some states, the statement is mandatory and automatic; in other states, the judgment creditor needs to request it by serving a blank form on the judgment debtor.

As you can see, the statement of assets makes an inquiry into the debtor's employment and wages, bank accounts, cash, real estate, automobiles, and other personal property.

If the judgment debtor refuses to provide a statement of assets, or provides inadequate or incomplete responses (as is often the case), a judgment creditor's next move should be to call the judgment debtor in for a debtor's examination (we cover debtor's examinations just below). If the judgment debtor does provide a statement of assets with meaningful information, it may not be necessary to call the debtor in for a face-to-face examination. As a judgment creditor, you'll need to decide if the information on the statement of assets is sufficient to move forward with collections.

How to Compel and Conduct a Debtor's Examination

One of a judgment creditor's most powerful tools is the debtor's examination, or order of examination. A debtor's examination is the final and most powerful (and most invasive) step in the asset discovery process. It is an effective tool, but be warned: Debtors don't like examinations and the debtor is likely to be extremely nasty. We have included a copy of the form used in California to order a judgment debtor to appear for examination in Figure 12-4.

Each state will have an equivalent form. Your state's court clerk will provide the form to you, and help you pick a date for the hearing. The order will state that the debtor must either pay the judgment in full, or appear at the court and answer questions about income and assets. A judgment creditor must "apply" for the order compelling the judgment creditor to appear, but

FIGURE 12-3. **Sample Judgment Debtor's Statement of Assets**

MAIL TO THE JUDGMENT CREDITOR
DO NOT FILE WITH THE COURT

SC-133

JUDGMENT CREDITOR (the person or business who won the case) *(name):*

JUDGMENT DEBTOR (the person or business who lost the case and owes money) *(name):*

SMALL CLAIMS CASE NO.:

NOTICE TO JUDGMENT DEBTOR: You *must* (1) pay the judgment or (2) appeal or (3) file a motion to vacate. If you fail to pay or take one of the other two actions, you must complete and mail this form to the judgment creditor. If you do not, you may have to go to court to answer questions and may have penalties imposed on you by the court.	AVISO AL DEUDOR POR FALLO JUDICIAL: Usted debe (1) pagar el monto del fallo judicial, o (2) presentar un recurso de apelación o (3) presentar un recurso de nulidad. Si usted no paga el fallo o presenta uno de estos dos recursos, deberá llenar y enviar por correo este formulario a su acreedor por fallo judicial. Si no lo hace, es posible que deba presentarse ante la corte para contestar preguntas y pagar las multas que la corte le pueda imponer.

INSTRUCTIONS

The small claims court has ruled that you owe money to the judgment creditor.

1. You may appeal a judgment against you only on the other party's claim. You may *not* appeal a judgment against you on *your* claim.
   a. If you appeared at the trial and you want to appeal, you must file a *Notice of Appeal* (form SC-140) within 30 days after the date the *Notice of Entry of Judgment* (form SC-130) was mailed or handed to you by the clerk.
   b. If you did not appear at the trial, before you can appeal, you must first file a *Notice of Motion to Vacate Judgment and Declaration* (form SC-135) and pay the required fee within 30 days after the date the *Notice of Entry of Judgment* was mailed or handed to you. The judgment cannot be collected until the motion is decided. If your motion is denied, you then have 10 days after the date the notice of denial was mailed to file your appeal.
2. Unless you **pay the judgment or appeal the judgment or file a motion to vacate, you must fill out this form and mail it to the person who won the case** within **30 days** after the *Notice of Entry of Judgment* was mailed or handed to you by the clerk. Mailing this completed form does not stay enforcement of the judgment.
3. If you lose your appeal or motion to vacate, you must pay the judgment, including postjudgment costs and interest. As soon as the small claims court denies your motion to vacate and the denial is not appealed, or receives the dismissal of your appeal or judgment from the superior court after appeal, the judgment is no longer suspended and may be immediately enforced against you by the judgment creditor.
4. Unless you have paid the judgment, complete and mail this form to the judgment creditor within **30 days** after the date the clerk mails or delivers to you (a) the denial of your motion to vacate, or (b) the dismissal of your appeal, or (c) the judgment against you on your appeal.

If you were sued as an individual, skip this box and begin with item 1 below. Otherwise, check the applicable box, attach the documents indicated, and complete item 15 on the reverse.

a. ☐ *(Corporation or partnership)* Attached to this form is a statement describing the nature, value, and exact location of all assets of the corporation or the partners, and a statement showing that the person signing this form is authorized to submit this form on behalf of the corporation or partnership.

b. ☐ *(Governmental agency)* Attached to this form is the statement of an authorized representative of the agency stating when the agency will pay the judgment and any reasons for its failure to do so.

JUDGMENT DEBTOR'S STATEMENT OF ASSETS

EMPLOYMENT

1. What are your sources of income and occupation? *(Provide job title and name of division or office in which you work.)*

2. a. Name and address of your business or employer *(include address of your payroll or human resources department, if different):*

   b. If not employed, names and addresses of all sources of income *(specify):*

3. How often are you paid?
   ☐ daily ☐ every two weeks ☐ monthly
   ☐ weekly ☐ twice a month ☐ other *(explain):*
4. What is your gross pay each pay period? $
5. What is your take-home pay each pay period? $
6. If your spouse earns any income, give the name of your spouse, the name and address of the business or employer, job title, and division or office *(specify):*

Page 1 of 2

Form Adopted for Mandatory Use
Judicial Council of California
SC-133 [Rev. January 1, 2004]

JUDGMENT DEBTOR'S STATEMENT OF ASSETS
(Small Claims)

Code of Civil Procedure,
§§ 116.620(a), 116.830

American LegalNet, Inc.
www.USCourtForms.com

FIGURE 12-3. **Sample Judgment Debtor's Statement of Assets** (continued)

CASH, BANK DEPOSITS

7. How much money do you have in cash? . . . . $
8. How much other money do you have in banks, savings and loans, credit unions, and other financial institutions either in your own name or jointly *(list)*:

Name and address of financial institution	Account number	Individual or joint?	Balance
a.			$
b.			$
c.			$

PROPERTY

9. List all automobiles, other vehicles, and boats owned in your name or jointly:

Make and year	License and vehicle identification (VIN) numbers	Value	Legal owner if different from registered owner	Amount owed
a.		$		$
b.		$		$
c.		$		$
d.		$		$

10. List all real estate owned in your name or jointly:

Address of real estate	Fair market value	Amount owed
a.	$	$
b.	$	$

OTHER PERSONAL PROPERTY (*Do not list household furniture and furnishings, appliances, or clothing.*)

11. List anything of value not listed above owned in your name or jointly *(continue on attached sheet if necessary)*:

Description	Value	Address where property is located
a.	$	
b.	$	
c.	$	

12. Is anyone holding assets for you? ☐ Yes. ☐ No. If yes, describe the assets and give the name and address of the person or entity holding each asset *(specify)*:

13. Have you disposed of or transferred any asset within the last 60 days? ☐ Yes. ☐ No. If yes, give the name and address of each person or entity who received any asset and describe each asset *(specify)*:

14. If you are not able to pay the judgment in one lump sum, you may be able to make payment arrangements with the person or business who won the case (the judgment creditor). State the amount that you can pay each month: $, beginning on *(date)*: . If you are unable to agree, you may also ask the court for permission to make installment payments by filing a *Request to Pay Judgment in Installments* (form SC-106).

15. I declare under penalty of perjury under the laws of the State of California that the foregoing is true and correct.

Date:

▶

_____   _____
(TYPE OR PRINT NAME)   (SIGNATURE)

Mail or deliver this completed form to the judgment creditor at the address shown on the Notice of Entry of Judgment form.

SC-133 [Rev. January 1, 2004]	**JUDGMENT DEBTOR'S STATEMENT OF ASSETS** (Small Claims)	Page 2 of 2

the order will be automatically awarded by the judge. Keep in mind that there are some jurisdictional limits to this procedure. For example, you won't be able to make the debtor travel long distances, or travel from another state.

On the day of the debtor's examination, do not be surprised if the debtor fails to appear. If the debtor fails to appear, ask the judge to issue a bench warrant for the debtor's arrest; the judge likely will not issue the warrant, but it is worth a try. For example, the informal policy in San Francisco courts is to not issue a bench warrant for the debtor's arrest until the debtor misses *two* scheduled examinations—the first failure to appear is forgiven. I suspect most judges would hesitate to issue a bench warrant for one missed examination. So, if the debtor fails to appear, ask the judge or the clerk to schedule a second hearing.

If the debtor does show up, all parties will be shown to a hearing room or empty courtroom. The judge won't be present, but will be available if a dispute arises, such as the debtor's refusal to answer certain questions. In the examination, the judgment creditor will want to ask the following questions. Consider the answers carefully; the answers may lead to new lines of inquiry.

- What is your home address? Do you own any other homes anywhere either inside or outside of the state?
- What is your home telephone number? Please list all other telephone numbers, fax numbers, or VOIP numbers that you have used.
- Are you married or do you have registered domestic partnership? If so, what is the first name, maiden name, and last name of your spouse or domestic partner?
- Do you live in a rented apartment? A single family home? A condo? A mobile home? What is the address?
- If you live in a single family home, condo, or mobile home, do you own it?
- If you live in a rented apartment, who pays the rent? To whom is it paid?
- Is the rent paid by check? Is your rent/mortgage up to date? Did you pay a security deposit on the rental property, and if so, what is the amount and who holds it?

- Do you have any boarders or subtenants? If so, what are their names and how much do they pay you each month?
- Do you have a vacation home, recreational vehicle, or boat?
- What is your social security number? What is your spouse or domestic partner's social security number?
- What is your occupation?
- Are you presently employed? If so, by whom? At what address? Where is the payroll office located?
- What is your work telephone number?
- What is the name of your supervisor?
- What is your gross salary? What is your net salary? What payroll deductions are made?
- Do you receive commissions? When are you paid?
- How much is owed to you now?
- Do you have any part-time employment? If so, please explain.
- Is your spouse or domestic partner employed or in business? If so, what is his or her salary? What is the address of his or her workplace?
- Do you own any stock or any interest in the business where you work? If so, please explain.
- In what companies or businesses do you own stock or a percentage interest?
- Do you or your spouse or domestic partner have any bank checking or savings accounts? If so, what is the name of the bank branch, and what are the account numbers and present balances?
- Do you, or have you in the last three years, receive any royalties, rents, spousal support, government support, or alimony payments?
- Please describe any expenditures you have made in excess of $50 in the past 60 days from today's date.
- Do you, your spouse, or domestic partner have a driver's license? For what state? What are the driver's license numbers?
- How did you get here today? What is the year and make of your car? Do you own it? Is it financed? By whom? How much remains to be paid on the car?

- Do you have any credit cards? What is the available cash advance balance on all of those cards?
- What type of retirement accounts do you have? Are you able to borrow against your retirement account?
- Do you have life insurance? Is it a whole life policy?
- Do you have any property, personal effects, cash, or other assets that you've not yet mentioned? If so, please explain.
- Do you understand that as long as the judgment remains unpaid, it accrues interest at the legal rate of interest in this state? Do you also understand that as long as the judgment remains unpaid, it is probably damaging to your credit rating? Do you understand that if the judgment remains unpaid, I have the right to examine you periodically?

A judgment creditor has the right to re-examine the debtor periodically. In California, the rule is 120 days. This period differs from state to state; the court clerk will know the rule in your state. At the end of this step, you should have a full picture of the debtor's financial condition. If the debtor is judgment proof, or close to judgment proof, you may need to take a hard look at letting the judgment go. There is very little point in going through the time, expense, and hassle of attaching property, if the attachments yield nothing. If there are assets available, though, in the following steps we will discuss how to attach the debtor's assets to satisfy the outstanding judgment.

Step 7: Attachments, Liens, and Garnishments

In a sense, the most productive assets for collection are not always the most valuable assets or the most liquid assets, but they are the assets that pose the greatest *inconvenience* to the judgment debtor. Consider the following: a small lien on a piece of real estate, while it is unlikely to trigger a sale of the home, can prevent the owner from refinancing the property or selling the property. The lien may also show up on the judgment debtor's credit report.

Wage garnishments are similarly inconvenient to judgment debtors. Wage garnishments, even in small amounts, are a nuisance and an embarrassment to judgment debtors; a wage garnishment announces to a debtor's employer that

FIGURE 12-4. **Sample Order Compelling Debtor's Examination**

SC-134

Name and Address of Court:

| PLAINTIFF/DE MANDANTE *(Name, street address, and telephone number of each)*: | SMALL CLAIMS CASE NO.: |
| | DEFENDANT/DEMANDADO *(Name, street address, and telephone number of each)*: |

Telephone No.:

Telephone No.:

☐ See attached sheet for additional plaintiffs and defendants.

**ORDER TO PRODUCE STATEMENT OF ASSETS
AND TO APPEAR FOR EXAMINATION**

1. TO JUDGMENT DEBTOR *(name)*:

2. YOU ARE ORDERED

   a. to pay the judgment and file proof of payment (a canceled check or money order or cash receipt, and a written declaration that shows full payment of the judgment, including postjudgment costs and interest) with the court before the hearing date shown in the box below, **OR**

   b. to (1) personally appear in this court on the date and time shown in the box below, and (2) bring with you a completed *Judgment Debtor's Statement of Assets* (form SC-133). (At the hearing you will be required to explain why you did not complete and mail form SC-133 to judgment creditor within 30 days after the *Notice of Entry of Judgment* (form SC-130) was mailed or handed to you by the clerk, and to answer questions about your income and assets.)

HEARING DATE		DATE	DAY	TIME	PLACE	COURT USE
	1.					
FECHA DEL JUICIO	2.					
	3.					

| If you fail to appear and have not paid the judgment, including postjudgment costs and interest, a bench warrant may be issued for your arrest, you may be held in contempt of court, and you may be ordered to pay penalties. | Si usted no se presenta y no ha pagado el monto del fallo judicial, inclusive las costas e intereses posteriores al fallo, la corte puede expedir una orden de detención contra usted, declararle en desacato y ordenar clue pague multas. |

3. This order may be served by a sheriff, marshal, or registered process server.

Date:

▶

(SIGNATURE OF JUDGE)

APPLICATION FOR THIS ORDER

A. Judgment creditor (the person who won the case) *(name)*:   applies for an order requiring judgment debtor (the person or business who lost the case and owes money) *(name)*:

to (1) pay the judgment or (2) personally appear in this court with a completed *Judgment Debtor's Statement of Assets* (form SC-133), explain why judgment debtor did not pay the judgment or complete and mail form SC-133 to judgment creditor within 30 days after the *Notice of Entry of Judgment* was mailed or delivered to judgment debtor, and answer questions about judgment debtor's income and assets.

B. Judgment creditor states the following:

   (1) Judgment debtor has not paid the judgment.

   (2) Judgment debtor either did not file an appeal or the appeal has been dismissed or judgment debtor lost the appeal.

   (3) Judgment debtor either did not file a motion to vacate or the motion to vacate has been denied.

   (4) More than 30 days have passed since the *Notice of Entry of Judgment* form was mailed or delivered to judgment debtor.

   (5) Judgment creditor has not received a completed *Judgment Debtor's Statement of Assets* form from judgment debtor.

   (6) The person to be examined resides or has a place of business in this county or within 150 miles of the place of examination

I declare under penalty of perjury under the laws of the State of California that the foregoing is true and correct.

Date:

▶

. . . . (TYPE OR PRINT NAME) . . . .   (See Instructions on reverse)   (DECLARANT)

— The county provides small claims advisor services free of charge. —

Page 1 of 2

| Form Adopted for Mandatory Use Judicial Council of California SC-134 [Rev. January 1, 2007] | **APPLICATION AND ORDER TO PRODUCE STATEMENT OF ASSETS AND TO APPEAR FOR EXAMINATION** (Small Claims) | Code of Civil Procedure §§ 11 6.820,116.830 www.courtinfo.ca.gov |

American LegalNet, Inc.
www.FormsWorkflow.com

he or she has been sued and has not paid the judgment. Incidentally, employers are forbidden by federal law from retaliating against employees because a wage garnishment has been placed upon the employee's earnings.

Finally, a judgment creditor can lien a judgment debtor's cash bank account. Such a lien can be very effective even if the amount in the debtor's bank account is not enough to satisfy the judgment. The judgment debtor, once their account has been attached by lien, cannot use the money to pay for housing, groceries, or anything else. The general rule suggests that the end of the month is the best time to lien a debtor's bank account because most housing payments are due on the first of the month.

The Writ of Execution

Before you can garnish a debtor's wages, or levy or attach bank accounts or other property, you must get a document from the court called a "writ of execution." A writ of execution (in some states it's called by a slightly different name) is court-ordered "permission" to attach the debtor's property. We have included a sample copy of a writ of execution form as Figure 12-5.

The court clerk will have a writ of execution form and will help you complete it. Keep in mind that a writ of execution carries a fee, but it's a recoverable cost and just gets added to the judgment. As you can see from the sample writ of execution, there is a line titled "fee for issuance of writ" where the fee for the writ is added to the total amount of the judgment. Once the writ of execution is filled out, present it to the court clerk for signature. The clerk will have you correct any errors. If the writ is complete and properly filled out, the court clerk will present you with a stamped copy of the writ.

Once the writ of execution is stamped by the court, a judgment creditor then uses the writ in connection with any one of several attachment devices, such as a garnishment of wages or a lien of bank account or personal property.

How to Levy a Bank Account

First, make sure you have your writ of execution completed and stamped by the court clerk. To make any attachment of property to satisfy your judgment,

FIGURE 12-5. **Sample Writ of Execution**

EJ-130

ATTORNEY OR PARTY WITHOUT ATTORNEY *(Name, State Bar number and address):*	FOR COURT USE ONLY

TELEPHONE NO.:   FAX NO. *(Optional):*

E-MAIL ADDRESS *(Optional):*

ATTORNEY FOR *(Name):*

☐ ATTORNEY FOR   ☐ JUDGMENT CREDITOR   ☐ ASSIGNEE OF RECORD

SUPERIOR COURT OF CALIFORNIA, COUNTY OF

STREET ADDRESS:

MAILING ADDRESS:

CITY AND ZIP CODE:

BRANCH NAME:

PLAINTIFF:

DEFENDANT:

WRIT OF	☐ **EXECUTION (Money Judgment)** ☐ **POSSESSION OF** ☐ **Personal Property** ☐ **Real Property** ☐ **SALE**	CASE NUMBER:

1. **To the Sheriff or Marshal of the County of:**

   You are directed to enforce the judgment described below with daily interest and your costs as provided by law.

2. **To any registered process server:** You are authorized to serve this writ only in accord with CCP 699.080 or CCP 715.040.

3. *(Name):*

   is the ☐ judgment creditor ☐ assignee of record   whose address is shown on this form above the court's name.

4. **Judgment debtor** *(name and last known address):*

   ☐ Additional judgment debtors on next page

5. **Judgment entered** on *(date):*

6. ☐ **Judgment renewed** on *(dates):*

7. **Notice of sale** under this writ
   a. ☐ has not been requested.
   b. ☐ has been requested *(see next page).*
8. ☐ Joint debtor information on next page.

[SEAL]

9. ☐ See next page for information on real or personal property to be delivered under a writ of possession or sold under a writ of sale.
10. ☐ This writ is issued on a sister-state judgment.
11. Total judgment . . . . $
12. Costs after judgment (per filed order or memo CCP 685.090) . . . . $
13. Subtotal *(add 11 and 12)* . . . . $
14. Credits . . . . $
15. Subtotal *(subtract 14 from 13)* . . . . . . $
16. Interest after judgment (per filed affidavit CCP 685.050) (not on GC 6103.5 fees). . . $
17. Fee for issuance of writ . . . . $
18. **Total** *(add 15, 16, and 17)* . . . . $
19. Levying officer:
    (a) Add daily interest from date of writ (at the legal rate on 15) (not on GC 6103.5 fees) of. . . . . . $
    (b) Pay directly to court costs included in 11 and 17 (GC 6103.5, 68511.3; CCP 699.520(i)) . . . . $
20. ☐ The amounts called for in items 11–19 are different for each debtor. These amounts are stated for each debtor on Attachment 20.

Issued on *(date):*   Clerk, by _____, Deputy

NOTICE TO PERSON SERVED: SEE NEXT PAGE FOR IMPORTANT INFORMATION.

Page 1 of 2

Form Approved for Optional Use
Judicial Council of California
EJ-130 [Rev. January 1, 2006]

WRIT OF EXECUTION

American LegalNet, Inc.
www.USCourtForms.com

Code of Civil Procedure, §§ 699.520, 712.010,
Government Code, § 6103.5
www.courtinfo.ca.gov

you'll need the assistance of the local sheriff. Often, their office is very near the courthouse. The writ of execution serves as "permission" for the sheriff in your jurisdiction to execute levies and garnishments on the debtor's property. One thing that the writ of execution does not do is tell the sheriff where the property is; sheriffs will not search for assets for you. You'll need to inform the sheriff of where the debtor maintains a bank account.

In some states, such as California, there is a specific form used to levy a bank account. In California, the form is called a "notice of levy." In other states, the sheriff has a one-page form that you'll need to fill out. The notice of levy (separate from the writ of execution) is an instruction to the bank to withhold and deliver the judgment debtor's funds to the sheriff. Once a notice of levy is served on the bank, the judgment debtor or the bank has a certain period of time (usually around 30 days) to claim an exemption for the property. In many states, the proceeds of wages are protected from levy just as the wages themselves would be protected from garnishment.

However, don't let a potential claim of exemption by a judgment debtor deter you from making the attachment. The judgment debtor may make a claim of exemption, but for whatever reason, the judgment debtor may fail to do so. If the debtor fails to raise a proper claim of exemption, the judgment creditor gets to take possession of the levied funds. If you have any concerns or difficulties with preparing a notice of levy, check with the sheriff's office. They are usually quite helpful and can assist you in preparing the notice of levy.

Interest on Judgments

Judgments earn interest while they remain unsatisfied. After all, the judgment debtor's obligation to pay is absolute—and so the law imposes an interest rate on the judgment. What interest rate will apply to a judgment depends on the state. Each state has its own legal rate for judgments. See the Appendix for an outline of the legal rate of interest in all 50 states. Whenever you execute on a judgment, make sure that you calculate the interest correctly.

How to Garnish a Debtor's Wages

First, make sure you have your writ of execution completed and stamped by the court clerk. Second, be mindful of your state's rules on wage garnishment—wages are often subject to substantial protections and cannot be garnished. To impose a wage garnishment, you'll need the assistance of the local sheriff. Keep in mind that a wage garnishment is a blunt instrument: You must always be careful not to push a debtor into bankruptcy. A wage garnishment can be a very traumatic episode for a debtor living on a tight budget. You can garnish a debtor's wages without difficulty if all of the following is true:

- The debtor does not quit the job, contest the garnishment, or file for bankruptcy (a bankruptcy filing "freezes" all collection efforts, and will most likely ultimately result in the discharge of the judgment).
- The debtor is a regular wage-based worker in the state where the writ of execution is issued.
- The debtor's pay is above the minimum poverty level.
- The debtor is not already burdened with existing garnishments or child or spousal support obligations.

If all the above is true and you are reasonably certain that you won't trigger the debtor to quit his or her job or declare bankruptcy, you can move forward with the garnishment. The process for obtaining a wage garnishment again requires you to see the services of the sheriff. You simply give the sheriff a copy of the writ of execution, and information regarding where the debtor works. The sheriff will inform the employer that the debtor's wages are subject to garnishment. The employer must comply with the garnishment—refusal is not an option. The sheriff will then collect the appropriate portion of the wages and deliver the funds to you.

How to Levy a Debtor's Automobile

Levying an automobile is rarely effective. In fact, I have never heard a first-hand account of a successful levy of an automobile. Here are a few reasons why levying an automobile is difficult:

- The automobile must be in a public place. If the automobile is in a locked garage, the sheriff cannot knock the door down to take possession of the automobile, but would need to secure a separate court order.
- Automobiles are exempt from levy in many states, or are subject to partial exemption in other states. In a state that exempts a portion of an automobile, an ultimate sale of the vehicle often yields a payment to the bank for the amount owed, and a payment to the debtor for the amount of the exemption, leaving little or nothing for the judgment creditor.
- The judgment debtor's car may be leased or financed, in which case the car is subject to the bank's interest.

The statement of assets that the judgment debtor provided to you should tell you who owns the debtor's car. In some states, you can search the motor vehicle department's records, but most motor vehicle departments are restricting the public availability of such information because it is commonly misused. If you are successful in determining how much "equity" is available in the automobile, you can ask the sheriff to take the car and sell it. Some warnings: The sheriff will charge high fees for delivery and storage of the automobile, and in connection with the sale. The sheriff's fees, however, will be added to the judgment. Consider also that the sale of the car in a sheriff's sale will garner far less than an open market sale.

How to Place a Lien on Real Estate

Placing a lien on real estate is a fairly sure way to satisfy a judgment—eventually. The problem with a lien on real estate is that a real estate lien only "clouds" title to the property, it does not deliver immediate money like a levy or garnishment. On the other hand, a debtor cannot object to a real estate lien as easily as he can object to say, a wage garnishment.

A lien on real property is not a levy—you will almost never be able to force a sale of the property, so the sheriff will not deliver any funds to you. Liens are effective, though, because they "tie up" the property. The judgment debtor cannot sell the property nor refinance the property without removing the lien. Ultimately, most real estate liens wind up being satisfied by judgment debtors.

You may not need to do anything to record your lien on real property. In a minority of states, a court judgment in a county automatically creates a lien on any real property in that county. Again, check with the court clerk, who will know that rule by heart. Otherwise, you can record the lien on your own. To record a lien, visit the court clerk and obtain an "abstract of judgment." An abstract of judgment is a summary of the material provisions of a court judgment that, when recorded in the county recorder's office, creates a lien upon the property of the defendant in that county, both presently owned or after acquired. You can then deliver the abstract of judgment to the county recorder's office in each county where the judgment debtor owns real estate. The recorder will record the lien, and send a notice to the judgment debtor.

A Note on Multi-State Collections

Some readers may have wondered, "What if the judgment debtor moves to another state, or has property in another state?" Collecting a judgment across state lines requires extra work, to be sure, but is not impossible. Most states have enacted a uniform law of foreign judgments called the Uniform Enforcement of Foreign Judgments Act that sets forth general guidelines for enforcing judgments across state lines. Even in the states that have not adopted the uniform law, the "Full Faith and Credit" clause of the U.S. Constitution requires that states give credence to court rulings in other states.

Here is how it works in practice: A judgment or a writ of execution from a California court has no effect in Nevada—the California judgment is only effective up to the California border. The key to enforcing a California judgment in Nevada is to file the judgment in a Nevada court (preferably in the county where the judgment debtor has property). You need to check with the clerk in the foreign state to learn about the procedure for filing out-of-state judgments. Typically, the procedure involves little more than mailing a certified copy of the original judgment to court clerk in Nevada with an affidavit showing the judgment creditor's and judgment debtor's names and addresses.

When the court files the judgment in the foreign state, you now have a judgment through which you can utilize levies, liens, and garnishments in the foreign state.

How to Levy on Business Assets

In some states, a procedure exists whereby a sheriff's office employee is sent to a judgment debtor's place of business to collect any available cash. This is familiarly referred to as a "till tap," and is well used in California. A variation is a "keeper," a sheriff's office employee that visits a place of business for a set period of hours or days and collects all receipts that come in. A keeper is expensive because she or he has to be paid an hourly wage while waiting at the debtor's place of business. If you feel a till tap would be effective, contact the sheriff's office in your county to learn more about the cost.

Non-Monetary Collection Devices

There are ways to induce a debtor to pay on a judgment without levying or garnishing property. These rules will vary by state, but usually they involve some threat to the driver's license or professional license of the judgment debtor. In some states, a judgment creditor in a case involving a car accident can notify the department of motor vehicles. In turn, the department of motor vehicles will suspend the license of any judgment debtor in a motor vehicle case until the judgment debtor satisfies the outstanding judgment. Check with the court clerk or DMV in your state to see if such a program is available.

Another variation is the possible suspension of a judgment debtor's professional license if the judgment debtor does not satisfy an outstanding judgment. You'll need to research this rule in your state to determine if this manner of relief is available.

A Note on Levy of Retirement Accounts

The process for levying a retirement account is the same as levying a bank account. After all, a retirement account is simply a bank account with special tax treatment. The difficulty with levying a retirement account is that retirement accounts are often exempt from levy by federal or state law. Federal law prohibits the levy of any retirement pension—pensions are sacrosanct under the Employment Retirement Income Security Act (ERISA), and are among the most protected assets under our legal system.

State laws sometimes go farther, protecting all forms of retirement accounts, including 401K and Roth plans. Texas and Florida lead the nation in protecting all forms of retirement accounts, while most other states offer some degree of protection. These exemption laws serve a valuable purpose: They ensure that we are not a nation with a class of destitute retirees.

In my practice, I once levied the self-employment retirement account of a 56-year old woman in California on behalf of a client of mine. California allows a judgment debtor to exempt self-employment IRAs "only to the extent necessary to provide for the support of the judgment debtor when the judgment debtor retires and for the support of the spouse and dependents of the judgment debtor." This is a fairly common construct in some states, the rule that allows levy of an IRA only to the extent that judgment debtor will not need the funds for maintenance. We were seeking about $35,000 of a total account of $55,000. Naturally, the judgment debtor argued that she needed the money for her retirement. The judge agreed, and ruled that the IRA was exempt from levy. As far as I know, that $35,000 judgment was never satisfied. One lesson from this case is that if the judgment debtor was further from retirement age, the court would be more likely to allow a levy of a retirement account.

Step 8: After the Judgment Is Paid: Filing the Satisfaction of Judgment and Removing Liens

After a judgment debtor pays the entire amount of the judgment, the judgment creditor should file a "Satisfaction of Judgment" with the court. This document tells the world (including, importantly, credit reporting agencies) that the judgment debtor has paid the judgment, and no longer owes the debt. The judgment creditor should also be sure that any liens placed against property are removed once the judgment is satisfied.

A former judgment creditor that leaves liens in place and fails to file a Satisfaction of Judgment after a judgment has been fully satisfied violates the

FIGURE 12-6. **Sample Satisfaction of Judgment Form**

EJ-100

ATTORNEY OR PARTY WITHOUT ATTORNEY (Name, State Bar number, and address):
After recording return to:

TELEPHONE NO.:
FAX NO. (Optional):
E-MAIL ADDRESS (Optional):
ATTORNEY FOR (Name):

SUPERIOR COURT OF CALIFORNIA, COUNTY OF
STREET ADDRESS:
MAILING ADDRESS:
CITY AND ZIP CODE:
BRANCH NAME:

FOR RECORDER'S OR SECRETARY OF STATE'S USE ONLY

PLAINTIFF:

DEFENDANT:

CASE NUMBER:

ACKNOWLEDGMENT OF SATISFACTION OF JUDGMENT
☐ FULL ☐ PARTIAL ☐ MATURED INSTALLMENT

FOR COURT USE ONLY

1. Satisfaction of the judgment is acknowledged as follows:
   a. ☐ Full satisfaction
      (1) ☐ Judgment is satisfied in full.
      (2) ☐ The judgment creditor has accepted payment or performance other than that specified in the judgment in full satisfaction of the judgment.
   b. ☐ Partial satisfaction
      The amount received in partial satisfaction of the judgment is $
   c. ☐ Matured installment
      All matured installments under the installment judgment have been satisfied as of (date):

2. Full name and address of judgment creditor:*

3. Full name and address of assignee of record, if any:

4. Full name and address of judgment debtor being fully or partially released:*

5. a. Judgment entered on (date):
   b. ☐ Renewal entered on (date):

6. ☐ An ☐ abstract of judgment ☐ certified copy of the judgment has been recorded as follows (complete all information for each county where recorded):

COUNTY	DATE OF RECORDING	INSTRUMENT NUMBER

7. ☐ A notice of judgment lien has been filed in the office of the Secretary of State as file number (specify):

NOTICE TO JUDGMENT DEBTOR: If this is an acknowledgment of full satisfaction of judgment, it will have to be recorded in each county shown in item 6 above, if any, in order to release the judgment lien, and will have to be filed in the office of the Secretary of State to terminate any judgment lien on personal property.

▶

Date: _____

_____
(SIGNATURE OF JUDGMENT CREDITOR OR ASSIGNEE OF CREDITOR OR ATTORNEY**)

Page 1 of 1

*The names of the judgment creditor and judgment debtor must be stated as shown in any Abstract of Judgment which was recorded and is being released by this satisfaction. ** A separate notary acknowledgment must be attached for each signature.

Form Approved for Optional Use
Judicial Council of California
EJ-100 [Rev. January 1, 2005]

ACKNOWLEDGMENT OF SATISFACTION OF JUDGMENT

American LegalNet, Inc.
www.USCourtForms.com

Code of Civil Procedure, §§ 724.060, 724.120, 724.250

rights of a judgment debtor. It is also possible that a judgment creditor's failure to remove liens and file a Satisfaction of Judgment could expose the judgment creditor to liability under the Fair Credit Reporting Act or under state laws that protect judgment debtors. Imagine if a former judgment debtor is denied a home loan because a former judgment debtor fails to remove a lien on property? In some states, the former judgment debtor can be awarded consequential damages or a set amount of money. The bottom line: it's sound practice to file a Satisfaction of Judgment when the judgment is satisfied.

California's Satisfaction of Judgment Form (Figure 12-6) is fairly representative of Satisfaction of Judgment forms used in other states. See the clerk of the court, he or she will have forms available. Some states may even post their forms on the internet.

Some judgment creditors will fail to file the Satisfaction of Judgment; some judgment creditors (especially unrepresented creditors in small claims cases) will not even be aware of the requirement to file the Satisfaction of Judgment. For this reason, defendants should always take the upper hand and insist that the creditor file the Satisfaction of Judgment. A simple letter such as found in Figure 12-7 will suffice.

Sometimes, however, the judgment creditor disappears, moves away, or dies without filing the Satisfaction of Judgment. In that case, the judgment creditor is obviously not available to file the form. If this happens, you, as the former judgment debtor, will have to contact the court to find out the procedure for submitting proof that the judgment was satisfied. The court will have a procedure whereby you can submit proof that the judgment was satisfied and proof that the judgment creditor failed to file the Satisfaction of Judgment form, and cannot be located. Thereby, you can have the court enter a satisfaction of judgment on your behalf.

Step 9: Know When to Give Up

Not all judgments can be collected. Some judgments languish for years without ever being paid. Every year, billions of dollars in judgments expire when judgment debtors pass away, and billions more are discharged in bankruptcy.

FIGURE 12-7. **Sample Letter to Creditor**

September 19, 2008

Bill Watanabe
123 Entrepreneur Way
Irvine, CA

Dear Mr. Watanabe,
Enclosed you will find the final payment of $150 to be applied to the judgment in
the case of Watanabe v. Miller, in the Irvine small claims court.

Please be sure to file the Satisfaction of Judgment—the form that you are legally
required to file when a judgment is satisfied. The clerk has copies of the form.

Thank you,

Bill Miller

Some debtors are actually too unsophisticated to either declare bankruptcy or
understand the need for bankruptcy. Some debtors languish in poverty and
debt their entire lives.

As a plaintiff and a judgment creditor, you must resist the common temptation to fight your case forever. Your judgment may not be collectible. All the
collection efforts available to a judgment creditor take time and money, and
chasing a losing judgment may be a waste of both. You need to know when to
cut your losses and write off a judgment.

Appendix
Information and Resources for Each State

W hat follows is a brief but informative summary of small claims rules and procedures in each state. Keep in mind that rules and laws change. It's always a good idea to confirm the rules with the court or with further research.

The tables direct you to state statutes for all 50 states. In the state statutes, you'll find all the codified law that governs courts and lawsuits. Also, the state-specific tables set forth, for each state, the maximum amount you can sue for in small claims court, a description of the proper county where the suit may be brought, a description of the proper manner in which to serve process upon the defendant, and how the small claims hearing date is selected. The state-specific tables set for the attorney representation rule for each jurisdiction, the special rules regarding the transfer of cases, the availability of an appeal from a small claims case, and other special rules and notes.

TABLE A-1. **Finding State Statutes Online**

State	Where to Find State Statutes
Alabama	www.legislature.state.al.us/CodeofAlabama/1975/coatoc.htm
Alaska	http://touchngo.com/lglcntr/akstats/statutes.htm
Arizona	www.azleg.state.az.us/ArizonaRevisedStatutes.asp
Arkansas	www.arkleg.state.ar.us/data/ar_code.asp
California	www.leginfo.ca.gov/calaw.html
Colorado	www2.michie.com/colorado/lpext.dll?f=templates&fn=fs-main.htm&2.0
Connecticut	www.cga.ct.gov/asp/menu/Statutes.asp
Delaware	http://michie.lexisnexis.com/delaware/lpext.dll?f=templates&fn=main-h.htm&cp=
District of Columbia	http://dccode.westgroup.com
Florida	www.flsenate.gov/statutes/
Georgia	www.lexis-nexis.com/hottopics/gacode/default.asp
Hawaii	www.capitol.hawaii.gov/site1/docs/docs.asp
Idaho	www3.state.id.us/idstat/TOC/idstTOC.html
Illinois	www.ilga.gov/legislation/ilcs/ilcs.asp
Indiana	www.in.gov/legislative/ic_iac/
Iowa	www.legis.state.ia.us/IowaLaw.html
Kansas	www.kslegislature.org/cgi-bin/statutes/index.cgi
Kentucky	www.lrc.state.ky.us/Statrev/frontpg.htm
Louisiana	www.legis.state.la.us/lss/tsrssearch.htm
Maine	http://janus.state.me.us/legis/statutes/
Maryland	http://michie.lexisnexis.com/maryland/lpext.dll?f=templates&fn=main-h.htm&cp=
Massachusetts	www.mass.gov/legis/laws/mgl/
Michigan	www.michiganlegislature.org/mileg.asp?page=ChapterIndex
Minnesota	www.leg.state.mn.us/leg/statutes.htm
Mississippi	www.mscode.com/

TABLE A-1. **Finding State Statutes Online** (continued)

State	Where to Find State Statutes
Missouri	www.moga.state.mo.us/homestat.htm
Montana	http://data.opi.state.mt.us/bills/mca_toc/index.htm
Nebraska	www.nlc.state.ne.us/bestofweb/currentstatutes.html
Nevada	www.leg.state.nv.us/nrsindex/index.html
New Hampshire	http://gencourt.state.nh.us/rsa/html/indexes/default.html
New Jersey	www.njlawnet.com/njstatutes.html
New Mexico	www.conwaygreene.com/nmsu/lpext.dll?f=templates&fn=main-h.htm&2.0
New York	http://public.leginfo.state.ny.us/menugetf.cgi?
North Carolina	www.ncga.state.nc.us/gascripts/Statutes/statutestoc.pl
North Dakota	www.legis.nd.gov/information/statutes/cent-code.html
Ohio	http://codes.ohio.gov/orc
Oklahoma	www.lsb.state.ok.us/osStatuesTitle.html
Oregon	www.leg.state.or.us/ors
Pennsylvania	www.legis.state.pa.us/cfdocs/legis/LI/PUBLIC/cons_index.cfm
Rhode Island	www.rilin.state.ri.us/Statutes
South Carolina	www.scstatehouse.net/code/statmast.htm
South Dakota	http://legis.state.sd.us/statutes/index.aspx
Tennessee	www.michie.com
Texas	http://tlo2.tlc.state.tx.us/statutes/statutes.html
Utah	www.le.state.ut.us/Documents/code_const.htm
Vermont	www.michie.com
Virginia	www.virginia.gov/cmsportal/government_881/virginia_1048/
Washington	http://apps.leg.wa.gov/rcw/
West Virginia	www.courts.state.va.us/legallinks/va.html
Wisconsin	www.legis.state.wi.us/rsb/stats.html
Wyoming	http://legisweb.state.wy.us/titles/statutes.htm

TABLE A-2. **Statutes of Limitations for All 50 States**

The following table sets forth the statutes of limitations (expressed in years) under the legal theories of written and oral contracts for injury to person and injury to property.

	Written Contracts and Book/Open Accounts	Oral Contracts and Agreements	Negligence: Injury to Person	Negligence: Property Damage
Alabama	6	6	2	6
Alaska	3	3	2	6
Arizona	6	3	2	2
Arkansas	5	5	3	3
California	4	2	2	3
Colorado	6	6	2/3	2
Connecticut	6	3	2	2
Delaware	3	3	2	2
District of Columbia	3	3	3	3
Florida	5	4	4	4
Georgia	6	4	2	4
Hawaii	6	6	2	2
Idaho	5	4	2	3
Illinois	10	5	2	5
Indiana	10	6	2	2
Iowa	10	5	2	5
Kansas	5	3	2	2
Kentucky	15	5	1	2
Louisiana	10	10	1	1
Maine	6	6	6	6
Maryland	3	3	3	3
Massachusetts	6	6	3	3
Michigan	6	6	3	3
Minnesota	6	6	6	2
Mississippi	3	3	3	3

TABLE A-2. **Statutes of Limitations for All 50 States** (continued)

	Written Contracts and Book/Open Accounts	Oral Contracts and Agreements	Negligence: Injury to Person	Negligence: Property Damage
Missouri	4/5/10	5	5	5
Montana	8	5	3	2
Nebraska	5	4	4	4
Nevada	6	4	2	3
New Hampshire	3	3	3	3
New Jersey	6	6	6	2
New Mexico	6	4	3	4
New York	6	6	3	3
North Carolina	3	3	3	3
North Dakota	6	6	6	6
Ohio	15	6	2	2
Oklahoma	5	3	3	2
Oregon	6	6	2	6
Pennsylvania	4	4	2	2
Rhode Island	10	10	3	10
South Carolina	3	3	3	3
South Dakota	6	6	3	6
Tennessee	6	6	1	3
Texas	4	4	2	2
Utah	6	4	4	3
Vermont	6	6	3	3
Virginia	5	3	2	5
Washington	6	3	3	3
West Virginia	10	5	2	2
Wisconsin	6	6	3	6
Wyoming	10	8	4	4

TABLE A-3. **Small Claims Court Summaries for All 50 States**

Alabama	
Maximum Jurisdictional Dollar Amount	The maximum dollar amount is $3,000.
Where Suit May Be Brought	Case may be brought where the defendant resides, or injury or property damage occurred. A corporation is deemed to reside where it does business.
Proper Manner of Service of Process upon Defendant	Service may be made by certified mail, sheriff or court-approved adult.
How the Hearing Date is Selected	The hearing date is set by the court.
Attorney Representation Rule	Attorneys are allowed, and are required for assignees (collection agencies).
Special Provisions Regarding Transfer or Jurisdiction of Cases	There is no provision.
Availability of Appeals	Either litigant may appeal for a new trial to circuit court within 14 days.
Special Rules and Notes	Injunctive relief is available. Defendant must answer within 14 days or lose by default. Small claims court cannot hear eviction cases.

TABLE A-3. **Small Claims Court Summaries for All 50 States** (continued)

Alaska	
Maximum Jurisdictional Dollar Amount	The maximum dollar amount is $10,000.
Where Suit May Be Brought	Case may be brought where the defendant resides, is employed, or where injury or property damage occurred.
Proper Manner of Service of Process upon Defendant	Service may be made by certified or registered mail (binding on defendant who refuses to accept), peace officer, or court-appointed individual.
How the Hearing Date Is Selected	Not less than 15 days from service.
Attorney Representation Rule	Attorneys are allowed and are required for assignees (collection agencies).
Special Provisions Regarding Transfer or Jurisdiction of Cases	Either the defendant or a plaintiff against whom a counterclaim has been filed, or the judge may transfer case to regular district court.
Availability of Appeals	For claims over $50, either litigant may appeal for a review of law but not of the facts to superior court within 30 days.
Special Rules and Notes	Injunctive relief is available. Defendant must file written answer within 20 days of service or lose by default. Arbitration may be ordered in counterclaim for less than $3,000. The court may order installment payments. No cases against the state.

TABLE A-3. **Small Claims Court Summaries for All 50 States** (continued)

Arizona	
Maximum Jurisdictional Dollar Amount	The maximum dollar amount is $2500 in the small claims division and $5,000 in regular justice court.
Where Suit May Be Brought	Case may be brought where the defendant resides. Intentional torts cases are heard where the act occurred. Cases to recover personal property are heard where the property is. Contract cases may be brought where the performance expected. Cases against nonresident defendants are brought where plaintiff resides.
Proper Manner of Service of Process upon Defendant	Service may be made by certified or registered mail with return receipts requested, sheriff, deputy, court-approved adult or private process server.
How the Hearing Date Is Selected	The hearing date is set by the court within 60 days of the filing of the answer.
Attorney Representation Rule	Attorneys are not allowed unless both sides agree in writing.
Special Provisions Regarding Transfer or Jurisdiction of Cases	Counterclaims over $2,500 or objections at least ten days before hearing (for right of appeal and jury), transfers to justice court. For counterclaims over $5,000, transfer is allowed to superior court.
Availability of Appeals	Appeals are not allowed in Small Claims Division, but are allowed following decisions in justice court.
Special Rules and Notes	Injunctive relief is available. Defendant must answer within 20 days or lose by default. No discovery is allowed. Jury trials are not available. No cases for libel or slander, forcible entry or unlawful detainer, specific performance, prejudgment remedies, injunctions, cases against the state or cases involving ownership of real estate. Right to sue may not be transferred.

TABLE A-3. **Small Claims Court Summaries for All 50 States** (continued)

Arkansas	
Maximum Jurisdictional Dollar Amount	The maximum dollar amount is $5,000.
Where Suit May Be Brought	Cases may be brought in the county in which a defendant currently resides or in the county where he or she was to perform an obligation. When the action is for injury to persons or to personal property, you can file a lawsuit in the county in which the injury occurred or in the county where the defendant currently resides. In all other cases, the case may be brought in the county in which the defendant resides.
Proper Manner of Service of Process upon Defendant	Complaints are usually served in one of three ways: by certified mail; by personal delivery of a summons by the sheriff; or in some counties, by a private process server. A summons is a Writ of Process directed to the sheriff or other proper officer requiring him to notify the person named that an action has been commenced against him and that he is required to answer the complaint in the action or have a judgment entered against him.
Attorney Representation Rule	Attorneys are not allowed in small claims courts, but are allowed in Justice of the Peace courts.
Special Provisions Regarding Transfer or Jurisdiction of Cases	In small claims, if party represented by an attorney or if defendant files compulsory counterclaim for more than $5000, the case shall be tried under regular civil procedure of municipal court. No transfer provision in Justice of Peace courts.
Availability of Appeals	By either side for new trial to circuit court within 30 days.
Special Rules and Notes	Collection agents and commercial lenders may not sue. Corporations limited to 12 claims a year. Right to sue may not be transferred. Defendant must file written answer within 20 days of service if he or she is in the state, within 30 days if outside the state.

TABLE A-3. **Small Claims Court Summaries for All 50 States** (continued)

California	
Maximum Jurisdictional Dollar Amount	An individual cannot seek more than $7,500 in a claim. Corporations and other entities (like government entities) cannot ask for more than $5,000. You can file as many claims as you want for up to $2,500 each. But you can only file two claims in a calendar year that ask for more than $2,500. One can only sue a guarantor for up to $4,000 ($2,500 if they don't charge for the guarantee). But if one is a natural person filing against the Registrar of the Contractors' State License Board, you can sue a guarantor for up to $7500. A guarantor is a person who promises to be responsible for what another person owes.
Where Suit May Be Brought	Cases should be brought where the defendant resides or injury occurred. Contract cases may be brought where the performance expected. Consumer Contract cases may be brought where the signed. A corporation is deemed to reside where it does business.
Proper Manner of Service of Process upon Defendant	Service may be made by certified or registered mail, sheriff or court-approved disinterested adult.
How the Hearing Date Is Selected	Defendant in country: 10-40 days after summons issued. One or more defendants outside country: 30-70 days after summons issued. All other cases: 90 days after summons issued.
Attorney Representation Rule	Attorneys are not allowed unless attorney represents self.
Special Provisions Regarding Transfer or Jurisdiction of Cases	If defendant counterclaims for more than $5,000, counterclaim removed to higher court if judge permits.
Availability of Appeals	A defendant may appeal for a new trial to superior court within 30 days. Lawyers are allowed to appear in appeals.
Special Rules and Notes	Injunctive relief is available. Right to sue may not be transferred. Judge may determine payment schedule. Interpreters are available. Small claims advisor is available at no cost. The court may order arbitration. Assignees (collection agencies) cannot sue in small claims court. Small claims court cannot hear eviction cases.

TABLE A-3. **Small Claims Court Summaries for All 50 States** (continued)

Colorado	
Maximum Jurisdictional Dollar Amount	The maximum dollar amount is $7,500.
Where Suit May Be Brought	Case may be brought where the defendant resides, is employed, or does business.
Proper Manner of Service of Process upon Defendant	Service may be made by certified mail, return receipt requested, or by a disinterested adult or a sheriff.
How the Hearing Date Is Selected	The hearing date is set by the court, and will be at least 21 days after summons issued.
Attorney Representation Rule	Attorneys are not allowed unless attorney represents self or as full-time employee of partnership or corporation involved in the case. If attorney appears, other side may also have attorney.
Special Provisions Regarding Transfer or Jurisdiction of Cases	If defendant counterclaims for more than $5,000 or wants to use an attorney, the case shall be tried under regular civil procedure of court.
Availability of Appeals	Either litigant may appeal for a review of law but not of the facts to district court within 15 days.
Special Rules and Notes	No Injunctive relief is available except for the nullification of contracts. Jury trials are not available. No cases for libel or slander, forcible entry or detainer, eviction, recovery of personal property, specific performance, prejudgment attachment, injunctions or traffic cases. Right to sue may not be transferred. No discovery is allowed. Limit of two claims a month per plaintiff or 18 claims a year. Referee may be appointed.

TABLE A-3. **Small Claims Court Summaries for All 50 States** (continued)

Connecticut	
Maximum Jurisdictional Dollar Amount	The maximum dollar amount is $5,000 (except in landlord-tenant security deposit claims).
Where Suit May Be Brought	Case may be brought where the defendant resides, does business, or where injury occurred. Contract cases may be brought where the breach occurred or obligation incurred. Landlord/tenant—where premises are located.
Proper Manner of Service of Process upon Defendant	Service may be made by registered or certified mail, sheriff, peace officer, disinterested adult.
How the Hearing Date Is Selected	The hearing date is set by the court.
Attorney Representation Rule	Attorneys are allowed. Attorneys are required for corporations.
Special Provisions Regarding Transfer or Jurisdiction of Cases	If defendant has a counterclaim over $3500 and requests and the court approves, the case may be heard according to regular civil procedure of superior court.
Availability of Appeals	Appeals are not allowed.
Special Rules and Notes	No injunctive relief is available in small claims court. Small claims court cannot hear libel or slander cases, or reputational damage cases. Litigants may submit the matter to County Commissioner for binding decision. Small claims court cannot hear eviction cases.

TABLE A-3. **Small Claims Court Summaries for All 50 States** (continued)

Delaware *(Note that Delaware does not have small claims courts. Cases are heard by the Justice of the Peace.)*	
Maximum Jurisdictional Dollar Amount	The maximum dollar amount is $15,000.
Where Suit May Be Brought	Any county.
Proper Manner of Service of Process upon Defendant	Service may be made by certified mail, sheriff, deputy, coroner, constable, or court-designated individual.
How the Hearing Date Is Selected	The hearing date is set by the court.
Attorney Representation Rule	Attorneys are allowed.
Special Provisions Regarding Transfer or Jurisdiction of Cases	There are no provisions.
Availability of Appeals	Either litigant may appeal for a new trial to superior court within 15 days.
Special Rules and Notes	Jury trials are generally not allowed.
	Defendant must file written answer within 15 days after service is made, or will lose by default. Interest due on any cause of action may be added to the claim, even if adding it will make the amount exceed $15,000.
	If defendant's counterclaim against plaintiff exceeds $15,000, plaintiff can still pursue the counterclaim in Justice of the Peace court since there is no provision for transfer to another court. If defendant wins the counterclaim, two options are available:
	1) the court will note the outcome on the record and defendant can prosecute the cause of action in higher court, or
	2) defendant may waive the excess over $15,000 and accept $15,000 as the judgment.

TABLE A-3. **Small Claims Court Summaries for All 50 States** (continued)

Florida	
Maximum Jurisdictional Dollar Amount	The maximum dollar amount is $5,000.
Where Suit May Be Brought	Cases should be brought where the defendant resides or where the injury occurred. Contracts cases can be heard where agreed, if contract provides so, where unsecured note was signed, or where maker of note resides, or where breach of contract occurred. In cases to recover property, cases should be heard where the property is. A U.S. corporation is deemed to reside where it maintains office for customary business. An out-of-state corporation resides where it has an agent.
Proper Manner of Service of Process upon Defendant	Service may be made by registered mail with return receipt (Florida residents only), or by a peace officer or court-approved disinterested adult.
How the Hearing Date Is Selected	Within 60 days after pre-trial conference set by the court.
Attorney Representation Rule	Attorneys are allowed; the court may require attorneys to appear for collection agents and assignees.
Special Provisions Regarding Transfer or Jurisdiction of Cases	If defendant counterclaims for more than $2,500, the case is tried under regular civil procedure of the county court.
Availability of Appeals	Appeals may be made by either side for review of law, but not for review of facts. Appeals are made to the circuit court within 30 days.
Special Rules and Notes	Injunctive relief is available. Jury trial is available. Party represented by attorney is subject to discovery. Defendant must file counterclaim in writing at least five days before appearance date. Eviction cases allowed.

TABLE A-3. **Small Claims Court Summaries for All 50 States** (continued)

Georgia *(Georgia has no small claims court. Cases are heard in magistrate court.)*	
Maximum Jurisdictional Dollar Amount	The maximum dollar amount is $15,000.
Where Suit May Be Brought	Case may be brought where the defendant resides.
Proper Manner of Service of Process upon Defendant	Service may be made by constable or court-approved adult.
How the Hearing Date Is Selected	The hearing date is set by the court.
Attorney Representation Rule	Attorneys are allowed.
Special Provisions Regarding Transfer or Jurisdiction of Cases	If defendant counterclaims for more than $15,000, the case may be transferred to an upper court.
Availability of Appeals	Either litigant may appeal for a new trial to superior court within 30 days.
Special Rules and Notes	Injunctive relief is available. Defendant must answer within 30 days or lose by default. Jury trials are not available. The court may order installment payments. Defendant must answer complaint (in writing or orally) within 30 days to avoid default.

TABLE A-3. **Small Claims Court Summaries for All 50 States** (continued)

Hawaii	
Maximum Jurisdictional Dollar Amount	In most cases, $3,500. Counterclaims enjoy a limit of $20,000. Cases for the return of residential rental security deposits have no limit.
Where Suit May Be Brought	The case can be brought where the defendant resides. If defendant resides outside of the judicial circuit, the case should be brought where the breach or injury occurred.
Proper Manner of Service of Process upon Defendant	Service may be made by certified or registered mail or otherwise by sheriff, deputy, chief of police or court-appointed process server, or by either party personally.
How the Hearing Date Is Selected	The hearing date is set by the court.
Attorney Representation Rule	Attorneys are allowed, except in landlord-tenant deposit cases.
Special Provisions Regarding Transfer or Jurisdiction of Cases	The case may be transferred if either party demands a jury trial or if the claim or counterclaim exceeds $5,000. Otherwise, the case may be transferred only if plaintiff agrees.
Availability of Appeals	Appeals are not allowed, although the losing party may ask the court to alter or set aside the judgment within 10 days after filing of the judgment.
Special Rules and Notes	No Injunctive relief is available except in landlord-tenant cases, in which jurisdiction is limited to certain orders.

TABLE A-3. **Small Claims Court Summaries for All 50 States** (continued)

Idaho	
Maximum Jurisdictional Dollar Amount	The maximum dollar amount is $4,000.
Where Suit May Be Brought	Cases should be brought where the defendant resides or where breach or injury occurred.
Proper Manner of Service of Process upon Defendant	Service may be made by certified or registered mail with return receipt, sheriff or court-approved disinterested adult.
How the Hearing Date Is Selected	The hearing date is set by the court.
Attorney Representation Rule	Attorneys are not allowed.
Special Provisions Regarding Transfer or Jurisdiction of Cases	There are no provisions.
Availability of Appeals	Either litigant may request a new trial within 30 days. New trial is assigned to new judge.
Special Rules and Notes	Jury trials are not available. Right to sue may not be transferred or assigned. The court cannot award punitive damages. The court cannot award damages for pain or suffering. Small claims court cannot hear eviction cases.

TABLE A-3. **Small Claims Court Summaries for All 50 States** (continued)

Illinois	
Maximum Jurisdictional Dollar Amount	The maximum dollar amount is $10,000.
Where Suit May Be Brought	Cases should be brought where the defendant resides or injury occurred. Contract case can be brought where performance expected.
Proper Manner of Service of Process upon Defendant	Service may be made by certified or registered mail with return receipt (if defendant resides within county of suit), sheriff or court-approved adult.
How the Hearing Date Is Selected	Between 14 and 40 days after summons issued.
Attorney Representation Rule	Attorneys are allowed, except in Cook County "Pro Se" branch. Attorneys are required for corporations and LLCs.
Special Provisions Regarding Transfer or Jurisdiction of Cases	Case may be transferred if the claim or counterclaim exceeds $10,000.
Availability of Appeals	Either litigant may appeal for a review of law but not of the facts to appellate court within 30 days.
Special Rules and Notes	Jury trial available at request of either party. The court may order installment payments. The court may order arbitration.

TABLE A-3. **Small Claims Court Summaries for All 50 States** (continued)

Indiana	
Maximum Jurisdictional Dollar Amount	The maximum dollar amount is $6,000.
Where Suit May Be Brought	Cases should be brought where the defendant resides or where injury occurred. Contract cases may be brought where the obligation incurred or performance expected.
Proper Manner of Service of Process upon Defendant	Service may be made by personal service. If personal service is not successful, then by registered or certified mail. In the alternative, service may be made by sheriff or peace officer.
Attorney Representation Rule	Attorneys are allowed.
Special Provisions Regarding Transfer or Jurisdiction of Cases	If defendant requests a jury trial, the case shall be tried under regular civil procedure of appropriate court.
Availability of Appeals	Either litigant may appeal for a review of law but not of the facts to a court of appeals within 60 days.
Special Rules and Notes	No injunctive relief is available in small claims court. Defendant may request jury trial within ten days following service of complaint if she or he can show questions of fact requiring a jury determination. In Marion County Small Claims Court, jury trials are not available. Case will be transferred to superior court if defendant request jury trial at least three days before trial date. The court may order installment payments.

TABLE A-3. **Small Claims Court Summaries for All 50 States** (continued)

Iowa	
Maximum Jurisdictional Dollar Amount	The maximum dollar amount is $5,000.
Where Suit May Be Brought	Cases should be brought where the defendant resides or injury occurred. Contracts cases can be heard, where the contractual obligation was incurred. Negotiable instruments where maker resides. Nonresident defendants can be sued where found. A corporation is deemed to reside where it has an office or agent.
Proper Manner of Service of Process upon Defendant	Service may be made by certified or registered mail, peace officer, or court-approved disinterested adult (except in eviction suits).
How the Hearing Date Is Selected	Defendant must appear within 20 days, the hearing shall be set within 5-20 days thereafter.
Attorney Representation Rule	Attorneys are allowed.
Special Provisions Regarding Transfer or Jurisdiction of Cases	If the defendant requests a jury trial or counterclaims for more than $4,000, the case shall be tried under regular civil procedure of the district court.
Availability of Appeals	Either litigant may appeal for a review of law but not of the facts to district court within 20 days.
Special Rules and Notes	No injunctive relief is available in small claims court. Jury trials are not available. Resident defendants have 20 days and nonresidents have 60 days to answer or lose by default. Written pleadings not required. The court may order installment payments including garnishments, where the amount sought does not exceed $4000. Replevin may be granted of value of property is $5,000 or less.

TABLE A-3. **Small Claims Court Summaries for All 50 States** (continued)

Kansas	
Maximum Jurisdictional Dollar Amount	The maximum dollar amount is $4,000.
Where Suit May Be Brought	Case may be brought where the defendant resides, does business, or where injury occurred. A corporation is deemed to reside where it does business or maintains registered office or resident agent.
Proper Manner of Service of Process upon Defendant	Service may be made by sheriff, deputy, attorney or court-approved adult, certified mail
How the Hearing Date Is Selected	The hearing date is set by the court.
Attorney Representation Rule	Generally attorney are not allowed, but if one party uses an attorney or is an attorney, all parties shall have the opportunity to have an attorney.
Special Provisions Regarding Transfer or Jurisdiction of Cases	If defendant counterclaims for more than $4,000 but less than dollar limit of district court, judge will decide case or allow defendant to transfer to court of competent jurisdiction.
Availability of Appeals	Either litigant may appeal for a new trial to district court within 10 days.
Special Rules and Notes	Limit of 10 claims a year per plaintiff. Right to sue may not be transferred. No discovery is allowed. Collection agents may not sue. Replevin may be granted if value of property is $4,000 or less. Jury trials are not allowed.

TABLE A-3. **Small Claims Court Summaries for All 50 States** (continued)

Kentucky	
Maximum Jurisdictional Dollar Amount	The maximum dollar amount is $1,500.
Where Suit May Be Brought	Cases should be brought where the defendant resides or does business.
Proper Manner of Service of Process upon Defendant	Service may be made by certified or registered mail. In the alternative, service may be made by sheriff or constable.
How the Hearing Date Is Selected	20-40 days from service.
Attorney Representation Rule	Attorneys are allowed.
Special Provisions Regarding Transfer or Jurisdiction of Cases	If defendant counterclaims for more than $1,500 or requests a jury trial or at judge's discretion, the case shall be tried under regular civil procedure of district court or circuit court.
Availability of Appeals	Either litigant may appeal for a review of law but not of the facts to circuit court within 10 days.
Special Rules and Notes	Limited injunctive relief is available. Limit of 25 claims a year per plaintiff. Collection agents and lenders of money at interest may not sue. No discovery is allowed. No libel, slander, alienation of affection, malicious prosecution, class action, or abuse of process actions. Jury trials are only allowed if defendant makes a written request within at least seven days before hearing date. Case is then transferred to regular court.

TABLE A-3. **Small Claims Court Summaries for All 50 States** (continued)

Louisiana	
Maximum Jurisdictional Dollar Amount	The maximum dollar amount is $3,000.
Where Suit May Be Brought	Case may be brought where the defendant resides. A corporation is deemed to reside where it has an office or business establishment.
Proper Manner of Service of Process upon Defendant	Service may be made in the following ways: by certified mail with return receipt, sheriff, marshal, or constable.
How the Hearing Date Is Selected	The hearing date is set by the court.
Attorney Representation Rule	Attorneys are allowed.
Special Provisions Regarding Transfer or Jurisdiction of Cases	City court: if defendant counterclaims for more than $3,000, (or if defendant files written request within time allowed), the case shall be tried under regular civil procedure of city court Justice of the Peace. If demand exceeds jurisdictional limit, case will be transferred to court of appropriate jurisdiction.
Availability of Appeals	City court: Appeals are not allowed. Justice of the Peace: Either litigant may appeal for a new trial to district court within 15 days.
Special Rules and Notes	In Louisiana's urban parishes, small claims cases are heard in City court. In rural parishes, cases are heard by the Justice of the Peace. Injunctive relief available in either court. Jury trials are not available. Case may be referred to arbitration if both sides consent. The court may order installment payments. Defendant must answer within ten days (15 if served through the secretary of state) or may loser by default. No real estate or family law cases. No class actions, summary proceedings, or incomplete proceedings allowed. Either party may request arbitration.

TABLE A-3. **Small Claims Court Summaries for All 50 States** (continued)

Maine	
Maximum Jurisdictional Dollar Amount	The maximum dollar amount is $4,500.
Where Suit May Be Brought	Case may be brought where the defendant resides, does business, or where transaction occurred. Cases against corporations may be brought where resident agent resides.
Proper Manner of Service of Process upon Defendant	Service may be made by certified mail, registered mail, sheriff, deputy, court-approved adult, or court clerk.
How the Hearing Date Is Selected	The hearing date is set by the court.
Attorney Representation Rule	Attorneys are allowed.
Special Provisions Regarding Transfer or Jurisdiction of Cases	Allowed.
Availability of Appeals	Either litigant may appeal to superior court within 30 days.
Special Rules and Notes	Limited injunctive relief is available. Jury trials are not available. The court may order mediation. Court cannot hear cases involving ownership of real estate.

TABLE A-3. **Small Claims Court Summaries for All 50 States** (continued)

Maryland	
Maximum Jurisdictional Dollar Amount	The maximum dollar amount is $5,000.
Where Suit May Be Brought	Case may be brought where the defendant resides, has regular business or is employed, or where injury occurred. Cases to recover personal property may be brought where the property is. Nonresident individual defendants may be sued in any county. A corporation is deemed to reside where principal office is. Nonresident corporate defendants may be sued where plaintiff resides.
Proper Manner of Service of Process upon Defendant	Service may be made by certified mail, sheriff, or non-party adult (may be an attorney for a party). If refused, clerk may re-mail and service is presumed.
How the Hearing Date Is Selected	The hearing date is set by the court, and is at least 60 days from filing of complaint (90 days for out-of-state defendants).
Attorney Representation Rule	Attorneys are allowed.
Special Provisions Regarding Transfer or Jurisdiction of Cases	If either side counterclaims for more than $2,500 or if defendant requests a jury trial, the case shall be tried under regular civil procedure of court.
Availability of Appeals	Either litigant may appeal for a new trial to circuit court within 30 days.
Special Rules and Notes	No injunctive relief is available in small claims court. No discovery is allowed. Jury trials are not allowed.

TABLE A-3. **Small Claims Court Summaries for All 50 States** (continued)

Massachusetts	
Maximum Jurisdictional Dollar Amount	The maximum dollar amount is $2,000, but there is no limit for property damage caused by motor vehicles.
Where Suit May Be Brought	Where plaintiff or defendant resides or where the defendant has regular business or is employed. Landlord-tenant cases: Where property is.
Proper Manner of Service of Process upon Defendant	Service may be made by certified or registered mail, sheriff, or constable.
How the Hearing Date Is Selected	The hearing date is set by the court.
Attorney Representation Rule	Attorneys are allowed.
Special Provisions Regarding Transfer or Jurisdiction of Cases	At judge's discretion, the case shall be tried under regular civil procedure of appropriate court.
Availability of Appeals	The defendant may appeal for a new trial to superior court within 10 days.
Special Rules and Notes	In Massachusetts, small claims is a division of the municipal court in Boston, and the district court in the remainder of the Commonwealth. Small claims court cannot hear libel and/or slander cases. Court may refer cases to mediation if both sides agree. For consumer complaints, plaintiff must make a demand 30 days before filing suit. Attorney's fees can be recovered, and triple damages are available.

TABLE A-3. **Small Claims Court Summaries for All 50 States** (continued)

Michigan	
Maximum Jurisdictional Dollar Amount	The maximum dollar amount is $3,000.
Where Suit May Be Brought	Cases should be brought where the defendant resides or where breach or injury occurred. If suing local government entity, suit must be brought in location of that entity.
Proper Manner of Service of Process upon Defendant	Service may be made by personal service or court clerk's certified mail with return receipt.
How the Hearing Date Is Selected	15-45 days from service.
Attorney Representation Rule	Attorneys are not allowed.
Special Provisions Regarding Transfer or Jurisdiction of Cases	If either side requests or defendant counterclaims for more than $3,000, the case shall be tried under regular civil procedure of court. Either party may transfer to regular district court procedure.
Availability of Appeals	If trial was before district court magistrate, either litigant may appeal for a new trial to a small claims district court judge within seven days. Otherwise, appeals are not available.
Special Rules and Notes	No injunctive relief is available in small claims court. Right to sue may not be transferred. No libel or slander, intentional torts or fraud cases. Jury trials are not available. Limit of five claims per plaintiff. A plaintiff may not file more than five claims in one week. Court may refer cases to mediation or arbitration.

TABLE A-3. **Small Claims Court Summaries for All 50 States** (continued)

Minnesota	
Maximum Jurisdictional Dollar Amount	The maximum dollar amount is $7,500, but only $4,000 in cases involving a commercial consumer credit transaction.
Where Suit May Be Brought	Cases should be brought where the defendant resides or where injury or property damage occurred. A corporation is deemed to reside where it does business or has a resident agent.
Proper Manner of Service of Process upon Defendant	Service may be made by first class mail (certified mail if claim exceeds $2,500), sheriff or court-approved adult.
Attorney Representation Rule	Attorneys are not allowed except with court's permission. Attorney representation is required for corporations.
Special Provisions Regarding Transfer or Jurisdiction of Cases	By either side on jury demand or if defendant counterclaims for more than $3,500, the case shall be tried under regular civil procedure of county court.
Availability of Appeals	Either litigant may appeal for a new trial to regular division of county court within 20 days. (Jury trial permitted upon appeal).
Special Rules and Notes	In Minnesota, small claims is known as "Conciliation Court." Disputes about ownership of real estate are not allowed. Libel or slander cases are not allowed. Medical malpractice claims are not allowed. Jury trials are not available. No pre-trial attachments or garnishments are allowed. A defendant must file counterclaim within five days of the trial date.

TABLE A-3. **Small Claims Court Summaries for All 50 States** (continued)

Mississippi	
Maximum Jurisdictional Dollar Amount	The maximum dollar amount is $2,500.
Where Suit May Be Brought	Case may be brought where the defendant resides. Nonresident defendants may be sued where breach or injury occurred.
Proper Manner of Service of Process upon Defendant	Service may be made by Sheriff, constable, or disinterested adult. Service by disinterested adult requires a showing of need and requires the court's permission.
How the Hearing Date Is Selected	The hearing date is set by the court.
Attorney Representation Rule	Attorneys are allowed.
Special Provisions Regarding Transfer or Jurisdiction of Cases	There are no provisions.
Availability of Appeals	Either litigant may appeal for a new trial to circuit court within 10 days.
Special Rules and Notes	In Mississippi, small claims cases are heard in justice court. Some help to collect judgments is available.

TABLE A-3. **Small Claims Court Summaries for All 50 States** (continued)

Missouri	
Maximum Jurisdictional Dollar Amount	The maximum dollar amount is $3,000.
Where Suit May Be Brought	Case may be brought where the defendant resides, where breach or injury occurred or where plaintiff resides and defendant is found. A corporation is deemed to reside where it has office or agent.
Proper Manner of Service of Process upon Defendant	Service may be made by certified mail with return receipt. If not possible, sheriff will serve.
How the Hearing Date Is Selected	The hearing date is set by the court.
Attorney Representation Rule	Attorneys are allowed.
Special Provisions Regarding Transfer or Jurisdiction of Cases	If defendant files compulsory counterclaim for more than $3,000, the case shall be tried under regular civil procedure of court, unless both sides agree not to transfer case.
Availability of Appeals	Either litigant may appeal for a new trial to regular circuit court judge within 10 days.
Special Rules and Notes	No discovery is allowed. Jury trials are not available. Right to sue may not be transferred. Limit of six claims a year per plaintiff. Defendant may file counterclaim against plaintiff any time up to 10 days after service of process and before the hearing date.

TABLE A-3. **Small Claims Court Summaries for All 50 States** (continued)

Montana	
Maximum Jurisdictional Dollar Amount	The maximum dollar amount is $3,000.
Where Suit May Be Brought	Case may be brought where the defendant resides. Contract cases may be brought where the performance expected.
Proper Manner of Service of Process upon Defendant	Service may be made by Sheriff or constable. (Justice court only: disinterested adult).
How the Hearing Date Is Selected	District court: 10-30 days from filing of claim. Justice court: 10-40 days.
Attorney Representation Rule	Not allowed, unless all sides represented by attorneys.
Special Provisions Regarding Transfer or Jurisdiction of Cases	District court: There are no provisions. Justice court: If defendant files notice within 10 days of receipt of complaint, the case shall be tried under regular civil procedure of court.
Availability of Appeals	Allowed by either party within 30 days (from justice or city court to district court) for new trial. Within ten days (from small claims court to justice or district court) on law, not facts.
Special Rules and Notes	A jury trial is available to the defendant unless a counterclaim is filed. The right to sue may not be transferred or assigned. No personal injury or property damage cases are allowed. Plaintiffs are restricted to a limit of ten claims a year. Defendant's counterclaim of up to $2500 arising out of the same transaction or occurrence must be served on plaintiff at least 72 hours before the hearing date.

TABLE A-3. **Small Claims Court Summaries for All 50 States** (continued)

Nebraska	
Maximum Jurisdictional Dollar Amount	The maximum dollar amount is $2,700.
Where Suit May Be Brought	Case may be brought where the defendant or agent resides or does business or where breach or injury occurred. A corporation is deemed to reside where it does business or has agent.
Proper Manner of Service of Process upon Defendant	Service may be made by certified mail or sheriff sent according to court instructions.
How the Hearing Date Is Selected	The hearing date is set by the court.
Attorney Representation Rule	Attorneys are not allowed.
Special Provisions Regarding Transfer or Jurisdiction of Cases	Defendant may request transfer of case from small claims court to county court docket. Must request transfer at least two days before the hearing time and must pay the difference in fees between the small claims court and the regular docket of county court. By law, plaintiff cannot object to transfer. After transfer, both the defendant and plaintiff may have an attorney. Jury trial must be requested when transfer is requested.
Availability of Appeals	Either litigant may appeal for a new trial to district court within 30 days. Attorneys are allowed, but a jury trial is not permitted.
Special Rules and Notes	Injunctive relief is available. Right to sue may not be transferred. Limit of two claims a week; up to ten claims a year per plaintiff.

TABLE A-3. **Small Claims Court Summaries for All 50 States** (continued)

Nevada	
Maximum Jurisdictional Dollar Amount	The maximum dollar amount is $5,000.
Where Suit May Be Brought	Cases should be brought where the defendant resides or does business. A corporation is deemed to reside where it does business or maintains an office.
Proper Manner of Service of Process upon Defendant	Service may be made by certified or registered mail with return receipt mailed by clerk, sheriff, constable or court-approved adult or licensed process server.
How the Hearing Date Is Selected	Within 90 days from service.
Attorney Representation Rule	Attorneys are allowed.
Special Provisions Regarding Transfer or Jurisdiction of Cases	There are no provisions.
Availability of Appeals	An appeal is available by either litigant for a review of law, not of facts to district court within five days. At court's discretion, there may be a new trial.
Special Rules and Notes	No equitable relief.

TABLE A-3. **Small Claims Court Summaries for All 50 States** (continued)

New Hampshire	
Maximum Jurisdictional Dollar Amount	The maximum dollar amount is $5,000.
Where Suit May Be Brought	Where plaintiff or defendant resides. Nonresident defendants may be sued where breach or injury occurred.
Proper Manner of Service of Process upon Defendant	Service may be made by certified mail sent by court or other court approved method with return receipt, sheriff or constable.
How the Hearing Date Is Selected	At least 14 days from service.
Attorney Representation Rule	Attorneys are allowed.
Special Provisions Regarding Transfer or Jurisdiction of Cases	If either party requests a jury trial or if claim plus counterclaim exceeds $2,500, the case shall be tried in superior court.
Availability of Appeals	By either side for review of law, not facts to supreme court within 30 days.
Special Rules and Notes	No real estate cases.

TABLE A-3. **Small Claims Court Summaries for All 50 States** (continued)

New Jersey	
Maximum Jurisdictional Dollar Amount	The maximum dollar amount is $3,000.
Where Suit May Be Brought	Case may be brought where the defendant resides. Nonresident defendants may be sued where breach or injury occurred.
Proper Manner of Service of Process upon Defendant	Service may be made by certified mail, sheriff, sergeant-at arms, court- approved adult, or Officers of the Special Civil Part.
How the Hearing Date Is Selected	The hearing date is set by the court.
Attorney Representation Rule	Attorneys are allowed.
Special Provisions Regarding Transfer or Jurisdiction of Cases	If defendant requests a jury trial or counterclaims for more than $2,000, the case shall be tried under regular civil procedure of Civil Part.
Availability of Appeals	Either litigant may appeal for a review of law but not of the facts to appellate division of superior court within 45 days.
Special Rules and Notes	Only contract, property damage caused by motor vehicles and landlord-tenant security deposit cases. Right to sue may not be transferred. Jury trials are available by written demand or court order.

TABLE A-3. **Small Claims Court Summaries for All 50 States** (continued)

New Mexico	
Maximum Jurisdictional Dollar Amount	The maximum dollar amount is $10,000.
Where Suit May Be Brought	Where plaintiff or defendant resides or where breach or injury occurred. Recovery of property is where property is located, A corporation is deemed to reside where it has an office or agent.
Proper Manner of Service of Process upon Defendant	Service may be made by mail, and if no response, personal service by sheriff or court-approved adult.
How the Hearing Date Is Selected	The hearing date is set by the court.
Attorney Representation Rule	Attorneys are allowed and are required for corporations.
Special Provisions Regarding Transfer or Jurisdiction of Cases	There are no provisions.
Availability of Appeals	Either litigant may appeal for a review of law but not of the facts to district court within 15 days.
Special Rules and Notes	Jury trial is available. Voluntary mediation programs are available in all metropolitan courts. Metropolitan court also has jurisdiction over contested parking violations or vehicle operation regulations. Eviction cases are allowed.

TABLE A-3. **Small Claims Court Summaries for All 50 States** (continued)

New York	
Maximum Jurisdictional Dollar Amount	The maximum dollar amount is $5,000. However, justice court (upstate town and village courts) have a limit of $3,000.
Where Suit May Be Brought	Case may be brought where the defendant resides, is employed or maintains a business office.
Proper Manner of Service of Process upon Defendant	Service may be made by certified or registered mail. If after 21 days the certified letter is not returned as undeliverable, then service is presumed. If mail service is not available, personal delivery upon the defendant must be made.
How the Hearing Date Is Selected	The hearing date is set by the court.
Attorney Representation Rule	Attorneys are allowed and are required for most corporations.
Special Provisions Regarding Transfer or Jurisdiction of Cases	Within court's discretion to appropriate court.
Availability of Appeals	By defendant only for review of law, not facts or by plaintiff if "substantial justice" was not done; to county court or appellate terms within 30 days.
Special Rules and Notes	In some courts, only individuals can bring suits. In other courts, partnerships may bring suit, but corporations and LLCs cannot bring suit. Check the local court for rules. In New York City, Small claims cases are heard in city civil court; in Nassau and Suffolk Counties in district court, except 1st District, in other cities in city court. In rural areas, cases are heard in justice court. No injunctive relief is available in small claims court. Non-appealable arbitration is available. Corporations and partnerships may not sue. Right to sue may not be transferred. Jury trial is available to defendant. Defendant must file affidavit stating the issues that require a jury trial. Business judgment-debtors must pay within 35 days of the entry of judgment or $100 may be added to the judgment. Businesses that fail to pay judgments may face a refusal of renewal of grant of business license from state authorities. No counterclaims are allowed in small claims unless within the dollar limit.

TABLE A-3. **Small Claims Court Summaries for All 50 States** (continued)

North Carolina	
Maximum Jurisdictional Dollar Amount	The maximum dollar amount is $5,000.
Where Suit May Be Brought	Case may be brought where the defendant resides. A corporation is deemed to reside where it has place of business.
Proper Manner of Service of Process upon Defendant	Service may be made by certified or registered mail, sheriff or court- approved adult. For evictions, sheriff may use ordinary first-class mail and then telephone or visit to arrange time to personally serve.
How the Hearing Date Is Selected	Within 30 days of filing claim.
Attorney Representation Rule	Attorneys are allowed.
Special Provisions Regarding Transfer or Jurisdiction of Cases	No provisions unless question of land title.
Availability of Appeals	Either litigant may appeal for new trial to district court within ten days. A jury trial is available if requested within ten days of appeal's notice.
Special Rules and Notes	No Injunctive relief is available except enforcement of liens. No counterclaims allowed in small claims unless within the dollar limit.

TABLE A-3. **Small Claims Court Summaries for All 50 States** (continued)

North Dakota	
Maximum Jurisdictional Dollar Amount	The maximum dollar amount is $5,000.
Where Suit May Be Brought	Case may be brought where the defendant resides. A corporation is deemed to reside where it does business or where breach or injury occurred.
Proper Manner of Service of Process upon Defendant	Service may be made by certified mail or court-approved adult.
How the Hearing Date Is Selected	10-30 days from service.
Attorney Representation Rule	Attorneys are allowed.
Special Provisions Regarding Transfer or Jurisdiction of Cases	If defendant requests, the case shall be tried under regular civil procedure of court.
Availability of Appeals	Appeals are not allowed.
Special Rules and Notes	No Injunctive relief is available except to cancel agreements obtained by fraud or misrepresentation. Jury trials are not available. Right to sue may not be transferred. No prejudgment attachment. Plaintiff's withdrawal of case results in dismissal with prejudice.

TABLE A-3. **Small Claims Court Summaries for All 50 States** (continued)

Ohio	
Maximum Jurisdictional Dollar Amount	The maximum dollar amount is $3,000.
Where Suit May Be Brought	Case may be brought where the defendant resides, has a place of business or where breach or injury occurred. Suit against a nonresident defendant may be brought where plaintiff resides. A corporation is deemed to reside where it has principal place of business or an agent.
Proper Manner of Service of Process upon Defendant upon Defendant	Service may be made by certified mail by clerk with a return receipt, or by sheriff, bailiff or court-approved adult.
How the Hearing Date Is Selected	30 days from filing of complaint.
Attorney Representation Rule	Attorneys are allowed. A corporation may proceed through an officer or employee, but may not cross-examine, argue or advocate except through attorney.
Special Provisions Regarding Transfer or Jurisdiction of Cases	If either side requests, if defendant counterclaims for more than $3,000 or at court's discretion, the case shall be tried under regular civil procedure of appropriate court.
Availability of Appeals	An appeal is available by either litigant for review of law, but not facts to court of appeals within 30 days.
Special Rules and Notes	No injunctive relief is available in small claims court. Jury trials are not available. No discovery is allowed. Small claims court cannot hear libel and/or slander cases. Right to sue may not be transferred. Limit of 24 claims a year per plaintiff. The court may order arbitration. Mediation is available in some jurisdictions. Municipal court cases limited to recovery of personal property, taxes, and money. No assignees (except to recover taxes).

TABLE A-3. **Small Claims Court Summaries for All 50 States** (continued)

Oklahoma	
Maximum Jurisdictional Dollar Amount	The maximum dollar amount is $6,000.
Where Suit May Be Brought	Case may be brought where the defendant resides, debt arose or contract signed. Cases concerning damage to land or buildings should be brought where property is. Corporations may be sued where its principal office is located, where an officer resides, where any co-defendant is sued or where the injury occurred. Nonresident corporations may be sued where it has property or debts due, where an agent is found, where any co-defendant is sued, where the injury occurred or where the plaintiff resides.
Proper Manner of Service of Process upon Defendant	Service may be made by certified mail by court clerk with return receipt, sheriff or court-approved disinterested adult.
How the Hearing Date Is Selected	10-60 days from filing of complaint.
Attorney Representation Rule	Attorneys are allowed, but can't charge more than 10% of judgment in uncontested cases.
Special Provisions Regarding Transfer or Jurisdiction of Cases	If defendant counterclaims for more than $4,500 or if court grants defendants request, the case may be tried under regular civil procedure of district court, unless both parties agree in writing to stay in small claims court.
Availability of Appeals	Either litigant may appeal for a review of law but not of the facts to supreme court within 30 days.
Special Rules and Notes	Only cases to recover money, personal property or debt-payment distribution to several creditors. Small claims court cannot hear libel and/or slander cases. Jury trial is available. Collection agents may not sue. Right to sue may not be transferred.

TABLE A-3. **Small Claims Court Summaries for All 50 States** (continued)

Oregon	
Maximum Jurisdictional Dollar Amount	The maximum dollar amount is $5,000.
Where Suit May Be Brought	Cases should be brought where the defendant resides or is found or where injury occurred. Contract cases may be brought where the performance expected.
Proper Manner of Service of Process upon Defendant	Service may be made by certified mail with return receipt, sheriff, constable, or court-approved adult.
How the Hearing Date Is Selected	The hearing date is set by the court.
Attorney Representation Rule	Attorneys are not allowed unless court consents.
Special Provisions Regarding Transfer or Jurisdiction of Cases	If defendant counterclaims for more than $5,000, case goes to regular docket of appropriate court. If defendant's claim is greater than $750 and she or he requests a jury trial, case goes to circuit court.
Availability of Appeals	Circuit court cases cannot be appealed. Justice court cases can be appealed by defendant for a new trial to circuit court within ten days.
Special Rules and Notes	Defendant must answer within 14 days or lose by default. Cases may be referred to mediation or arbitration.

TABLE A-3. **Small Claims Court Summaries for All 50 States** (continued)

Pennsylvania	
Maximum Jurisdictional Dollar Amount	The maximum dollar amount is $8,000 in district or justice court, but $10,000 in Philadelphia Municipal Court.
Where Suit May Be Brought	Cases should be brought where the defendant resides or is found or where breach or injury occurred. A corporation is deemed to reside where it has principal place of business.
Proper Manner of Service of Process upon Defendant	Service may be made by certified or registered mail, sheriff or court-approved disinterested adult.
How the Hearing Date Is Selected	Municipal court: The hearing date is set by the court. District or justice court: 12-60 days from service.
Attorney Representation Rule	Attorneys are allowed and are required for corporations, except when corporation is defendant and claim is for more than $2,500 (Philadelphia Municipal Court).
Special Provisions Regarding Transfer or Jurisdiction of Cases	Municipal court: If defendant counterclaims over jurisdictional limit, the case shall be tried in court of common pleas. District or justice court: There are no provisions.
Availability of Appeals	Either litigant may request an appeal in the court of common pleas within 30 days.
Special Rules and Notes	In Philadelphia, small claims cases are heard in municipal court. Elsewhere, cases are heard in district or justice court. In district or justice court, real estate cases are not allowed. The court may order installment payments, or the court may order arbitration. In municipal court, jury trials are not available.

TABLE A-3. **Small Claims Court Summaries for All 50 States** (continued)

Rhode Island	
Maximum Jurisdictional Dollar Amount	The maximum dollar amount is $1,500.
Where Suit May Be Brought	Case may be brought where either plaintiff or defendants resides. A corporation is deemed to reside where it does business.
Proper Manner of Service of Process upon Defendant	Service may be made by certified or registered mail (note: service is binding on defendant who refuses to accept), or service may be made by sheriff, deputy, constable or court-approved adult.
How the Hearing Date Is Selected	The hearing date is set by the court.
Attorney Representation Rule	Attorneys are allowed and are required for corporations, except close and family corporations with less than $1 million in assets.
Special Provisions Regarding Transfer or Jurisdiction of Cases	If defendant counterclaims for more than $1,500 and court approves, the case may be tried under regular civil procedure of district court.
Availability of Appeals	Defendant may appeal only for new trial. Appeals are to superior court for new trial.
Special Rules and Notes	No personal injury or property damage cases. The court may order installment payments. Consumers may bring actions for contracts (including sale of personal property) and for damages resulting from a retail sale or delivery service.

TABLE A-3. **Small Claims Court Summaries for All 50 States** (continued)

South Carolina	
Maximum Jurisdictional Dollar Amount	The maximum dollar amount is $7,500, but no limit in landlord-tenant cases.
Where Suit May Be Brought	Case may be brought where the defendant resides. Cases to recover personal property may be brought where the property is. A corporation is deemed to reside where it does business.
Proper Manner of Service of Process upon Defendant	Service may be made by certified or registered mail, sheriff, deputy, attorney in case or court-approved disinterested adult.
How the Hearing Date Is Selected	The hearing date is set by the court.
Attorney Representation Rule	Attorneys are allowed.
Special Provisions Regarding Transfer or Jurisdiction of Cases	If defendant counterclaims for more than $7,500, the case may be tried under the docket of common pleas.
Availability of Appeals	Either litigant may appeal for a review of law, not a review of facts to circuit court within 30 days.
Special Rules and Notes	Jury trial is available. Defendant must answer within 20 days or lose by default. Cases for more than $100 against the state and real estate cases are not allowed.

TABLE A-3. **Small Claims Court Summaries for All 50 States** (continued)

South Dakota	
Maximum Jurisdictional Dollar Amount	The maximum dollar amount is $8,000.
Where Suit May Be Brought	Cases should be brought where the defendant resides or injury occurred. A corporation is deemed to reside where it does business.
Proper Manner of Service of Process upon Defendant	Service may be made by certified or registered mail first, return receipt (note: service is binding on defendant who refuses to accept certified mail). Or, in the alternative, by a sheriff or court-approved adult, who is a county resident.
How the Hearing Date Is Selected	The hearing date is set by the court.
Attorney Representation Rule	Attorneys are allowed.
Special Provisions Regarding Transfer or Jurisdiction of Cases	Transfers are allowed at judge's discretion if defendant requests a jury trial at least five days before the small claims hearing. The defendant must provide an affidavit justifying transfer because the facts of the case are too complex.
Availability of Appeals	Appeals are not allowed.
Special Rules and Notes	Small claims court cannot hear libel and/or slander cases. Small claims court cannot hear eviction cases.

TABLE A-3. **Small Claims Court Summaries for All 50 States** (continued)

Tennessee	
Maximum Jurisdictional Dollar Amount	The maximum dollar amount is $15,000. However, in counties of more than 700,000 in population, the limit is $25,000 (Anderson County and Shelby County). There is no limit in forcible entry and detainer cases or to recover specific personal property, except $25,000 limit for alternative money judgments in personal property cases in counties of less than 700,000.
Where Suit May Be Brought	Cases should be brought where the defendant resides or is found or where injury occurred. Cases to recover personal property may be brought where the property is. A corporation is deemed to reside where it maintains an office.
Proper Manner of Service of Process upon Defendant	Service may be made by certified mail, sheriff, deputy or constable.
How the Hearing Date Is Selected	The hearing date is set by the court.
Attorney Representation Rule	Attorneys are allowed.
Special Provisions Regarding Transfer or Jurisdiction of Cases	Before hearing, defendant may request transfer to circuit court (must provide affidavit explaining why defense warrants transfer).
Availability of Appeals	Either litigant may appeal for new trial to circuit court within 10 days.
Special Rules and Notes	Injunctive relief is limited to restraining orders. Jury trials are not available. No formal pleadings are required.

TABLE A-3. **Small Claims Court Summaries for All 50 States** (continued)

Texas	
Maximum Jurisdictional Dollar Amount	The maximum dollar amount is $5,000.
Where Suit May Be Brought	Case may be brought where the defendant resides. Contract cases may be brought where the performance expected.
Proper Manner of Service of Process upon Defendant	Service may be made by certified mail by clerk of court, sheriff, constable, or court-approved adult.
How the Hearing Date Is Selected	The hearing date is set by the court.
Attorney Representation Rule	Attorneys are allowed.
Special Provisions Regarding Transfer or Jurisdiction of Cases	Defendant may file a written motion to transfer as provided by the rules governing justice courts.
Availability of Appeals	Either litigant may appeal for a new trial to county court within 10 days.
Special Rules and Notes	No injunctive relief is available in small claims court. Jury trial available if requested at least one day before trial. Right to sue may not be transferred. Collection agents and commercial lenders may not sue.

TABLE A-3. **Small Claims Court Summaries for All 50 States** (continued)

Utah	
Maximum Jurisdictional Dollar Amount	The maximum dollar amount is $7,500.
Where Suit May Be Brought	Cases should be brought where the defendant resides or where breach or injury occurred.
Proper Manner of Service of Process upon Defendant	Service may be made by sheriff, deputy, constable or disinterested adult.
How the Hearing Date Is Selected	The hearing date is set by the court.
Attorney Representation Rule	Attorneys are allowed.
Special Provisions Regarding Transfer or Jurisdiction of Cases	There is no provision.
Availability of Appeals	Either litigant may appeal for a new trial to district court within ten days. District court will try the appeal in accordance with small claims court procedures, except that a record of the trial will be maintained.
Special Rules and Notes	Parties may request jury trial. The right to sue may not be transferred. Evening sessions are available. Defendant must counterclaim at least two days before trial.

TABLE A-3. **Small Claims Court Summaries for All 50 States** (continued)

Vermont	
Maximum Jurisdictional Dollar Amount	The maximum dollar amount is $3,500.
Where Suit May Be Brought	Where either side resides or where breach or injury occurred.
Proper Manner of Service of Process upon Defendant	Service may be made by first class mail, or by sheriff or court-approved adult.
How the Hearing Date Is Selected	The hearing date is set by the court.
Attorney Representation Rule	Attorneys are allowed.
Special Provisions Regarding Transfer or Jurisdiction of Cases	Appeals are not allowed.
Availability of Appeals	Either litigant may appeal for a review of law but not of the facts to superior court within 30 days.
Special Rules and Notes	No injunctive relief is available in small claims court. Defendant must file a written answer within 20 days of service or lose by default. Defendant may counterclaim for more than $3,500, but the small claims court may not award more than $3,500. In the event the counterclaiming defendant's claim exceeds the small claims jurisdictional limit, the defendant may later sue in separate action for the difference. Defendant may request a jury trial. Small claims court cannot hear libel and/or slander cases.

TABLE A-3. **Small Claims Court Summaries for All 50 States** (continued)

Virginia	
Maximum Jurisdictional Dollar Amount	The maximum dollar amount is $5,000 in damages, or for the recovery of personal property valued up to $5,000.
Where Suit May Be Brought	Case may be brought where the defendant resides, is employed or regularly transacts business, or where breach or injury occurred. Actions to recover property should be brought where the property is.
Proper Manner of Service of Process upon Defendant	Service may be made by sheriff or court-approved adult.
How the Hearing Date Is Selected	The hearing date is set by the court.
Attorney Representation Rule	Attorneys are not allowed.
Special Provisions Regarding Transfer or Jurisdiction of Cases	If defendant counterclaims for more than $5,000 and requests transfer, the case may be transferred to an upper court.
Availability of Appeals	Either litigant may request a new trial on claims exceeding $50 to circuit court within ten days.
Special Rules and Notes	Eviction cases can be heard. Jury trials are not allowed except on appeals.

TABLE A-3. **Small Claims Court Summaries for All 50 States** (continued)

Washington	
Maximum Jurisdictional Dollar Amount	The maximum dollar amount is $4,000.
Where Suit May Be Brought	Case may be brought where the defendant resides. A corporation is deemed to reside where it does business or has an office.
Proper Manner of Service of Process upon Defendant	Service may be made by certified or registered mail, sheriff, deputy, constable or disinterested adult.
How the Hearing Date Is Selected	The hearing date is set by the court.
Attorney Representation Rule	Attorneys are not allowed unless court consents.
Special Provisions Regarding Transfer or Jurisdiction of Cases	At judge's discretion, following a hearing.
Availability of Appeals	Either litigant may appeal when the amount in dispute exceeds $250 for new trial to superior court within 30 days.
Special Rules and Notes	No injunctive relief is available in small claims court. Either party has the right to demand a jury trial.

TABLE A-3. **Small Claims Court Summaries for All 50 States** (continued)

West Virginia	
Maximum Jurisdictional Dollar Amount	The maximum dollar amount is $5,000.
Where Suit May Be Brought	Cases should be brought where the defendant resides or where injury occurred. Contract cases may be brought where the breach occurred. Property insurance claims may be brought where the property is. Cases against nonresident defendants may be brought where plaintiff resides or where the defendant has property or debts due. A corporation is deemed to reside where it has principal office or where chief officer resides. Cases against nonresident U.S. corporate defendants may be brought where the corporate defendant does business or where plaintiff resides.
Proper Manner of Service of Process upon Defendant	Service may be made by sheriff. If that fails any credible disinterested adult or attorney in the case may personally serve the defendant.
How the Hearing Date Is Selected	Defendant has 20 days to appear (five days in entry and detainer cases). Trial date set after defendant notifies court of intention to defend against claim.
Attorney Representation Rule	Attorneys are allowed and are required for collection agents.
Special Provisions Regarding Transfer or Jurisdiction of Cases	Transfers are allowed at magistrate's discretion if defendant requests transfer in answer or within a reasonable time.
Availability of Appeals	Either litigant may appeal for a new trial to circuit court within 20 days.
Special Rules and Notes	No injunctive relief is available in small claims court. Defendant must answer within 20 days or lose by default. No libel or slander, real estate, false imprisonment, or eminent domain cases. Claims against the state must be brought in the court of Claims at the state capitol. Eviction cases are allowed but time limit for action is five days.

TABLE A-3. **Small Claims Court Summaries for All 50 States** (continued)

Wisconsin	
Maximum Jurisdictional Dollar Amount	The maximum dollar amount is $5,000, no limit in eviction cases.
Where Suit May Be Brought	Cases should be brought where the defendant resides or does substantial business or where breach or injury occurred. Consumer credit claims may be brought where the customer resides, where collateral is located or where governing document is signed. A corporation is deemed to reside where it has principal office or where it does business.
Proper Manner of Service of Process upon Defendant	Service may be made by certified or registered mail, or by any disinterested adult resident. For evictions, personal service is required.
How the Hearing Date Is Selected	The hearing date is set by the court.
Attorney Representation Rule	Attorneys are allowed. Attorney representation is mandatory for assignees.
Special Provisions Regarding Transfer or Jurisdiction of Cases	If either side requests a jury trial or if the defendant files a compulsory counterclaim for more than $5,000, case is tried under regular civil procedure.
Availability of Appeals	Either litigant may appeal for a review of law, but not a review of facts to court of appeals within 45 days, or 15 days in eviction cases.
Special Rules and Notes	The prevailing party may be awarded attorney fees of up to $100 on judgments of more than $1,000. A jury trial is available. Evening and Saturday sessions are available. A motion for a new trial must be made within 20 days of judgment.

TABLE A-3. **Small Claims Court Summaries for All 50 States** (continued)

Wyoming	
Maximum Jurisdictional Dollar Amount	The maximum dollar amount is $7,000
Where Suit May Be Brought	Cases should be brought where the defendant resides or is found. A corporation is deemed to reside where it has principal place of business. Cases against nonresident defendants may be brought where the breach or injury occurred.
Proper Manner of Service of Process upon Defendant	Service may be made by certified or registered mail, or by sheriff, deputy, deputized process-server or court-approved adult.
How the Hearing Date Is Selected	3-12 days from service.
Attorney Representation Rule	Attorneys are allowed.
Special Provisions Regarding Transfer or Jurisdiction of Cases	Allowed
Availability of Appeals	Either side may appeal for a review of law, but not facts to upper court within 10 days.
Special Rules and Notes	A jury trial is available. No formal pleadings are required. Arbitration is available in some circumstances.

Glossary

Actionable. An actionable claim is one that affords grounds for legal action.

Agent for service of process. The person or entity that is authorized to receive legal papers on behalf of a corporation, LLC or other business entity.

Alter ego liability. Doctrine that attaches liability to corporate shareholders in cases of commingling of assets and failure to observe corporate formalities.

Answer. The formal written response to a complaint that is filed in a lawsuit.

Bank levy. The process whereby a judgment creditor attaches and takes possession of property of a judgment debtor that exists at a bank or financial institution; a bank levy is used by judgment creditors following a successful civil suit against a defendant.

Bench warrant. A warrant of arrest issued by a presiding judge to a party who fails to appear at a court-ordered hearing or debtor's examination.

Business judgment rule. The rule that shields directors, officers, and managers from liability for mismanagement of the corporations and LLCs that they serve.

Case law. Case law refers to the collective body of written court decisions that comprise the common law of a jurisdiction.

Certificate of good standing. A document issued by the secretary of state or equivalent department certifying that a corporation or LLC is validly existing and in compliance with all periodic and taxation requirements. The failure of a corporation or LLC to maintain good standing may be cause to extend liability to owners of the entity.

Common law. Common law is the collective body of law that is established by precedent, from judicial court cases and judicial decisions within a jurisdiction.

Complaint. The complaint is the formal, written notice and explanation of a set of facts that describes a claim or claims brought by a plaintiff; a complaint initiates a lawsuit.

Compromise. A plaintiff is said to compromise a claim when he or she reduces the amount of a perfectly valid claim in order to secure the defendant's cooperating in resolving the case.

Contract. A contract is a legally binding exchange of promises or an agreement between parties to deliver goods, money, services or other consideration. Contracts can be oral or written. Typically, one party is to receive money, but not always. At its core, a contract requires that one party make an offer, and that the other party accept that offer.

Counterclaim. A counterclaim is a claim brought by the defendant against the plaintiff that is filed and served following the plaintiff's original claim.

Debtor's examination. A court-supervised inquiry at which a judgment debtor is compelled to appear and answer questions about his or her assets. The debtor's examination is initiated and conducted by a judgment creditor.

Defamation. Defamation is the issuance of a false statement about another person, which causes that person to suffer harm.

Default. Default is relief granted by a court when an opposing party fails to answer a complaint or appear for trial.

Defendant. The Defendant is the party that opposes a plaintiff in a lawsuit. The plaintiff in a lawsuit seeks compensation from a defendant.

Deposition. A deposition is the oral examination of a witness, taken under oath and recorded for use in court at a later date.

Discovery. Discovery is the phase of the pre-trial litigation process during which each party requests relevant information and documents from the other side in an attempt to "discover" pertinent facts. Such devices include depositions (oral interviews), interrogatories (written questions), requests for admissions, document production requests and requests for inspection. Discovery is limited in small claims court.

Doing business as (DBA). A company whose operating name differs from its legal name is said to be doing business as the operating name. Some states require DBA or fictitious business name filings to be made for the protection of consumers conducting business with the entity.

Evidence. Evidence is testimony, documents, material objects, or other tangible objects or things that are legally admissible in court to prove the existence or nonexistence of a fact.

Judgment creditor. The plaintiff becomes a judgment creditor if and when his or her case proceeds to victory over the opponent.

Judgment debtor. A judgment debtor is a party against whom a judgment has been entered in a civil case or small claims case. The defendant becomes a judgment debtor when he or she loses the case.

Judgment lien. The right to take and hold or sell the property of a judgment debtor as payment for a judgment awarded in a civil case.

Jurisdictional limit. The jurisdictional limit in small claims court is the maximum dollar amount that a small claims court is empowered to award. Cases that exceed the jurisdictional limit can typically be brought in small claims court, but the amount of the award in excess of the jurisdictional limit cannot be awarded and will be permanently waived.

Levy. To confiscate the property of a judgment debtor in accordance with a legal judgment following a civil case.

Lien. The right to take and hold or sell the property of a debtor as security or payment for a debt or duty.

Liability shield. The protection from liabilities, debts, and lawsuits enjoyed by the owners of a well-operated LLC or corporation that maintains its good standing. The owners of such an LLC or corporation are said to be "shielded from liability."

Libel. Libel is the making of defamatory statements in a fixed medium, such as a magazine, newspaper or the internet.

Limited liability company (LLC). A new and flexible business organization that offers the advantages of liability protection and the simplicity of a partnership.

Limited partnership. A business organization that allows limited partners to enjoy limited personal liability while general partners have unlimited personal liability.

Order of examination. The order under which a judgment debtor is ordered to appear at a debtor's examination. A debtor's examination is a court-supervised inquiry at which a judgment debtor is compelled to appear and answer questions about his or her assets. The debtor's examination is initiated and conducted by a judgment creditor.

Negligence. The doing of an act which a reasonably prudent person would not do, or the failure to do something which a reasonably prudent person would do under like circumstances, that causes harm to another person.

Personal jurisdiction. Personal jurisdiction refers to the ability and authority of a court in a state to have jurisdiction over the parties to a dispute. A small claims court, like any court, must have personal jurisdiction over the parties in order to render a decision.

Pierce the veil. Doctrine that attaches liability to corporate shareholders in cases of commingling of assets and failure to observe corporate formalities.

Plaintiff. A plaintiff in a lawsuit—small claims or otherwise—is the party that is seeking relief by bringing the legal action.

Pleadings. The collective body of documents submitted to a court by all parties in connection with a lawsuit.

Punitive damages. Punitive damages are monetary awards made to a victim that are intended to punish a defendant and deter the defendant from repeating the conduct that injured a victim. Punitive damages are intended to deter others from similar conduct.

Resident agent. The person or entity that is authorized to receive legal papers on behalf of a corporation or LLC.

Service of process. The procedure employed to give legal notice to a defendant of a court case concerning a person, which is accomplished by delivery, or purported delivery, of written notice of the suit upon the defendant.

Slander. Slander is the making of defamatory statements by a spoken representation.

Statute of frauds. Laws that require that some contracts be committed to a writing signed by the party against whom enforcement is sought in order to be enforceable. The term statute of frauds comes from an English law passed in 1677 called the Statute of Frauds and Perjuries.

Statute of limitations. A statute of limitations is a law that dictates the number of years in which a claim must be brought for liability to attach to a defendant. If a plaintiff waits beyond the expiration of the statute of limitations to bring his claim, the claim is lost forever.

Subject-matter jurisdiction. Subject-matter jurisdiction refers to the authority of a court to hear cases dealing with a particular subject matter.

All courts are bound to hear only those cases within their subject matter jurisdiction.

Subpoena. A subpoena is a written command to a witness to appear at a time and place to give testimony.

Subpoena duces tecum. A variation of a subpoena is a *subpoena duces tecum*, which is a written command to produce tangible evidence (usually documents) for use at a hearing or trial.

Tort. A civil wrong or breach of a duty to another person, as outlined by law.

Venue. The doctrine that dictates that the locality or region where a court sits must be the same locality or region that bears a meaningful connection to the underlying facts of a lawsuit.

Wage garnishment. Wage garnishment is the process whereby a judgment creditor obtains, directly from an employer, part of the salary of an employee who has failed to fully satisfy a judgment. The wages of American workers are partially protected from garnishment by both federal and state laws. In general, federal wage garnishment protection limits the amount of garnishment to either 25 percent of the disposable earnings of an employee, or 30 times the minimum wage per week, whichever is less.

Writ of attachment. A writ of execution (in some states it's called by a slightly different name) is court-ordered "permission" to attach a judgment debtor's property. Once the writ of execution is stamped by a court, a judgment creditor then uses the writ in connection with any one of several attachment devices, such as a garnishment of wages, or a lien of bank account or personal property.

About the Author

M ichael Spadaccini is a business law author and semi-retired attorney. He practiced business law for small businesses and startups in San Francisco and Silicon Valley since 1993, and more recently in Austin, Texas. He is the author of numerous business law books for Entrepreneur Press. From 1991 to 1992, he was the Editor-in-Chief of *The Connecticut Probate Law Journal*—an academic publication operated at his Alma Mater, Quinnipiac University School of Law. He has been sought for comment on business law and intellectual property issues in publications such at *USA Today*, *The San Francisco Examiner*, and *Women's Wear Daily*.

Index

C